Counseling 21st Century Students for Optimal College and Career Readiness

Counseling 21st Century Students for Optimal College and Career Readiness

A 9th–12th Grade Curriculum

Corine Fitzpatrick and *Kathleen Costantini*

Routledge
Taylor & Francis Group
New York   London

Routledge
Taylor & Francis Group
711 Third Avenue
New York, NY 10017

Routledge
Taylor & Francis Group
27 Church Road
Hove, East Sussex BN3 2FA

© 2011 by Taylor & Francis Group, LLC
Routledge is an imprint of Taylor & Francis Group, an Informa business

Printed in the United States of America on acid-free paper
10 9 8 7 6 5 4 3 2 1

International Standard Book Number: 978-0-415-87612-4 (Paperback)

Library of Congress Cataloging-in-Publication Data

Fitzpatrick, Corine.
    Counseling 21st century students for optimal college and career readiness : a 9th-12th grade curriculum / Corine Fitzpatrick and Kathleen Costantini.
        p. cm.
    Includes bibliographical references and index.
    ISBN 978-0-415-87612-4 (pbk. : alk. paper)
    1. Vocational guidance--Handbooks, manuals, etc. 2. Educational counseling--Handbooks, manuals, etc. 3. Career development.
I. Costantini, Kathleen. II. Title. III. Title: Counseling twenty-first century students for optimal college and career readiness.

HF5381.F58 2011
373.14'2--dc22   2011003325

Visit the Taylor & Francis Web site at
http://www.taylorandfrancis.com

and the Routledge Web site at
http://www.routledgementalhealth.com

Contents

SECTION III THE COUNSELOR AS CREATOR AND MANAGER

Preface

Counseling 21st Century Students for Optimal College and Career Readiness was many years in the making, starting with our professional experience as teachers together in New York, and continuing in our work together as college advisors. Its completion is truly a culminating experience for us professionally. As educators who believe in the potential of all students to achieve academic and personal success, we know how critical it is to prepare students to be optimally successful and how critical the role that college advising plays in that development is.

What is unique about our vision is the intertwining of psychological theory and best practices with a practical hands-on counseling curriculum that actively engages the student as a participant not only in the planning of college and career goals but also in learning a methodology to achieve them. We have developed a step-by-step curriculum designed to achieve that goal.

Another essential component of our book focuses on the counselor. We encourage the counselor to act as both advocate and leader in assisting students. From the development of study skills to college and career counseling and the financial aid process, the role of the counselor as advocate and leader has enormous potential to impact students. We live in an increasingly complex and fast-changing global society. If our students are to compete, they must be equipped with the requisite skills and education. Using this curriculum, the counselor can take the lead in helping students understand their goals and aspirations, and find the ways to achieve them.

We have also included a CD with the tables, exercises, and charts contained in the book for easy access for the counselor or teacher. In this way, materials may be reproduced so that students may benefit from the practical, hands-on experience that is essential in our approach to an effective college and career readiness curriculum. The CD is an essential tool for counselors and teachers in the vital work of helping students understand and achieve their collegiate and career goals.

Together then, we decided to write this book, develop the curriculum, and challenge counselors to strengthen their roles in advancing the lives of their students.

Kathleen Costantini and Corine Fitzpatrick

Acknowledgments

We are indebted to many people who graciously contributed their ideas and efforts to our work. Most importantly, we want to thank Rose Fairweather-Clunie, the principal of IN-Tech Academy (a technology-focused public 6–12 school in the Bronx borough of New York City), for her passion for wanting the best for children, academically and otherwise. As a result, she allowed us to pilot our curriculum at IN-Tech, to work with her faculty and students, to allow counselors-in-training and undergraduate students from Manhattan College to work with her students, and, finally, to provide all necessary support for the development of college advising activities. In the spring of 2010, she received an achievement award from *Education Update* (see Additional Resources), a 14-year-old award-winning Web-based newspaper focused on education. Each year the newspaper honors several outstanding leaders in New York City Schools. She is truly an exceptional person. She is our partner and our friend.

UNDERSTANDING THE CHALLENGE

Chapter 1

Counseling for College and Career Readiness in the 21st Century: The Challenges of a Changing World

In this chapter we attempt to address the challenges facing educators in the 21st century that relate to college and careers. We then describe the unique role that counselors play in helping students become empowered learners for their own future economical and educational benefit. The chapter will draw on the impact of the changing global landscape, on relevant findings in cognitive and psychosocial development, and on themes present in the National School Counselor Standards.

The work of college counselors has never been more important than it is today. With the increasing costs of college, the explosion in the number of applications made, and the choices of college and major more numerous than ever, the work of counselors is more demanding as well. More importantly, providing college counseling in the 21st century will continue to play a critical role in helping students become self-actualized and successful in their lives. Never before has a college degree been seen as absolutely essential, indeed as almost a prerequisite to fulfillment in an individual's personal and professional life. Helping students to be prepared, to be admitted, and to be successful both academically and psychologically in college has always been the goal of college counselors. We have been very successful in this endeavor. Counselors by nature bring their caring, their passion, and their professional discipline to their work; we are deservedly proud.

Yet the world has radically changed in the last 10 years, and those whom we would counsel have experienced the impact of that changing world on their lives economically and in their learning experiences. The world has become "flat," knowledge has become more complex, and learning has truly been effectively transformed through the Internet and media. Adding to those millennial changes is a declining international view of American K–12 education as seen on international tests. Therefore, it is imperative for counselors to take on an increased role in infusing best practices into the work of college advising, including broadening what we mean by *college advising*. The National School Counselor Standards clearly advocate for counselors to take on leadership roles in schools. Leading the way in the development of students who are optimally ready for college has never been more critical than now. We believe our book makes a serious contribution to this critical effort. We have designed this book to enhance the work you do with your students to help them be prepared for, be admitted to, and be reasonably confident that they will be successful in college. We believe that this work begins much earlier than when students take the Preliminary Scholastic Aptitude Test (PSAT) in their junior year. Our vision is to see college and career advising integrated into all of high school. The design of the book centers on a college advising curriculum that includes all 4 years in high school, addresses development in learning skills and developmental transitions, and provides timelines and plans for college and career explorations. Its uniqueness lies in the fact that it is a curriculum with fully developed aids for use in working with the students.

Before we can move into the curriculum chapters, we must first review some of the challenges facing those who counsel for college and career readiness. Specifically, we see the need for a twofold reflection on the challenges of the 21st century: (1) on changes internationally, and (2) on changes in our understanding of the learning process in the digital age. These challenges provide the overview and rationale for the curriculum work that is the main focus of this book.

The Postglobalization World

A Faster Growing and More Complex World

How much faster and more complex is our world today? Between 2000 and 2007 the world economy grew at a faster pace than in the past 4 decades and income per person rose at a faster rate than in any other period in history—at 3.2% (Zakaria, 2008). This economic leap was fueled by the free movement of capital once Western countries gave up monetary controls. That change allowed more and more investment capital to move around the world. At the same time, enormous political changes in countries moved them toward democracy and the freedom to make use of this capital (e.g., Brazil, Russia, India, and China). Technology further pushed the world in a faster and more complex direction. In the 1970s on Wall Street, a broker traded either bonds or stocks; there were no computers, just the ticker tape, and rarely was a trade outside of the domestic United States. Today, a complexity of financial instruments exists, and trading occurs instantaneously across the globe.

Everything is not only faster but also, more importantly, more complex. In 1907, when the United States was an emerging industrial society, 10% of

American children graduated from high school; currently about 70% finish high school in the expected 4 years (Wise, 2008). Today, experts predict that almost 90% of the fastest growing jobs of the future will require some postsecondary education and training with expertise in technologies (U.S. Department of Labor, 2006). Most jobs now require more complexity and, in particular, technology literacy. Think about the skills required for work in the medical fields, the financial world, and education. Not only will we be faced with the demand for better technology skills, but we will also have to have better cognitive skills with which to develop those technology skills. Brooks (2008) forcefully connects the two by describing a new period called "the cognitive age," a period in his view that is as revolutionary as the impact of globalization.

Globalization and a Shrinking World

We live in a smaller world due to the forces of globalization; recent advances in technology have further shrunk the world. Globalization has been referred to as a process of integration and interaction among different countries driven by trade, investment, and technology advances (Globalization101, 2007). However, today's globalization is farther, faster, cheaper, and deeper according to Friedman (2005), who identified stages of globalization and labeled the most recent stage globalization 3.0. The dynamic force for globalization 1.0 was countries globalizing; for globalization 2.0, companies globalizing; and now for globalization 3.0, the power of *individuals* to compete and collaborate globally (Friedman, 2005). Some examples include YouTube, Web 2.0, Twitter, Facebook, and lesson plan development between teachers from the United States and China. We are clearly embracing a level of globalization that touches all of us personally.

Our shrinking world, in which other countries are improving the education of their children, has also provided competition for us educationally and in careers. China has provided funding for the development of 14 national universities in the hope of competing with major U.S. research universities. Furthermore, international students are much more likely than American students to pursue technical fields. "More people will graduate in the United States in 2006 with sports/exercise degrees than with electrical engineering degrees," says General Electric's former CEO (Immelt, 2006, p. 1). We must educate American children to participate meaningfully and competitively in that world, and counselors must strive to help them optimize their college and career readiness for this world.

Learning in the Digital Age

Information and technology have significantly impacted the development of American children. Children growing up in the 1950s were primarily influenced in the preschool years by their families and little media. Children born in the 1980s had those influences plus the media of television and movies. Today, the

Internet has contributed a whole new dimension to cognitive and psychosocial development. Kao (2007, p. 103) sees the profound influence of the Internet: "To my mind, the Internet is the most significant learning tool since Gutenberg invented moveable type in the 15th century." It has been noted that movies, television, and even books are one-way propositions that push their content on us. In contrast, the Internet is two-way—it combines push and pull and is a powerful influence on development because of that interaction (Seely, 2000). Counselors, teachers, and parents must all be concerned about the impact of media on cognitive and psychosocial development. Counselors must maintain their understanding of these developmental changes and how the breadth of information and technology impact them.

Learning, Cognitive Development, and Critical Thinking

The ways in which children learn and the complexity of knowledge that they must gain has changed significantly even in the past 10 years. Counselors must consider the breadth of information that bombards students when they are gaining knowledge not only about their school subjects but also about complex careers, college majors, and in essence all of the parts of the college advising process.

Furthermore, due to potential cognitive overload that may well threaten students' capacities as learners and studiers, counselors need to increase their understanding of self-regulated cognitive and metacognitive strategies so that they can help students become better learners with better study skills; this is not just the purview of teachers. Recent cognitive development studies have focused on enhancing the cognitive processing necessary to gain more information in this oversaturated world of technology. In a review of some of the best practices in fostering these strategies in learning and in the use of study skills, for example, Fitzpatrick (2008) focused on the importance of students' gaining academic self-discipline and, in particular, better study skills in light of the expansive use of technology, the enormous amounts of knowledge available to them, and the increasingly demanding collegiate experience.

Moreover, the need for critical thinking will grow in the future. American educators pride themselves on the teaching and learning of higher-order thinking skills. Brooks (2008) believes that we are moving beyond globalization and into a more demanding age, where people must be able to learn to think more complexly and apply their thinking to novel problems. So how are we doing? Well, we do not do well on international tests, and not only in mathematics. However, in a review of comparative performance on the Trends in International Mathematics and Science Study (TIMSS), Zakaria (2008, p. 193) notes: "Other educational systems teach you to take tests; the American system teaches you to think." Parents of Korean children are increasingly sending their young children to the United States and Canada so that they can not only learn English but also learn how to think. "South Korean parents believe the [Korean] schools are failing not only to teach English but also other skills crucial in the era of globalization, like creative thinking" (Onishi, 2008, p. 2).

Many people believe that our present educational system provides the environment to develop critical and creative thinking—thinking outside the box such as engaging in analysis and synthesis. Zakaria believes it is being done well with our best students in our best schools, but not everywhere. Wise (2008) agrees but suggests that because as of 2005 approximately 30% of our high school students do not graduate, there must be a disconnect between what we expect and what most of our schools are actually delivering.

The development of academic self-discipline, better study skills, and critical thinking are areas where we believe counselors have taken and must continue to take a leadership role. The curriculum that is the major focus of the book is full of best practice ideas to further enhance this counselor role in its focus on these strategies as part of the development of optimal college readiness.

Our challenge as counselors has always been to inculcate our students with a sense of respect for knowledge and information, and the ethics of learning and achieving. Conveying a love of knowledge, an ethical approach to one's work, a respect for learning, and a respect for others in all of these endeavors through modeling, is one of our most empowering roles. These are our greatest gifts to our students and will not change—even in the 21st century.

Learning and Psychosocial Development

Some important findings in recent emotional and social development research also ground our work. The capacity to understand emotions, express them, and relate to others is one of the most important aspects of optimal, healthy personality development. In addition, the ability to recognize fear, anxiety, and anger and to learn appropriate coping skills, norms, rules, and values is critical to children's psychological development. Future predictions indicate that children and adolescents will learn more about emotions and shape their own ability to deal emotionally from media rather than from others, including their families (Roberts & Foehr, 2008; Wilson, 2008).

Bandura (1986) opened the world's eyes with "Bobo Doll" research, in showing that children learn from what they see modeled. There is nothing to suggest that this kind of learning will change in the future. The amount of exposure to media will increase, and the degree to which content can be controlled will in all likelihood decrease. Roberts and Foehr (2008) report that children under the age of 6 spend more time watching television than they do playing outdoors. He believes that the United States has reached the point where children's social interactions are no longer face-to-face. Researchers note that most, if not all, studies on the relationship between psychosocial development and the media are correlational and not longitudinal, which should caution all generalizations about the possible relationship (Shore, 2008; Wilson, 2008). Nevertheless, Facebook usage has supported the further development of non-face-to-face interactions as part of social development.

One of the more troubling areas of research that should be noted is related to *cultivation theory*, which has found that people who watch a great deal of television will come to perceive or "cultivate" the real world as being consistent with what they see on the screen. Thus, people who watch a lot of violence on TV or in other media forms, such as video games, see the world as more fearful or violent and then react with anxiety or aggression in their own lives. The enormous popularity of reality TV suggests that adolescents in particular may connect in this manner. The increasing number of aberrant violent events in our country is another example (e.g., Columbine).

Much of what was stated above regarding emotional development is also true of social development. There are both positive and negative aspects of the relationship between media exposure and the social development of children and adolescents. However, it is our view that the future direction of media influence on social development will be even greater given technological advances. Web 2.0, YouTube, Facebook, blogs, cell phones, text messaging, and the many other "socializing" technologies will continue to change the way children, adolescents, and adults interact. This use of technologies reflects a profound change in human relations (Kao, 2007). More and more, we will see adolescents use these tools not only to reinforce existing relationships but also to gain more information about those whom they want to be a part of their off-line world (Subrahmanyam & Greenfield, 2008). This is a good thing.

Pontin (2008), in speaking of the future of the Web, refers to its renewed emphasis on collaboration and communication—its socializing role. He reminds us that an entire generation of young people has come of age using the Internet as its "dominant means of socializing" (p. 1). We expect this engagement to continue in the future. Subrahmanyam and Greenfield (2008) believe that the benefits of these socializing enterprises to normal optimal development far outweigh the negative concerns. So, what's in the future for counselors? First and foremost, counselors must recognize that we must be valuable consumers of research and be actively involved in understanding the changing world of socialization for our students.

Brooks (2008, p. A21) points out what must go hand-in-hand with the use of media:

> In order to thrive, people are compelled to become better at absorbing, processing and combining information. The globalization paradigm emphasizes the fact that information can now travel 15,000 miles in an instant. But the most important part of information's journey is the last few inches—the space between a person's eyes or ears and the various regions of the brain. Does the individual have the capacity to understand the information? Does he or she have the training to exploit it?

Counselors have always played a critical role in the development of their students. As the world becomes more complex and as students are increasingly exposed to many forces during their developmental years, our many roles take on even more importance. Providing best college advising practices in helping them to develop college readiness in its broadest sense including their learning and their psychosocial development is our primary goal. Providing best practices in college advising in light of the global economic changes in the demand for skilled workers is our second goal.

Chapter 2

School–College Partnerships: Why They Are Important to College and Career Readiness and to the Challenge

This chapter explores the role that college partnerships should have in the development of a successful program and how counselors can develop these relationships to further foster the impact of this curriculum on student success. Specifically, this chapter describes the development of a professional partnership between an urban 6–12 school and a School of Education at a local college with a particular emphasis on the ability of each partner to provide meaningful input into developing plans. Ideas on how to develop and foster such a partnership, including a section on mutual grant proposal writing and the development of a college student outreach program, are included.

The goal of this chapter is to convince counselors of the valuable rationale for fostering partnerships with colleges, of the value of these partnerships for students, and of the emerging importance of themselves as the major leaders in these partnerships. We first explore some of the general background in partnerships between K–12 schools and colleges. Next, we examine the link to the American School Counselor Association (ASCA) and how it compels us to be more proactive in partnerships. Finally, we describe a real-life example of such a partnership.

K–12/College Partnerships

Most educators and counselors are familiar with K–12/college partnerships. The rationale for Professional Development Schools (PDS), a form of school–college collaborations, began to be formulated in the reform movement of the 1980s that was motivated by a concern for economic competitiveness in a global market. In the early 1990s the focus turned to standards for children and teachers. These standards in turn led to reexamination of standards for accreditation of Schools of Education. The concept of PDSs emerged from within this call for change. The National Council for the Accreditation of Teacher Education PDS Standards Project identified three characteristics of successful PDSs: the nurturing of a learning community, a true collaboration both within and between partners, and accountability for teaching and learning. According to Levine (1997), this learning community is one in which professionals engage in knowledge-based practice, collegial interaction and an inquiry-based orientation. The collaboration is based on the needs and practices of both school and college. Most importantly, PDSs and all partnerships must "break ground, build a foundation, and keep house" in order to renew their place in education in the 21st century (Fitzpatrick, Mucciardi, & Sierra, 2002 p. 9).

In the last several years, collaborative efforts between school districts and institutions of higher education (IHEs) have expanded to address college access, retention, and achievement issues, particularly for underrepresented students. Often times the lead is taken by the university or college (Ravitch, 2000; Timpane & White, 1998). Most of these collaborations focus on teachers, students, or staff and rarely focus on the work of counselors in helping students, yet these issues are clearly the domain of anyone who works in college advising.

Since the millennium, more foundations have become the leads in partnerships. Among others, the W. K. Kellogg Foundation (New Options for Youth), the Bill and Melinda Gates Foundation (Model High Schools, including Early College High Schools), the Carnegie Corporation of New York (Teachers for a New Era), and the Ford Foundation (Collaboration for Education Reform Initiative) have funded a variety of long-term projects in which universities have been critical partners, but not the lead institution (Bodilly, Chun, Ikemoto, & Stockly, 2004; Sanders, 2005; W. K. Kellogg Foundation, 2005). Counselors have not been involved in most if not all of these partnerships partially because those efforts have focused on teachers.

Recent researchers have indicated that the kinds of partnerships described above have not been greatly successful in addressing the educational needs of underrepresented students: "The critical issue is that students who are most at risk of dropping out of high school or, if they are able to gain entrance into a postsecondary institution, will most likely not complete their first year of study" (Collins, Weinbaum, Ramon, & Vaughan, 2009, p. 398). These collaboration models either are incapable of fulfilling this role or were not designed to fulfill them (Bodilly et al., 2004; Oliva, 2004; Ostrower, 2005; Sanders, 2005; W. K. Kellogg Foundation, 2005).

Such a finding is a compelling argument for reexamining the models of some of these partnerships, who should be in them, and where we should go in the 21st century. Quite simply, counselors need to be at the forefront of these endeavors. Few, if any, partnerships include counselors let alone spend funding on their efforts, yet we are informed by studies funded by foundations about our work. In a recent study funded by the Bill and Melinda Gates Foundation surveying high school students about their guidance counselors, the researchers found that many young people give the high school guidance system "stunningly poor reviews," thus leading those researchers to say this about the state of high school counseling: "As education focuses its attention on bringing today's high schools into the 21st century, the guidance counseling system is a prime candidate for innovation and reform" (Johnson, Rochkind, Ott, & DuPont, 2009, p. 74). Well, we say the time has come for counselors to be proactive in developing partnerships related to their work with students and in taking leadership positions. Counselors need to be purposeful in finding these partnerships. Such partnerships need to be enacted in places where there is a commitment to change, both in the school and in the college and with any foundations if involved. School and university faculty working together find solutions to problems and develop better ways of optimizing student development and preparedness when students go to college. Each faculty group brings a different set of skills and perspectives to this effort. University partners might facilitate counselors learning from each other and working collegially. University faculty also have expert knowledge to bring to bear on school problems. As members of this learning community, they have a role to share this expertise. This process creates different ways of doing things and a new culture. Norms of privacy and isolation are replaced by norms of public practice and collegiality.

Yet collaboration is critical to development of these professional development partnerships (Fitzpatrick, 2001). College counseling faculty are not the experts and the K–12 school counselors are not the learners. Rather, each member of the learning community brings certain strengths to the relationship. College faculty should participate on committees of the schools and contribute their expertise. School counselors likewise advise college faculty on best practices. The point is that these partnerships are collaborative and through their interaction and sharing of best practices they can further enhance college advising counseling services.

The ASCA National Model: Calling Counselors to Be Leaders in Educational Reform

The ASCA has developed a model for the standardization of the practice of school counseling. That model is now our National Model for practice as school counselors. The ASCA National Model was formed by compiling theory, practices, documents, and writings from national leaders in the field of school counseling (ASCA, 2005). The model supports a school's mission by focusing on the integration of three themes: academic, career, and personal/social development. Equally as important is their view of the role of counselors in supporting best practices in the school community. "ASCA encourages school counselors to become catalysts for educational change and to assume or accept a leadership role in educational reform" (ASCA, 2005, p. 15).

The model further describes the role of counselors as collaborators with many stakeholders to ensure a quality program, including teachers, administrators, parents, students, and community members. Aligning schools with these national standards takes a commitment on the part of many of these stakeholders, but most importantly school administrators. The importance of the partnership between principals and counselors to prepare students for the 21st century by implementing these standards has been noted as critical. "The principals' vision for their students and their commitment to student success are motivations to tap the talent and training of school counselors, their partners in preparing students to meet the challenges of the new millennium" (Dahir, 2000, p. 76). The standards are quite clear on what our role should be; it is time to step up and take our place as leaders and directors of these partnerships.

We would like to describe to you one such partnership that has been in existence since 2001 and has most recently shifted more focus to the counseling department.

An Urban Partnership: IN-Tech Academy (MS/HS 368) and Manhattan College

Manhattan College is a private coeducational college with a graduate division, situated in Riverdale, a section of the Bronx borough of New York City. The School of Education has always addressed the needs of the community for teachers and counselors as well as of urban educators who looked for advanced degrees and in-service training. There is a commitment on the part of the faculty to encourage its students to consider a career (e.g., teacher, counselor, principal) in an urban school setting.

IN-Tech Academy is a 6–12 New York City public school. The vision of those who worked from the beginning on this school was that of a school focusing on technology, and in particular, information and network technology. The partnership with Manhattan College began at the earliest stages of development in 2000 with faculty representation on the original committee that developed the vision and the curriculum. Manhattan College continues to play an active role in the development of the school with faculty representation on the Leadership Committee and because of the inclusion of IN-Tech in TITAN (Transforming Instruction through Technology and Networking), a technology grant received by Dr. Fitzpatrick and the college in 2000 and that ran through 2004.

At the core of this continually developing relationship are the people who engage in this work, both at IN-Tech and Manhattan College. Early collaborative efforts focused on traditional shared experiences such as the placement of student teachers and counselors-in-training at IN-Tech. Due to the TITAN grant, technology began to strengthen the collaboration. One of the projects of TITAN was the development of *curriculum revision teams*, which were made up of faculty from the School of Education, professional educators from the schools, and graduate and undergraduate students from the college. The teams were assigned review of their curriculum, both the college and the 6–12 school. In that way, no one was an expert; rather they were a community of learners sharing ideas of how to infuse technology into their work. Surprisingly, counselors were part of this project; they were part of teams along with school counseling professors. In many cases, the school counselors were the experts informing the counseling faculty of school practice needs.

Since 2004, the partnership has been running a Manhattan College outreach program including Manhattan College undergraduate and graduate students engaging in a variety of experiences. In some cases the Manhattan College students receive work-study funding, and in some cases they volunteer. Engineering students help with a robotics club, communications majors help with student media presentations, and special education majors help learning-disabled students. Counselors-in-training have on-site experiences organized by the counseling department that are very often academic in nature. Manhattan College students also help IN-Tech faculty, and as a result, the Manhattan College students learn from the faculty.

Faculty from Manhattan College's School of Education continue to seek placements for their preservice teachers and counselors-in-training at the school, not only because the School of Education is committed to urban education but also because of the atmosphere that has been sustained by the partnership, a community of learners. The partnership has developed grants together, worked together on corporate-sponsored programs for mentoring, and developed opportunities for the counseling students to become more involved at the school.

In 2009–2010, the partnership reached a whole new level. Together and along with two local community partners, Manhattan College received the Optimal College Readiness (OCR) grant that had as its main focus counseling for college success. This grant is at the forefront in its response to a number of the suggestions in the Gates Foundation–funded review of student perception of high school counselors (Johnson et al., 2009). In the review, those authors described what kinds of changes they thought might be needed for counselors. They suggested improving student–counselor ratios and relieving guidance counselors of some of the other chores they now assume. We agree. This suggestion has been forever at the forefront of most professional counseling revitalizing ideas and yet has rarely been implemented. Furthermore, they noted that counseling education programs do not include instruction or coursework on how to help parents and students navigate the financial aid system or on how to advise students about college selection, apprenticeships, or other postsecondary options. Finally, they cited research suggesting that relatively few public high schools require ongoing professional development for counselors.

We believe that the current grant, which was made possible due to the strength of the existing partnership, has developed some innovative practices that we now share with you. The grant was awarded to the School of Education at Manhattan College by the Higher Education Services Corporation (HESC) of New York State.

It focuses on *empowering students for optimal college readiness* ($S + C^3 = OCR$; that is, students + counselors + college mentors + curriculum = optimal college readiness). There are two goals: one focused on students and their families and one focused on counselor development in the area of college advising:

1. A multifaceted college readiness program includes family activities, outreach from college and graduate students, and two financial resource centers to serve this population in its aspirations.
2. Professional development builds the capacity of local counselors and teachers to better serve these needy students (including middle schoolers) in preparing for and paying for college. Dr. Fitzpatrick is the co-author of the grant, along with one of the faculty from IN-Tech, and Ms. Costantini provides services authorized by the grant to IN-Tech.

The grant provides workshops to parents and students that build college awareness, enhance their knowledge of the requirements for getting into college, and help them to finance their education. We have brought together experienced people to provide these workshops and have made an effort to include those from minority groups themselves; we have done this strategically to enhance the comfortability of families and therefore make them feel connected. We have developed two financial resource centers (somewhat akin to what colleges have), one in a school and one in a community center. Parents, families, and students may get aid and resources for researching colleges, searching for scholarships, and applying for aid. We want to bring the help to the families where they are most likely to participate. Manhattan College outreach undergraduate and graduate counseling students assist parents and students with their research at both centers; they are role models, tutors, and mentors for students and are first-hand informants about their college majors. The outreach program has students from all majors including among others engineering, science, education, and arts. We consider it to be a critical part of the program.

The professional development goal uses grant funding to begin to provide best 21st century practices in college advising to practicing counselors and teachers who work with poor families and to counselors-in-training who are committed to counseling in less-advantaged schools. We wanted teachers and guidance counselors at all partnering schools and counselors-in-training (who want to service these people) to attend existing and newly developed graduate classes at Manhattan College that specifically focus on preparing students for college, such as Counseling the College Applicant, Professional Writing and Student Grant Research, and Counseling At-Risk and Disabled Students and Their Families. Dr. Fitzpatrick has presented nationally on the development of one of the courses and has written on the critical need for this curriculum in counseling programs. Thirty vouchers per year were made available. Participants are counselors serving poor Bronx schools (those identified as having at least 50% of their students falling below the poverty line), counselors who are partners in the grant, and counselors-in-training who would make a 2-year commitment to inner city schools. Manhattan College already places many of its counseling graduates in city schools, particularly those who are bilingual.

A second objective is professional development in a middle school college readiness curriculum; the curriculum was developed by Ms. Costantini with a team of middle school teachers and the assistant principal for guidance this past year and will be piloted in the following year. The ASCA has made a compelling case for bringing the curriculum to middle schools. Indeed, starting college readiness work with middle school children has been endorsed nationally. The curriculum focuses on training teachers and counselors together to prepare students to be more academically rigorous in middle school, transition more robustly into high school, and perform better on the Preliminary Scholastic Aptitude Tests (PSATs). We want to help students early on to be motivated toward excellence by learning to be rigorous and more motivated to want to get into and remain in college. The grant provides a stipend for teachers and counselors to attend these workshops and courses.

Finally, the third objective of the second goal is professional development on the use of Naviance, a comprehensive college preparation software program. Naviance not only provides a management system for college advising, but it also includes programs on career advising and study skills. Manhattan College counselors-in-training who are part of the outreach program learn it and then prepare students in its use.

The point of describing this grant in detail is to show the power of this partnership, that everyone in the community is committed, and that counselors are leading the way. Finally, funding for counselors and for college advising has begun to emerge as a potential positive force in enhancing student expectation and performance.

Here are some tips on being active in developing partnerships and using them to fire up support for your program dreams:

1. Establish a good relationship with an institute of higher education.
   a. Find one that is close to you and has faculty who are eager to develop a "community of learners."
   b. Consider working with faculty from departments other than counseling (e.g., math, English, education).
2. Set up a counseling plan for getting and supporting counselors-in-training.
   a. IN-Tech has developed a space and a schedule for its interns.
   b. A number of their counselors have mentored counseling interns.
3. Continue to learn about best practices in the field by continuing your education.
4. Learn about foundations and how to write grants.
   a. Check out the Foundation Center (see Additional Resources).
   b. Take a grant-writing course.

Chapter 3

Addressing the Challenge: Overview of the Counseling Curriculum for Grades 9–12

Counseling 21st Century Students for Optimal College and Career Readiness addresses one of the most important issues facing our country: How do we ensure that students stay in school and that they are prepared for both college and possible careers? As of 2009, approximately one-third of our high school students do not graduate on time, if ever, and half of those who remain graduate without the skills for college or a job; the United States is confronted with a serious problem. While many new initiatives designed to foster excellence in our schools exist, very few of these plans have focused on counselors. Yet school counselors have an enormous impact on student achievement and postsecondary goals. Indeed, the National Center for Transforming School Counseling (see Additional Resources), part of the Education Trust Foundation, has found that counselors are often left unprepared to help students, in particular low-income students and students of color, who most need their help in striving for a meaningful future.

Counseling 21st Century Students for Optimal College and Career Readiness addresses this need. We have designed a comprehensive curriculum in the chapters that follow for high school counselors to engage in the college and career advising process in American schools in the 21st century. Not only is this a program created for counselors to assist students, but it is also an action-based curriculum that actively engages students in constructing a planned methodology to discover what they need to do to succeed beyond high school. Each curriculum chapter contains exercises and activities, making students active participants in their own preparation for post–high school. We expect that such engagement will also provide motivation to achieve and remain focused throughout high school. Our approach is comprehensive since valuable developmental work starts the first day of 9th grade. Therefore, our curriculum fully covers 9–12th grades, rather than focusing primarily on 11th and 12th grades for college advising. Each curriculum chapter begins with a Memo to Counselors, followed by an actual classroom curriculum plan spoken in the voice of the counselor. An added feature is that while this curriculum is designed for 9th–12th grade students, it can be adapted to the particular counseling structure of individual schools. Best practices are also explained where they are critical to implementing the curriculum.

Below is a brief chapter-by-chapter overview of the curriculum.

Chapter 4—The Move to High School: Making the Transition to 9th Grade Successful

This chapter reviews some of the most recent and important findings on the transitioning experience, including a brief overview of important research on psychosocial and cognitive modifications for the beginning high school student. We then discuss the importance of developing solid study skills and assist counselors in helping students make a successful transition to the academic demands of secondary school. Through the use of personality, learning style, and study skills inventories, counselors will deepen students' awareness of the learning process and their own growth in the transition process. In this chapter, we also discuss how technology has changed the ways in which students learn, and we present proven study skill techniques and methods of time management and long-term planning.

Chapter 5—Using Technology in the College and Career Advising Process

In this chapter we present the ways in which counselors and students can use innovative technologies throughout the 4 years of the curriculum. While most of the relevant technologies will be addressed in the individual chapters, this chapter provides an overview of important "big-picture" ideas that are crucial to understanding how students use technology and what students will face in this postglobalized world. Specifically, counselors need to consider two overarching changes: changes internationally and changes in our understanding of the learning process in the digital age. The challenge is not about innovation generally, but rather it is about being able to be innovative, efficient, and thorough; this challenge applies to both the practicing counselor and the student. Next, we focus on the student as the active user of the available technology tools in either career or college applications. This section includes ideas on how counselors can help students optimally maximize their *choices* and *uses* of technology in the college process. A final focus is to help counselors make their work less overwhelming and more productive.

Chapter 6—Motivation and Testing: Learning About Standardized Testing and Using It to Get Motivated About the College Process (10th–11th Grades)

In this chapter, we discuss recent work on developing motivation to do well on standardized assessments that influence students' post–high school goals. Researchers have found that unmotivated students do not perform as well on standardized tests. Lack of understanding about how these assessments influence their future has been cited by Segal (2010). We will assist counselors in presenting standardized testing as a means of motivating students to begin the college and career search. We also discuss the Preliminary Scholastic Aptitude Test (PSAT) format, methods of preparation, scoring, and uses of test results for the National Merit Scholarship Program. We then compare the SAT and ACT® programs and present counselors with useful advice to assist them in advising students about test choices. This chapter also explains the College Board's MyRoad and QuickStart programs as a method of exploring career possibilities and initiating college research and relating them to the importance of assessment.

Chapter 7—Assisting Students in Career Exploration

In this chapter we first present recent work on career development theories including Social Cognitive Career Theory (SCCT), which suggests that career choice is influenced by outcome expectancies, career interests, and career self-efficacy. We then provide practical methods to help students explore possible careers by first examining their interests and then expanding their knowledge of what kind of work particular careers entail. Students will use exercises to help them clarify their interests, discover actual work descriptions, and understand the necessary educational requirements for specific careers. We also explain the role of technology in career exploration, using specific Web sites and systems that enhance student research. Most importantly, we emphasize the importance of students maintaining an open mind to the career possibilities that lie ahead of them (Segal, 2010). This curriculum may be adapted to students who have taken the PSAT or the PLAN® in either their sophomore or junior year.

Chapter 8—Advising Students in College Research (11th Grade)

In this chapter, we explain the essentials of the college search and application process. Students actively engage the terminology of higher education: liberal arts colleges, universities, specialized institutes, community colleges, and the meaning of majors and minors. In addition, we explore relevant factors in college selection such as size, location, on-campus life, and commuting. Students also learn how to arrange a college visit and what to look for when on campus. Using the Common Application, students gather the necessary information to fill out an actual application. By the end of the academic year, students will have compiled an initial list of colleges that they believe are good matches for them. We then conclude with advice on profitable ways to spend the summer between the junior and senior years.

At the same time, counselors must remind and advise students about standardized testing discussed in Chapter 6. While it is the responsibility of students and parents to register for tests, it is imperative that the counselor assists in this process, making sure that students are on a course to prepare and take the necessary standardized testing for college admission and that they understand relevant information about fee waivers and reductions. Helpful forms for the counselor to gather essential information are included in this chapter.

Chapter 9—Empowering Students in Their Essay Writing (11th–12th Grades)

In this chapter, we explain why the personal statement is important in the college application process. Using the questions on the Common Application, we present exercises and activities designed to assist students in focusing on possible topics for their personal statement essay. We then show students different methods of developing their topics as well as provide sample personal essays from students. In this chapter, we also provide counselors with models for conducting Personal Essay Writing Workshops and follow-up activities for counselors and students. This chapter concludes with a sampling of what college admission officers across the country have to say about the personal essay.

Chapter 10—Assisting Students in Constructing the Final List of Colleges (12th Grade)

This chapter focuses on the necessary tasks that need to be accomplished in the college application process. This includes ongoing college research, a review of what to look for when visiting colleges, and a presentation of interview techniques. We also explain how to build a list of appropriate colleges and then how to narrow it down to a manageable number of schools. In addition, we provide practical suggestions for counselors to assist students in asking for teacher recommendations, registering for standardized testing, and completing applications. Again, helpful forms for counselors to ascertain student progress in the college process are included.

Chapter 11—Helping Seniors Make the Transition to College (12th Grade)

This chapter examines the separation issues, both affective and cognitive, that many seniors may be experiencing as they face the transition from high school to college. We also focus on issues that seem to be particularly problematic for urban adolescents. For example, students from low socioeconomic families who often help with younger siblings find it difficult to think they can leave their families or consider taking on loans for college. Some urban students become very comfortable in their schools, which can become second homes. There is some thinking that these students may sabotage graduating and moving on. Thus, this critical chapter focuses on how counselors can help students complete the necessary tasks for graduation. We also provide examples of leave-taking exercises to help students make this transition.

In the fast-changing global society of the 21st century, students need a framework in which they can explore college and career opportunities. This curriculum provides such a framework not only because it provides a wealth of essential information but also because it ensures that students are actively engaged in the process that will shape their future lives. Counselors will find this curriculum to be a godsend in helping assist their students in this all-important task.

MAKING THE COLLEGE AND CAREER ADVISING PROCESS OPTIMAL
The Curriculum

Chapter 4

The Move to High School: Making the Transition to 9th Grade Successful

Memo to Counselors

In this chapter we review some of the most recent and important findings on the transitioning experience to high school, including a brief review of important research on psychosocial and cognitive modifications for the beginning high school student. We include the development of study skills and assist counselors in helping students make a successful transition to the academic demands of secondary school. Through the use of personality, learning style, and study skills inventories, counselors will deepen students' awareness of the learning process and their own growth in the transition process. In this chapter, we also discuss how technology has changed the ways in which students learn as well as present proven study skills techniques and methods of time management and long-term planning.

Research on the Transition to High School

Most counselors, students, and their families recognize that there is a period of transition from grammar school to high school (8th to 9th grade) or from middle school to high school (9th to 10th grade). Educators focus on the academic leaps that students will have to make in high school. Researchers have documented that students often experience difficulty academically during the transition to high school (Chinien & Boutin, 2001; Forgan & Vaughn, 2000; George, 2000; Hertzog, Morgan, Diamond, & Walker, 1996; Mizelle & Irvin, 2000; Morgan & Hertzog, 2001; Newman, Lohman, Newman, Myers, & Smith, 2000; Reents, 2002).

This transition requires students to experience new environments, new and more difficult curricula, new class organizations, and new teachers at the same time when they are in a stage of transition in their own cognitive, physical, and psychosocial development. McIntosh, Flannery, Sugai, Braun, and Cochrane (2008) studied the relationships between academic performance and problem behavior in the transition from middle school to high school. They found that persistently low academic skills drastically modify the school experience. Academic problems restrict access to daily academic success and close teacher–student relationships, and persistent academic failure in middle school is clearly a risk factor for continued failure in high school (Finn & Rock, 1997; Slavin, 1999) even though cognitive ability has not been found to predict dropout (Bear, Kortering, & Braziel, 2006).

High school teachers pride themselves on the teaching and learning of higher-order thinking skills and recognize the higher level of academic work required of students. Students in the 21st century must be able to show skill development and knowledge to compete in our globalized world. We are moving beyond globalization into an even more demanding age where people must be able to learn to think more complexly and apply their thinking to novel problems (Brooks, 2008). Today's high school students are fast entering a world in which they will minimally need college to gain access to decent-paying careers.

As described by Wise (2008, p. 15), "The rest of the world's education has improved such that today the United States is increasingly competing for what used to be our constant triumph: the high-skilled, high-paying job." Herbert (2008) recently addressed the toll that high schools are imposing on America's future by noting that we cannot even keep our students in school—one-third do not complete school in 4 years, or drop out and half of those who remain graduate without the skills for college or a job. Of those who go on, we have fewer going into technical fields while other countries have more.

Many people believe that our present educational system provides the environment to develop critical and creative thinking—thinking out of the box such as engaging in analysis and synthesis. Wise (2008) agrees but suggests that since one-third of our high school students do not graduate, there must be a disconnect between what we expect and what most of our schools are actually delivering. We used to lead the world in graduation rates, and now we are 16th. Nationwide, only 70% of 9th graders make it to graduation, and that figure drops to 46% for Black males, 52% for Hispanic males, and 60% for Black and Hispanic females. Most telling for the focus of this chapter on the importance of *transitioning* is a finding of the 2010 edition of the *Diplomas 2010* report from Education Week. That edition reported that more than one-third of students lost from high school failed to make the transition from 9th to 10th grade. Far too many American students see a reality gap between their dreams and the real world. Overwhelming numbers of middle school students say they intend to go to college. Unfortunately, many do not graduate from high school, and those who do are often unprepared.

Thus, the preparation of students for college and careers must begin with more than just an understanding that students have to transition and that the work is harder. Whether students engage in a successful high school experience, particularly those who come to high school with weak academic skills and focus, depends on attitudes they develop in these transitioning times. There must be a structure developed that supports and enhances students in transition. If we reframe the idea of transition to one that might well span the next 10 years of their lives (4 years of high school, 4 years of college, 2 years of transition to the work world), then the importance of the counselors' and the schools' attention to transition is even more imperative. Students need to be made aware that they need a comparable level of skill whether they want to go to work or to college after high school. Furthermore, they need to understand what level of performance is "good enough" to demonstrate readiness for college.

Psychosocial and Cognitive Modifications

So, too, we must be aware of cognitive and psychosocial developmental changes that are more evident in the 21st century. For example, our students have to learn more every day than prior generations, so they need to be better learners. Consequently, many countries are seeking technology-enriched curricula and textbooks that develop these skills as opposed to overwhelming students with huge amounts of facts in large textbooks (Kao, 2007). It has been suggested that we should follow countries from Germany to Singapore that have extremely small textbooks that focus on the most powerful and generative ideas and supplement them with rich technologies (Wallis, 2006). We as counselors must explore even more effective ways for students to learn and how to study, especially during times of transition.

Psychosocial development also takes a gigantic leap during this period. The capacity to understand emotions, express them, and relate to others is one of the most important aspects of optimal, healthy personality development. In addition, the ability to recognize fear, anxiety, and anger and to learn appropriate coping skills, norms, rules, and values is critical to adolescent psychological development. Future predictions indicate that children and adolescents will learn more about emotions and shape their own ability to deal emotionally from media rather than from others, including their families (Roberts & Foehr, 2008; Wilson, 2008). Transition to high school is multifaceted, developmental, and pervasive.

The three primary sources of social support—family, peers, and school adults—are each likely to undergo changes as a result of the developmental transitions of adolescence combined with the transition to high school (Newman, Newman, Griffen, O'Connor, & Spas, 2007). Psychologically, adolescence is a critical and unique stage of human development. It is a time when individuals begin and are expected to develop their own identity; academically and socially prepare themselves for adulthood; and explore and contribute to their families, communities, and society. As students undergo these developmental changes, they experience many changes in their social contexts. Parents often expect more autonomy and self-sufficiency. New friendships must be made, and some old peer relationships are gone. Going into high school, adolescents lose familiar teachers, advisors, and routines. High schools are typically more anonymous settings than middle schools; they are typically larger buildings with more students in larger classes. As a consequence, high school students receive less individualized attention from teachers. Newman et al. (2007) found that parents, peers, and schools can play key roles in sustaining adolescents' sense of well-being during this transition. Most importantly, high schools provide more than an academic function. They offer a context through which adolescents experience a sense of group belonging that enables students to gain academic and psychosocial success. This research clearly suggests that the *transitional* focus of this chapter is critical to overall optimal adolescent development and to college and career readiness.

Transition activities might include transition classes for the 9th graders, study skills assessment (see below), regular class periods designed for transitional activities, and a focus on education and career plans for each student.

Transitional Classes

There are various outlines for the development of transitional classes for 9th graders including those that focus on using teachers (Dedmond, 2008), those that focus on the role of the entire school community (Achieve, 2008), and those that focus on the role of the school counselor (Akos, 2010). Development of these classes can often incorporate the elements developed separately in the rest of this chapter. Decisions as to whether to consider such classes should be based upon counselor review of these three possible approaches and upon the presentation to faculty and administrators of a strong rationale for inclusion of the approach in supporting the vision of the school.

What follows are activities deemed critical to this transitional period.

Study Skills Introduction

Memo to Counselors

The approach in presenting this information is that of the voice of the counselor speaking to students.

Table 4.1   Exercise on Establishing Goals for First Semester

Goals	How to Achieve
Academics	
Extracurricular Activities	
Sports	
Other	

As you enter high school, you will be meeting new challenges in all areas of your life:

- Academics
- Extracurricular activities
- Sports
- Community activities/service
- Social life

How do you begin to prioritize and balance all of the demands in your life?

What we will try to accomplish in this Study Skills group session is to give you some of the tools that can help you achieve success.

Goals

Let's think about the goals that you have for yourself as a 9th grader. It's always helpful to think about what and why you want to do something before you actually attempt it. Using the Goals Exercise sheet (Table 4.1), list your goals for this year, and then rank them in the chart. At the end of the first semester, look back and see what you were able to accomplish and where you need to work harder, and then rank your goals again. Look at what worked for you and what did not—this can make the second semester a more successful experience for you. Try to be as specific as possible in thinking about the How to Achieve column. For example, in the Academics section, do not simply say *study harder*, but say *nightly/weekly review of subject material* or *planning to study prior to the night before a test.*

Vocabulary

Now let's make certain terms part of your high school vocabulary. You may know their definitions, but think of them in a new way that is centered around *you*.

A you-centered vocabulary:
- *Active reader*
- *Active listener*

- *Engaged student*
- *Proactive student*

You will notice that the one word that is missing is *passive*. *Passive* and *student* do not belong in the same sentence!

An *active reader*:
- Notes bold headings and word sections in a textbook
- Looks for the topic sentence in paragraphs and supporting ideas
- Makes margin notes where possible

In effect, the active reader makes the most use of his or her abilities when reading.

An *active listener*:
- Pays attention throughout class
- Takes notes as the teacher explains
- Stays focused despite distractions

Again, the active listener makes the most of the classroom session.

An *engaged student*:
- Participates in class discussions
- Listens to what others have to say
- Is truly involved in the subject work

The engaged student learns the most because he or she is truly involved in the learning process.

Finally, a *proactive student*:
- Has clearly defined goals
- Has developed strategies to achieve success
- Is an active participant in the learning process

Proactive students assume responsibility for their own success.

Learning Styles

Now it Is Time to Talk About Learning Styles

Understanding what your preferred learning style is another way that you can achieve greater academic success. All of us feel more comfortable learning in certain ways that are essentially based on three of our key senses: seeing, hearing and touching. This does not mean that you cannot learn in other ways but only that it is helpful if you understand how you learn most easily. This way you will know that when you are in a class that requires another method of learning you may have to adapt in order to succeed. While most of us have a dominant preferred learning style, as we go through school we learn to develop the learning styles that are not our primary way of learning.

Learning styles fall into three categories: visual, auditory, and tactile/kinesthetic.

- Visual learners like to see; they prefer to have a textbook, an image on a computer screen, or words on a chalkboard—essentially, written images that appeal to vision. For them, taking notes for future study is another way of seeing the information.
- Auditory learners like to hear; they learn through listening and are often able to relate the pitch and tone of voice to what is being said. Frequently, they learn best by hearing lectures and discussions and find recordings of classes or books helpful.
- Tactile/kinesthetic learners like a hands-on approach. Taking the kind of notes that visual learners love may not be easy for them. However, completing that chemistry lab is exactly what they love. Tactile/kinesthetic learners enjoy experiential learning—they learn best by doing.

None of us are robots; we all have our learning strengths and weaknesses. The key is to know what these are and to approach our studies understanding that there will many times that we will have to work a little harder if the class presentation does not fall into our areas of strengths.

Students will now complete a Learning Styles Inventory using Naviance and/or the College Board's QuickStart and MyRoad (see Chapter 5 for further detail on these programs).

Now that you have:

- Established goals for your first semester
- Learned some you-centered vocabulary
- Learned your preferred learning style

Let's look at one more essential term: *executive functioning*.

Executive Functioning

Memo to Counselors

The term *executive function* describes a set of cognitive abilities that control and regulate other abilities and behaviors. Executive functions are necessary for goal-directed behavior (see Encyclopedia of Mental Disorders in Additional Resources).

What is executive functioning? Think of it as the boss of your brain. Executive functioning helps you to (1) prioritize and plan your work, (2) organize your thoughts and effectively complete your assignments, and (3) make efficient use of your time. These are essential components of good study skills:

1. Effective planning
2. Organization
3. Time management

How good is your executive functioning? Complete the Executive Functioning Exercise (Table 4.2) to see how you rate your executive functioning. After completing this chart, note how many times you marked a No or Sometimes. These

Table 4.2 Executive Functioning Exercise

Question	Yes	No	Sometimes
Do you look at your daily assignments and plan how you will complete them?			
Do you prioritize your assignments by thinking about what will take the most time or effort?			
Do you think about what is the most important task for you to complete?			
Do you use a planner to write down assignments?			
Do you break long-term assignments into smaller parts?			
Do you correctly estimate how long it will take you to complete an assignment?			
Do you have a nightly study schedule that you try to follow?			
Do you organize your schoolwork neatly in a binder or notebook?			
Do you review on a regular basis, not just before a test?			
Do you keep a record of your grades in each subject?			
Do you include the demands of your job, sports, and so forth in your planning to complete your schoolwork?			

are areas where you can improve your executive functioning to become a better student.

Now it's time to look at some practical tools that can help you achieve the success that you want. Effective planning and time management make all the difference in academic success. These are tools that once developed will enhance your success in college and career.

Let's Get Started: Using a Planner

Why Use a Planner?

A planner will help you:

- See what your assignments are
- Organize your time more effectively
- Schedule your time for long-term assignments
- Keep track of your grades for each quarter
- Include personal, extracurricular, and family events in your time schedule

How to Make Effective Use of Your Planner

1. Fill in the subjects on the left side of your planner. Do this for the first 4 weeks of school. Be sure that you keep the subjects in the same order for every week.

> **HELPFUL HINT**
>
> If you are assigned a long-term project or paper, write in the due dates now. This will remind you of future deadlines.

2. Many of the best planners available do not list the month and the dates because it gives students more flexibility in incorporating school activities into their planning. If you have a blank planner, fill in the month and date at the top of the planner page. Do this for at least the first 4 weeks of school. Make sure that you include the weekend dates—you will have homework over the weekend. Also note any days off and mark them in your planner. Note that some comprehensive online systems have planners too, such as Naviance.
3. At the bottom of the planner sheet, write in your own activities, such as extracurricular activities, sports, and family events. Remember, you are developing time-management skills as you plan for your homework and other commitments.

> **HELPFUL HINT**
>
> You have a life outside of school and homework. Include this in your planner so you can effectively allot your time.

4. Now go to the back of the planner where you will find pages designed to help you keep track of your grades. List your classes in the appropriate column. Beneath each subject, create a section for the components of your grade such as tests, quizzes, papers, class participation, and labs. As the quarter proceeds, write down your grades in each subject. You may not be able to estimate your class participation, but this will remind you to be involved in class discussions.

> **HELPFUL HINT**
>
> You should never be surprised by your quarter grade if you keep track of your grades. Not doing so well? Ask your teacher or another student for help before you receive a low grade on your report card.

Remember to fill in the rest of the dates for your planner.

Getting Organized and Staying Organized

Organization is a vital key to academic success, so let's talk about how you organize your schoolwork.

Different subject areas demand different kinds of organization, but the common theme is that you should have the necessary materials at your fingertips. Teachers may tell you how they want your work organized. For example, your math teacher may want all of your work in one notebook.

If your teacher allows you to decide how to organize, try this method. The materials needed are

- 2-inch binder
- Dividers with pockets
- Loose leaf paper

Sample Binder

As a sample, let's organize your English and Social Studies binder.

1. First, label a divider *English*.
2. Then label dividers—class notes, homework, tests and quizzes, and handouts.
3. Place loose leaf paper in appropriate dividers.
4. For vocabulary, you may want to use index cards so that you can quiz yourself on words. You may need another divider labeled *Vocabulary*.

5. Now label a divider *Social Studies*.
6. Then label dividers—class notes, homework, test and quizzes, and handouts.
7. You may also need a divider for maps.

HELPFUL HINT

Adapt this system to each class. For example, in science class, you may need a divider for labs.

If you follow this method of organizing your materials, you should be able to find whatever you need quickly.

HELPFUL HINT

At the end of a unit or a quarter, remove materials from your binder and place them in large envelopes or file folders for future use.

You do not need to carry 2 months' worth of notes in your daily binder, but you will need this material for midterm and final exams. Make sure that you label stored material, for example, English first-quarter materials. Then store it safely in your room at home.

HELPFUL HINT

Clean out your binders regularly. You will be amazed at how many unnecessary papers you will find. They will only get in the way of your effective studying.

Who Am I as a Student? What Are My Study Skills?

Now that you have filled out your planner and organized your binders and notebooks, let's talk about you as a student.

Remember, this is your primary job: to study and to achieve as much academic success as possible.

Ask yourself:

■ Who am I as a student?
■ What are my strengths?
■ Where do I need to improve?
■ How does this fit into knowing who I am and what I want to become?

Heavy questions, but you probably know many of the answers. Sometimes we all need to stand back and look at the bigger picture in order to understand the smaller details. Reexamine your answers to the Executive Functioning Exercise (Table 4.2). They also reveal your strengths and weaknesses in study skills. Use this knowledge to help you become a better student.

Doing That Nightly Homework

You know that homework varies from night to night, but there is always something to do. But before we begin, think about the following:

- What does it mean to prioritize and how can it help you?
- What does it mean to review and why is it important?
- What is the difference between doing homework and studying?

What Does It Mean to Prioritize?

To *prioritize* is to decide which assignments are the most demanding and important to you. Look over your assignments, and decide the order in which you will do your homework.

For some suggestions about completing your daily homework, look at the exercise below to help you plan how you will approach your assignments. While it is important to decide the order of your work, you should also give yourself some short breaks (10–15 minutes).

Exercise on Prioritizing and Planning Your Work

Answer the following questions then fill in the Prioritizing Schedule (Table 4.3) to plan your work for optimal effectiveness:

What assignment is most important?
Do I have a test or quiz to prepare for?
What assignment will take the most time?

Note the difference between your estimated time and the actual time that it took you to complete your assignments. This will help you in future planning and time management.

HELPFUL HINT

Turn off your cell phone and instant messaging when doing your homework. You can use your breaks to catch up with friends, but regard the time you have slated for your schoolwork as solid—no interruptions!

Table 4.3 Prioritizing Schedule

	Assignment	Estimated Time	Actual Time
5:00			
5:30			
6:00			
6:30			
7:00			
7:30			
8:00			
8:30			
9:00			
9:30			
10:00			
10:30			

Why Is It Essential to Review?

Think of your mind as a computer. If you work on an essay on your computer and then forget to save your work, you lose it. The same is true for your memory. We all have short-term memory and long-term memory. Unlike saving on a computer, getting information into your long-term memory is not so easy, but you can incorporate many techniques into your study habits that will help you remember information.

To review means to go over. As you do your homework each evening, spend 2 minutes going over your class notes from that day. Believe it or not, these few minutes can have a great impact.

Also, once a week review your class notes in each subject—this can go a long way in improving test grades.

HELPFUL HINT

Use a highlighter to mark key ideas in your class notes when you review. Don't overhighlight, but just mark essentials. This helps to make ideas stand out in your mind.

What Is the Difference Between Homework and Studying?

You are in high school now, and more is expected of you as a student. Doing your homework is important, but it is the minimum. Studying demands review and attempting to understand the subject material as thoroughly as possible.

HELPFUL HINT

If you have a long-term assignment, break it into pieces so that it does not become overwhelming. For example, do your lab report in segments, or prepare your English essay in sections by doing the outline, then a rough draft, and a final version.

HELPFUL HINT

Leave spaces in your class notes so you can write clarifying information texts.

How to Take Good Homework Notes

Doing your homework is the best way to be prepared for class. A common assignment, especially in social studies and science, is to read and take notes on a number of pages in your textbook. Taking good notes is great preparation and will ensure that you get the most out of class the next day.

- Preview the material that you are to read. Remember that most textbooks use boldface and larger fonts to show subdivisions in the material that you will be reading.
  - Look over the assigned pages, noting any boldface subdivisions.
  - Note any individual words that are boldfaced. This tells you that these are key terms you will need to know.
- Now it's time to read. Have questions in mind as you examine the material: Think about the five W's—the who, what, where, when, and why—of the passage. It will help you to understand what you are reading.
- Most paragraphs begin with topic sentences that express the meaning of the paragraph.
  - Be aware of the meaning of each topic sentence, and then look for the supporting details that explain the topic sentence.
- Take notes as you read.
  - Use the boldface subdivisions as a way of dividing your notes.

HELPFUL HINT

You do not need to do a formal outline; instead, use spacing and indentation in your note taking.

Sample Notes on the Civil War

The North had many advantages over the South in the Civil War:

> Larger population
> Strong industrial base
> Existing government
> Existing army and navy

Taking notes this way shows the main idea of Northern advantages. Indenting points out the specific points that support the main idea.

HELPFUL HINT

Don't crowd your note taking; give yourself plenty of space. This makes it easier to review and study for exams.

Remember always to:

- Preview
- Note boldfaced subdivisions
- Be aware of boldfaced terms
- Keep the five W's in mind as you read
- Take notes using space and indentation

HELPFUL HINT

While we have been talking about note taking in social studies and science textbooks, you can adapt this method to your other subjects such as math, foreign language, and English.

Taking Notes in Class

A rule to live by: Taking notes in class is always easier if you have done your homework. This helps you to know what the teacher is going to discuss and greatly enhances your understanding of the material.

1. Have your homework on your desk so that you know the order of the material.
2. Stay focused despite distractions.
3. Listen for key phrases such as *the key significance* or *the most important*. These signal ideas you want in your notes.

4. Be aware of what the teacher writes on the board—another signal for important material.
5. If you missed an important point, note it and make sure to check with a friend after class so that you are not missing any information.

HELPFUL HINT

If the lesson is closely related to your homework, take notes directly on your homework notes. That's one of the advantages of leaving lots of space. Use a different colored pen for class notes so that you know what the teacher emphasized. Do this with your teacher's permission. Some teachers may want to look at homework separate from your class notes.

HELPFUL HINT

Always take notes in pen, not pencil. Two months from now when you are studying for a midterm exam, that pencil may have faded.

---

6. Before beginning the next day's homework, make sure that your notes are complete. Always take a few minutes to review and highlight key terms.

Preparing for Tests—Large or Small

Taking tests is a fact of academic life. Now comes "The Big *If*"—If you have done nightly and weekly review, this will be much easier for you. If you haven't, don't panic—there is still time to prepare.

Remember how we talked earlier about how to get information into your long-term memory? Well, effective review is the answer.

- How to prepare for that unit test, midterm, or final exam?
  - First of all, know what material will be on the test.
  - Organize your notes, old tests, quizzes, and relevant handouts.
- Establish a realistic time schedule for studying for your test or exam. Do not leave all of your studying until the night before the test.
- Start to review materials in realistic amounts—for example, a chapter at a time for a midterm.
  - Use a highlighter to mark key ideas.
  - Box in key terms, names, places, and events with a red pen.

Doing this method of review will help ideas stand out when you take a test.

HELPFUL HINT

Make a cover sheet for each chapter or unit. For example, for a test on the American Civil War, use a chart to mark key people, places, events, and terms. Do not identify—simply list.

After you have reviewed your notes and listed items, use the cover sheet to quiz yourself.

HELPFUL HINT

Make sure to keep cover sheets with the appropriate materials. They can be invaluable in studying for major exams such as midterm and final exams.

While the cover sheet example is for a social studies test, you can adapt this method to other subjects. List short stories, authors, themes, characters, and so forth for English and terms for science or theorems for math.

HELPFUL HINT

For some subjects it is helpful to make flash cards for vocabulary. You may want to use index cards to help you master Spanish. On each card, print the word on the front and definitions on the back. Make sure to keep cards in a labeled envelope, for example, Spanish Chapter 2 vocabulary. Store these at home or in a pocket folder in your binder.

Review, review, review is what studying is all about!

Taking Tests

Some Do's and Don'ts About Test Taking

Definitely Do:

- Get a good night's sleep and eat breakfast.
- Be conscious of time allotted for the test.
- Look over the entire exam.
- Read directions. It is important that you know what you are being asked to do. If you are uncertain, ask for clarification.

- Work systematically. Do not jump around answering questions; you may end up leaving some questions blank.
- Be aware of the number of points attached to a question. Don't spend so much time on one question that you are unable to answer others.
- Stay focused during the entire exam.

Definitely Don't:

- Stay up all night trying to cram.
- Skip reading directions because you think it may take too much time.
- Answer some questions and not others thinking that you will be able to come back to them later. This usually ends up in blank answers.
- Spend too much time on one essay question or math problem and then are unable to finish other questions.
- Rush through the exam thinking that you will have time to check your answers.
- Finish early and relax rather than checking your answers.

We all know the fable about the tortoise and the hare. Remember who wins—consistent effort is what pays off.

Chapter 5

Using Technology in the College and Career Advising Process

Memo to Counselors

In this chapter we present thinking about how the counselor and the students can use innovative technologies throughout the 4 years of the curriculum. While most of the relevant technologies will be addressed in the individual chapters, this chapter provides an overview of important big-picture ideas that are crucial to understanding how students use technology and what students will face in this postglobalized world. Specifically, counselors need to consider two overarching transformations: changes internationally and changes in our understanding of the learning process in the digital age. The challenge is not about innovation generally, but rather it is about being innovative, efficient, and thorough; this challenge applies to both the practicing counselor and the student. Next, we focus on students as the active users of the available technology tools they will use in either career or college applications. This section includes ideas on how counselors can help students optimally maximize their choices and uses of technology in the college process. We will also discuss the increasing use of online applications and advise counselors about benefits and pitfalls of this process. A final focus is to help counselors make their work less overwhelming and more productive.

The 21st Century World: Considerations for Counselors and Students

Counselors

Henry Luce once proclaimed the 20th century as the "American Century" (Baughman, 1940). China surpassed the U.S. in Internet use in 2008 (Economic

Times, 2008) and some think that the 21st century will belong to China (Kao, 2007). Clearly, other countries are catching up. As described by Wise (2008, p.15), "The rest of the world's education has improved such that today the United States is increasingly competing for what used to be our constant triumph: the high-skilled, high-paying job." Herbert (2008) addressed the toll that high schools are imposing on America's future by noting that we cannot even keep our students in school. According to his information, one-third are dropping out and half of those who remain graduate *without the skills for college or a job*. What does this mean for college advising counselors?

The challenge is for us to convey to students and their families the importance of developing skills throughout high school and of developing their understanding that the working world is more competitive than ever. First of all, counselors must be their own best advocates for the importance of structuring 9–12th grade college and career advising; they must promote their work to principals, district leaders, and most importantly, students and their families. Moreover, counselors must provide the best and most efficient counseling advising process possible *throughout* the 4 years of high school. Finally, they must do everything possible to bring families into this communication loop.

Making our work on college and career advising more visible is critical in order to gain support from our leaders and have better interaction with students and parents. Technology can play a key role here by enabling us to reach students, parents, and principals. While there are many forms of media that can be used, they can all become part of an interactive Web site. A section of the School Web site should be devoted to the school counseling department; or counseling departments in schools that use a software management system (e.g., Naviance) can promote their work via that system Web site. Such a system will be described in more detail later in this chapter. The Web site should be advertised and it should be interactive. It could include:

- Multimedia presentations (MMP) on anything from how to start the college process to a list of best study skills for A.P. classes and exams could be made available.
- Articles of interest to parents and students on careers including, for example, data from the Occupational Outlook Handbook (OOH) http://www.bls.gov/oco/, could be made available.
- Biweekly short articles from the counselor's office on some relevant topic in college or career advising could begin to draw an audience to the site.
- Videotapes of important missed meetings (e.g., the first junior parent night on financial planning) can be uploaded to the Web site or can be developed in DVDs to be handed out to parents and students.
- The Web site can be made accessible to other counselors and educators thereby sharing best practices among peers and promoting any clear programs we have effectively used to help our students succeed.

Reaching out through the digital world to our constituencies (students, families, counselors, school and district leaders), and using it to convey our most creative and important ideas for our students and their families is crucial to their belief in the value of our work. It promotes us as powerfully embracing the 21st century world that we propose as so important for our students. We must be very smart in our choices to make sure they will be effective in targeting our audience, effective in helping us become more efficient in our work, and effective in promoting our image as leading an office that is integrally involved within the school community in promoting the vision of academic and personal growth.

Student Learning

We have to be more creative in guiding the learning process about colleges and postsecondary careers because students have to learn more every day and have to be open to a much broader and more complex variety of careers. To find out about a college's requirements, in the mid-1990s students had to learn so much less than what high school students today have to know. Taking in all this information and developing a knowledge base, however, can be much richer and therefore more easily learned because of technological advances and creative ways of representing information. The Internet has it all, right? College video? Semester abroad? Financial aid? Scholarships? Well, not so fast.

Students may be great users of the Internet, but surfing the Internet is not the same as being disciplined and organized in gaining information from the Internet. Kids are great recreational users of the Internet, but they are not academic users. Today, most colleges provide in-depth opportunities to learn not only about their campus look, majors, and weekend events but also, for example, about what college faculty are researching, how accessible the faculty are to students, and student evaluations of faculty. Since college is becoming an increasingly more expensive venture, it is imperative that students maximize their opportunities. That starts with good, solid exploration and considered thinking.

Considering these two themes, the changing global world and the increased complexity in student learning, counselors must keep the following in mind:

- Students need to learn about themselves and to develop their desires by exploring colleges and careers; such explorations should be made into projects, be very focused, in-depth, and involve critical thinking.
- Students' early exposure to college and career information from the Internet will help them develop stronger achievement motivation.
- Counselors should develop their own expertise in understanding the range and competitiveness of careers in the 21st century.
- Counselors must take some responsibility for teaching students to be strong researchers of the Internet.

Maximizing Opportunities for College and Careers Through the Use of Technology

Next, we focus on the student as the active user of the available technological tools they will use in either career or college applications. This section includes ideas on how counselors can help students optimally maximize their *choices* and *uses* of technology in the college process.

First and foremost, providing motivating experiences from 9th grade on is key in helping students maximize their opportunities. Of particular note are the following:

1. Explore financial aid and scholarships early in the process. If students know what kinds of grades and scores will enable them to get scholarships and grants, they have more incentive to do well academically. FinAid.org and FastWeb.com are two sample sites.
2. Plan a specific process for college and career exploration, and start early (9th grade). Have students keep electronic folders of each of their college and career explorations—year to year.
3. Plan specific learning sessions on Web searching regarding standardized testing. Provide such exposure early in the 9–12 process, and use *improvement* as a motivator.
4. Plan a specific process and activity for online applications. Too many students want to engage in the "I don't need to review my application" syndrome. Others ignore requests for forms to be filled out by counselors or teachers.
5. Infuse into practice a comprehensive technology support system for use by students to accomplish the above goals and to organize their work.

The following systems are offered as potential choices for school use.

Naviance

Naviance (see Additional Resources) is a leading provider of planning and advising systems for secondary schools. Nearly 100,000 educators and counselors serving more than 5.0 million students in schools across the United States and in 72 other countries use Naviance products to manage academic and postsecondary advising, to communicate with students and families, and to analyze data. Palos Verdes Peninsula High School named Naviance the 2010 Innovative Program of the Year (Naviance, 2010).

WorkspaceK12, a subsection of Naviance devoted to students and their families, includes a powerful Web service. Known as Family Connection, this service provides extensive, advertising-free services that each school can customize to meet its own unique needs. Here are just a few things schools can do with Family Connection:

- Conduct custom online surveys of parents and students
- Publish scholarship information and matching tools

- Post a schedule of visits by college representatives
- Share personalized status information about college applications
- Maintain a journal of interactions with parents and students
- Build multiyear plans and accept online course requests
- Provide online personality and career assessments
- Help students explore career options

Naviance is an expensive system that comprehensively meets all the needs for students as described above and includes a thorough, organized system for counselors and schools.

College Board

The College Board (see Additional Resources) is a not-for-profit membership association to connect students to college success and opportunity. Founded in 1900, the association is composed of more than 5,400 schools, colleges, universities, and other educational organizations. Each year, the College Board serves 7 million students and their parents, 23,000 high schools, and 3,500 colleges through major programs and services in college admissions, guidance, assessment, financial aid, enrollment, and teaching and learning. Among its best-known programs are the Scholastic Aptitude Test (SAT), the Preliminary SAT (PSAT)/National Merit Scholarship Qualifying Test (NMSQT®), and the Advanced Placement Program. The College Board is committed to the principles of excellence and equity, and this commitment is embodied in all of its programs, services, activities, and concerns. The Web site has specific sections available for students, parents, and professionals including counselors. It has sections that deal specifically with each academic year. For example, below is their listing for the sophomore year.

Plan for the Year Ahead
- Meet with your counselor to discuss your college plans. Review your schedule with him or her to make sure you're enrolled in challenging classes that will help you prepare for college. Colleges prefer 4 years of English, history, math, science, and a foreign language.
- Start a calendar with important dates and deadlines.
- Get more involved with your extracurricular activities.
- Use College Search to find out the required courses and tests of colleges that you might be interested in attending.
- Go to college fairs in your area.

Consider Taking the PSAT/NMSQT
- Sign up for the PSAT/NMSQT, which is given in October. Ask your counselor which date is offered at your school. Get free online PSAT/NMSQT practice.
- If you're taking the PSAT/NMSQT check *yes* for Student Search Service to hear about colleges and scholarships.

The College Board maps out the years for each student and focuses primarily on college and testing. Through its QuickStart and MyRoad programs, students are able to begin both college and career research and exploration. The service is free, unlike Naviance. There are real differences in terms of what the technologies offer and what is the primary focus. Naviance has a capacity to reach down to middle school data.

The ACT

The ACT® (see Additional Resources, http://www.act.org/aap) test (formerly called the American College Test Program) assesses high school students' general educational development and their ability to complete college-level work. Unlike the SAT, the ACT is a curriculum-based test that measures competence in four areas: English, mathematics, reading comprehension, and science. The writing test, which is optional, measures skills in planning and writing a short essay. Every 3 to 5 years, ACT conducts the ACT National Curriculum Survey initiative to ensure its curriculum-based assessment tools accurately measure the skills high school teachers teach and instructors of entry-level college courses expect. The ACT offers a variety of programs for parents, students, school administrators, and counselors, including the following:

■ ACT's College Readiness Test is for 8th and 9th graders.
■ The EXPLORE® program is designed to help 8th and 9th graders explore a broad range of options for their future. EXPLORE prepares students not only for their high school coursework but for their post–high school choices as well.
■ The PLAN® program helps 10th graders build a solid foundation for future academic and career success and provides information needed to address school districts' high-priority issues.
■ The QualityCore® instructional improvement program, designed to help ensure that the outcomes of high school preparatory courses are aligned with essential postsecondary skills, has shown that performance on the ACT is directly related to first-year college grade point average.
■ The College Readiness Standards Information Services offer a variety of report packages that allow schools to compare students' performance with that of others nationwide and to make decisions about students' future academic growth.
■ The WorkKeys System connects work skills, training, and testing for education and employers.
■ ACT's EPAS®, Educational Planning and Assessment System, was developed in response to the need for all students to be prepared for high school and the transitions they make after graduation. The EPAS system provides a longitudinal, systematic approach to educational and career planning, assessment, instructional support, and evaluation. The system focuses on the

integrated, higher-order thinking skills students develop in grades K–12 that are important for success both during and after high school.

Unlike the College Board, the ACT services require fees.

The Common Application

The Common Application (see Additional Resources, https:commonapp.org/ CommonApp/default.aspx) Membership Association was established in 1975 by 15 private colleges that wished to provide a common, standardized first-year application form for use at any member institution. With the administrative support of the National Association of Secondary School Principals (NASSP), the organization grew steadily throughout its first 30 years. Now in its fourth decade, the Common Application currently provides both online and print versions of its first-year and transfer applications. Their membership of nearly 400 institutions now represents the full range of higher education institutions in the United States: public and private; large and small; highly selective and modestly selective; and East Coast, West Coast, and every region in between.

The Common Application online is a powerful tool for students. If students are applying to colleges on the Common Application, they may use the online version to research and compare colleges and to prepare and submit their actual applications and supplements. In addition, most member colleges accept application fees through this Web site. Students simply create an account by supplying a user name and a password. Once this account has been established, they can use the search engine to research colleges and create a list of saved colleges that interest them. Students may also use the search engine to compare colleges on the Common Application. A list of My Colleges is automatically created, and students may then add or delete schools to their list. By clicking on a college on this list, students can easily see where they are in the application process. User-friendly symbols ascertain whether or not applications or supplements have been submitted. In addition, commonapp.org has an information bar that provides deadlines for submission, tests required, supplemental forms if necessary, and fee payment information—all of which may be completed online at this one Web site.

Counselor-O-Matic—Princeton Review

The Counselor-O-Matic Princeton Review (see Additional Resources) begins its commitment to student success on the student's first day of school, continuing through high school graduation and beyond. It uses formative assessments and research-based interventions to help students succeed. It evaluates students' chances for getting into various schools and provides a list of schools in three categories: good match, safety, and reach. It also provides a service to colleges looking for certain students. An online review of the Counselor-O-Matic tools is also available (see Counselor-O-Matic review in Additional Resources). The service is free.

For Counselors: Infusing Technology Professionally to Further Student Success in College and Career Choice Decisions

College admissions and career readiness advising is one of the most important responsibilities of counselors, yet many feel overworked and overwhelmed and thus find this important work to be their least enjoyed professional responsibility. Moreover, counselors find little support from the broader school community in understanding the high demands related to this kind of work.

Thus, counselors may be less likely to step forward to learn technologies that would ultimately make their work more efficient, thorough, and organized, thereby providing better services to their students. Likewise, counselors often will not advocate for and present the big picture of a 9–12 curriculum-based process that ultimately will impact positively all the other activities of a school's community academically. Yet the National School Counselor Standards indicate that this is exactly what we must do (ASCA National Model, 2005). Optimizing the role of technology in the everyday life of counselors is crucial in enabling counselors, particularly those in urban schools with large counselor–student ratios, to better serve their students and to feel they have control over their own professional life (Fitzpatrick & Lienert, 2009). The following sites are potential choices for aiding counselors in the development of a technologically enriched and organized office:

1. National Association for College Admission Counseling (NACAC) (see NACAC for counselors in Additional Resources). NACAC is the major organization linking the college admissions counselors to high school college advisors. It has striven to provide professionalism and inclusivity in the admission of the counseling field throughout its history. NACAC is committed to educating students, their families, the public, other education professionals, and themselves about the transition to and within postsecondary education. This organization makes every effort to practice professionalism and inclusion in the admission of the counseling field. The Web site is a wonderful source for new and upcoming changes that impact this process.

2. Naviance (see Naviance for counselors in Additional Resources). Naviance is a top provider of planning and advising systems for secondary schools. Naviance dedicates a personal support representative for each client and offers regional and on-site training options. Naviance is the most powerful online professional community of counselors with resources for counselors, teachers, administrators, students, and parents. It allows for counselors to provide customized secondary school reports, tracking transcripts and grades, and most importantly it can interact with the school's data system.

3. The American School Counselor Association (ASCA) (see Additional Resources). ASCA has created the National Model, which outlines a comprehensive, data-driven school counseling program to benefit students. School counselors create individualized activities to assist students in creating personal goals and in developing plans for the future.

4. The College Board (see College Board for counselors in Additional Resources). The College Board Web site provides tools that enable school counselors to have access to important dates and deadlines for the PSAT and SAT tests. This Web site includes links to hundreds of workshops with important information on programs, tools, and services that help prepare students for college success. The mission of the College Board Web site is reflected in their College Readiness System. This system serves to connect students to college success and opportunity, with a commitment to excellence and equity in education.

There are also many sites that directly relate to helping students with their college research work and their application process. Some sites include essay writing help and finding scholarships, among others. The following examples are listed in the Additional Resources section:

1. **College Admission Essay.** (http://www.college-admission-essay.com/comprehensive.html) This Web site matches applicants with writing specialists who guide them through every facet of the essay writing process. For students who are having trouble starting their essay, this Web site will help them brainstorm on essay topics as well as edit the final draft. Correspondence between the writer and the applicant occurs over the telephone or e-mail. This Web site also provides a detailed description of popular colleges, allowing the student to get a more personal feel of the college.

2. **Quintessential Careers.** (http://www.quintcareers.com/college-application-essay.html) This Web site is a how-to on college essay writing incorporated in a career readiness site. Students are able to tackle their application essay in three easy steps: brainstorming, selecting an essay topic, and tips for writing a successful essay. This Web site also includes links to financial aid resources, standardized testing resources, and overall college planning advice.

3. **College Admissions Essays.** (http://www.collegeadmissionsessays.com) This site gives the student tips and advice that can help them convey themselves as an intelligent, motivated, interesting person. The site instructs the student to first decide on a theme and then lists some questions the student should ask themselves. The site also gives ideas for essay topics and tells the student what colleges really want to see—and in the end, that is the "real you."

For some other well-known and useful scholarship Web sites, see the following in Additional Resources:

1. Fastweb
2. Mach 25
3. Scholarship Resource Network (SRN) Express
4. College Board Scholarship Search

The role of technology, both positively and negatively, in the education of the 21st century student has been well documented (e.g., Brooks, 2008; Fitzpatrick & Mucciardi, 2005). Indeed, Thomas Friedman, in *The World Is Flat*, raises many concerns about the need to apply such technologies effectively for our children to compete in the global world (Friedman, 2005). We are at the tipping point of figuring out how to optimize learning, including cognitive processing of our students through technology (Fitzpatrick, 2008). We must apply the same principles and research findings to our work as counselors so as to optimize our work, our attitude, and our satisfaction in knowing we have provided one of the most critical services in the developing lives of high school students.

Chapter 6

Motivation and Testing: Learning About Standardized Testing and Using It to Get Motivated About the College Process (10th–11th Grades)

Memo to Counselors

In this chapter, we first present recent work on developing motivation to do well on standardized assessments that influence students' post–high school goals. Researchers have found that unmotivated students do not perform as well on standardized tests. (Lack of understanding about how these assessments influence their future has been cited by Siegal, 2006.) We hope to assist you in presenting standardized testing as a means of motivating students to begin the college and career search. We discuss the Preliminary Scholastic Aptitude Test (PSAT) format, methods of preparation, scoring, and uses of test results for the National Merit Scholarship Program. We also compare the SAT and ACT programs and present useful advice to assist you in advising students about test choices. Should your school offer the PSAT only in 11th grade, you can easily adapt this to the junior year curriculum. If you are in a school that asks students to register with you to take the PSAT, we encourage you to be proactive in recruiting all students to take the PSAT so that they may see this test as the first step in planning their collegiate career.

Motivation

There is no question that standardized testing has continued to be a critical part of college-related work with high school students. Though in recent years several very competitive schools have not required SATs or ACTs, the fact is that most schools do consider it. Additionally, the PSAT's use as a factor in the National Merit Scholarship Competition suggests that it too has remained an important measure in many colleges' determination of who are the best high school students. Indeed, it has been suggested that there is more pressure, particularly among the most selective schools, to approach the admissions process from a very formulaic perspective. Leana (2009), writing in the *Journal for College Admissions*, attributes this formulaic perspective to pressure from boards of trustees to improve college ranks as well as to the sheer increase in numbers of applications. He points out that in 2007 applications to colleges increased somewhere between 8% and 30%. For example, Boston College reviewed 30,000 applications. Leana suggests that these factors have contributed to a more numerical approach to college admissions and a loss of the more creative surprise and imagination that used to characterize college admissions. Testing as a part of the high school–college application process is not going to go away. Accordingly, we need to become even more creative in helping students become more motivated in their practice for and in their desire to perform well in these assessments.

How can we help students be more motivated in their test taking? We have no doubt you already have some tried and true methods. What we hope to do in this chapter is offer a few you might not have considered. From a brief review of early and recent research on achievement, performance, and motivation, we advance some thinking. Wanting to achieve and what affects achievement have been researched extensively by Elliott and Dweck (1988). They showed that performance goals and learning goals affect achievement situations. Performance-goal-oriented individuals seek out positive judgment of their abilities (study to do well) while learning-goal-oriented individuals seek to increase their ability to master new tasks (learn something new for the sake of learning). Elliott and Dweck's research supports an approach to achievement behavior that emphasizes learning and performance achievement goals as the critical determinants of different achievement patterns. Some students do well on the SATs because they are performance oriented, while others might not do well because they see the SATs as unrelated to learning. If students could understand that just as one practices a sport to do well in games, one could practice the skills required of SAT takers.

Bandura's work provides another perspective. He found that self-efficacy or the belief in one's possession of and ability to access and use skills needed to accomplish a task is based on feedback that is received from significant others. Individuals obtain their *most powerful feedback* through enactive mastery or their ability to perform a task successfully (Bandura, 1986). Students may enhance their enactive mastery by performing well on tasks embedded within regular instruction that are similar to the test or on prior simulations of the test. This may sound like "teaching to the test," but it can be effective. There is no question—Bandura would agree.

Other research has found that student perceptions of high-stakes tests and their performance can vary by grade level (Wheelock, Bebell, & Haney, 2000a, 2000b). Wheelock et al. (2000a, 2000b) analyzed elementary and secondary students' drawings created shortly after high-stakes testing in Massachusetts. They found that approximately 40% of the 411 student self-portraits reflected either the students' willingness to comply with test demands without comment or their positive perceptions of the test and their confidence in their ability to perform successfully. However, the other 60% produced pictures that reflected anxiety, anger, pessimism, boredom, or loss of motivation as a result of their participation in the high-stakes testing. More importantly, Wheelock et al. (2000a) determined that these negative emotions were confined primarily to secondary students in the sample. Thus, somewhere between elementary school and high school, students in that sample become more negative about standardized testing.

Motivating students can be challenging, then, especially when dealing with high-stakes testing situations. Hoffman and Nottis (2008) designed a pilot of suburban, middle school students' strategies that helped them when taking a high-stakes test. They asked 8th graders: "What strategies do students perceive as influential in motivating them during a high-stakes testing situation?" (Hoffman & Nottis, 2008, p. 212). Of the 215 student participants from a suburban, mid-Atlantic state, 109 were males and 106 were female. A 20-item questionnaire with a 5-choice Likert scale was given to the students 2 weeks after taking a high-stakes test. Additionally, students were asked to write a letter to their principal with their thoughts on students' success on the test. The results from this study indicated that students were most motivated by extrinsic rewards, such as a promised grade-level picnic that followed the testing period. In addition, students were least motivated by student government announcements and posters (Hoffman & Nottis, 2008). Of course, these were 8th graders, not high school students, but a point can be taken from this study. Reinforcement and rewards work.

Lastly, Chan, Schmitt, DeShon, Clause, and Delbridge (1997) explored, among other constructs, test motivation and test performance in college freshmen. Similar to the Hoffman and Nottis (2008) work, they found that an extrinsic reward produced a better performance on a subsequent similar test. In other words, rewards work even for college students. Also, they found a direct link to performance on the tests and a perception that the content of a test is directly related to the content of a job or career. Researchers call it *face validity*.

So, what can we suggest from these findings as further ideas for motivating students to work harder in practice for and in performing on important standardized tests?

■ Individuals obtain their *most powerful feedback* through enactive mastery, or their ability to perform a task successfully; providing opportunities for embedding test type exercises in academic work is effective and should be encouraged.

- Counselors should recognize that students lose interest in doing well on standardized tests in high school; find creative ways to enable them to see the connection between the skills they master on these tests and the skills needed in college and beyond.
- Students are motivated by extrinsic rewards; try including ones for classes or groups of students (e.g., a free pizza lunch if 40% of the juniors show up and score at a certain level on a practice PSAT).
- Relating the SATs or the ACTs to the real world of careers is critical; engage them in understanding what is developed through practice on these tests. For example, review with them the skills of a broadcaster, including possessing a large vocabulary, reading quickly and accurately, etc.

Memo to Counselor

What follows is the curriculum section of this chapter, in the voice of the counselor speaking to students.

Initial Session with Students

In mid-October, you will be taking the PSAT/NMSQT (National Merit Scholarship Qualifying Test), and believe it or not, you are in the first step of the college process. Check with your counselor to make sure that you are registered for the PSAT.

It is essential that you understand why standardized testing is important and how it can affect your academic future. Most colleges want standardized test scores because these are one part of a picture of who you are as a student. Colleges need to see these scores because they want to know that you are capable of the work they will demand. The two commonly accepted tests for college entrance are the SAT and the ACT. At this point, we will focus on the SAT because it has a preliminary exam known as the PSAT, which you will be taking in a few weeks. The PSAT/NMSQT measures the skills that you have developed over the course of your education. These include skills in critical reading, math problem solving, and writing.

Good performance on this test requires practice and dedication to your goal of presenting the best picture of yourself to a college. Think of yourself as an athlete, a dancer, a musician, an artist—success is achieved through hard work and practice. It is no different for you as a student entering the world of standardized testing.

The PSAT/NMSQT

Officially, the PSAT/NMSQT (see College Board in Additional Resources) is given in the fall of your junior year. So why take this test as a sophomore? Taking the

PSAT now gives you the experience of sitting for a national exam. Once you receive your scores, you will understand what areas of the test need greater focus and study. You will also receive personalized feedback on your skill strengths and weaknesses and be able to compare your scores with those of other college-bound students around the country. Since the PSAT/NMSQT is the best preparation for the SAT, by taking the test before 11th grade, you have more time to develop your skills and to begin preparing for the SAT, which uses similar questions and directions. Also, you will now be qualified to use the College Board's MyRoad to explore career possibilities and the QuickStart program to begin college research. (More about these programs is included in Chapters 7 and 8.)

How to Prepare for the PSAT/NMSQT

Familiarize yourself with the five sections of the test, covering three areas of testing:

- Two sections of critical reading, which include sentence completion and reading comprehension.
- Two sections of mathematics. You may use a calculator. Make sure that you bring an approved calculator to the test—one that you are familiar using! Approved calculators generally include four-function calculators, scientific calculators, and graphing calculators.
- One section of writing skills, which measures your ability to determine correct language usage and expression.

There is no essay on the PSAT.

Use *The Official Student Guide to the PSAT* provided by the College Board to take practice questions in each area. This will help you to become familiar with the exact kinds of questions that you will be asked. The College Board also provides a free online service where students can answer questions in each area of the test. Go to the College Board's PSAT practice test page (www.collegeboard.com/student/testing/psat/prep.html) (see Additional Resources). Following the links at this Web site will lead you to questions, answers, and explanations for all five sections of the PSAT.

Taking a practice test should be your first step. Make sure that you time yourself for each section. Plan to take it on a day that you have enough time to complete an entire test. Turn off your cell phone and do not let anyone bother you. Don't eat during the test. After taking a practice test, complete the chart in Table 6.1. This will give you an initial indication of your strengths and weaknesses on this test.

Remember that you are just beginning to prepare for the PSAT. When you receive your actual PSAT score report, you will also receive detailed information about your performance as well as be able to view the actual test online. Your counselor will also give you a hard copy of your test booklet so that you may look at questions that you missed on the PSAT.

Table 6.1   Your Results on the Initial Practice PSAT

	# of Questions	# of Correct Answers	# of Omitted Answers
Critical Reading			
Sentence Completions			
Reading Comprehension			
Mathematics			
Algebra			
Data			
Geometry			
Number			
Writing Skills			
Improving Sentences			
Sentence Errors			
Improving Paragraphs			

How PSATs Are Scored

Questions range from easy to medium to hard. However, despite the difficulty level, each question is worth 1 point. There is no penalty for blank or omitted answers—for not answering a question; however, a one-quarter of a point penalty is taken for each wrong answer, excluding the student-produced answers in the math section. Although there is no penalty for leaving questions blank, you should try to answer as many questions as possible in order to achieve a better score. Never randomly guess, but if you can eliminate two or three possibilities, you are not guessing and should try to answer the question.

The raw scores from each of the three sections—Critical Reading, Mathematics, and Writing Skills—are then converted into scores ranging from 20 to 80. This converted score is what is reported as your score on your PSAT Score Sheet.

Table 6.2 contains some useful information for counselors prior to the administration of the PSAT.

PSAT scores are reported on a scale of 20 to 80. In 2006, the average score for 11th graders was about 48 in Critical Reading, 49 in Mathematics, and 46 in Writing Skills. The average score for 10th graders was about 43 in Critical Reading, 44 in Mathematics, and 41 in Writing Skills.

Beneath your scores are two boxes showing the range of your scores and the place of your score in a national percentile. These national percentiles allow you to compare your scores with other students in your grade level who

Table 6.2 Tips for Counselors

What to Do Prior to the PSAT
■ Go over PSAT practice questions.
■ Have students fill in the required biographical information on the PSAT Answer Sheet. This is somewhat time-consuming but can make the actual testing easier for many students.
■ When filling out the Answer Sheet, advise students to check the appropriate boxes to participate in the National Merit Scholarship Competitions.
■ Help students answer the Student Descriptive Questionnaire. Many students are confused by some of these questions.
■ Advise students about which calculators are approved.
■ Identify and meet with students with disabilities regarding their accommodations.
■ Remind students about #2 pencils.

have taken the PSAT/NMSQT. If you take the PSAT/NMSQT in the 11th grade, you receive junior percentiles. If you take the PSAT/NMSQT in 10th grade or younger, you will receive sophomore percentiles. For example, a student in 11th grade with a percentile of 55 has earned a score better than 55% of all 11th graders.

You will also receive your Selection Index in the upper right-hand side of the Score Report. The Selection Index is used to determine eligibility in the National Merit Scholarship Corporation (NMSC) programs. It is the sum of the scores in each of the three test sections. The Selection Index ranges from 60 to 240. The average Selection Index for students in 11th grade is about 147. Note: Only students in 11th grade are eligible to enter NMSC programs.

Student Descriptive Questionnaire and Student Search Service

The Student Descriptive Questionnaire is a great way to receive information from many colleges. When you take the PSAT, you will fill out a Student Descriptive Questionnaire. The answers to this questionnaire provide the Student Search Service with a way of introducing you to colleges that will then send you information about their schools, scholarship services, and financial aid. To participate, indicate "yes" to the Student Search Service on the registration form. The Student Search Service will use the information from your Student Descriptive Questionnaire through December of your senior year.

Student Search Service does not report your scores to colleges or scholarship services. The following information about you is sent to colleges, universities, and scholarship programs:

```
* Name
* Address
* Sex
* Birth date
* School
* Grade level
* Ethnic identification (if provided)
* Intended college major (if provided)
```

Colleges, universities, and scholarship programs sponsored by government and nonprofit organizations that use the Student Search Service receive your name and address if you have, for example, a specific grade average, score range, or intended major or if you live in a particular state or zip code. All who receive information from the Student Search Service are required to maintain strict confidentiality. The College Board and ETS (Educational Testing Service) actively review all uses to ensure adherence to guidelines.

How PSAT Scores Are Reported

In approximately mid-December, your scores will be reported to your school. Your counselor will then give you your score report.

This score report will give your answers in each category, the correct answer, and the level of difficulty of each question (easy, medium, hard). The score report will also show if you omitted a question. You will also receive your scores in each category at the top of the page.

How to Interpret the Scores and Make Them Work for You

The most important part of the PSAT test *process* is that you will learn what your strengths and weaknesses are. Then it becomes easier to prepare for both the PSAT and the SAT that you may take in your junior year. At the bottom of the Score Sheet, you will find the number of questions that you answered correctly in each area of testing: Critical Reading, Mathematics, and Writing Skills. Included here will also be a breakdown of whether the questions were easy, medium, or hard. You will also see the number of questions that you omitted in each category. Note the pattern of omitted answers. Did you not complete some sections? You may need to work on your pacing when taking the test.

Let's look at your subtest scores. Using your copy of the PSAT that your counselor has returned to you and your Score Sheet, analyze your performance in the three areas of testing.

1. Critical Reading. How did you do in the Critical Reading? Remember that this section has two components: sentence completions and reading comprehension. How many blanks or errors did you have in the Sentence Completion section? Look at the vocabulary in this section. Whether you had a correct or wrong answer or left the question blank, make a list of the vocabulary words that you do not know. Making flashcards for these words is a great way to increase your vocabulary. Note how many errors or blanks you had in the Passage-Based Reading section. You may want to review reading comprehension techniques such as the following:

   a. Underline topic sentences in your reading (main ideas questions).
   b. Look for details that support or develop the main idea (detail questions).
   c. Circle the vocabulary word in vocabulary-in-context questions where a word may have a slightly different twist in the passage.
   d. Be aware of which questions are inferential—where you interpret what you have read—words such as *suggest, imply,* and *infer* are usually the verbs in these questions.

2. Mathematics. Four areas of math are tested on the PSAT: Number and Operations; Algebra and Functions; Geometry and Measurement; and Data Analysis, Statistics, and Probability. Looking at your score sheet, see what kinds of questions you left blank or where you entered a wrong answer. Next to each answer is the content area tested. By analyzing questions by content area, you will know what you need to review or learn. If you are a 10th-grade student, you may have not yet had enough geometry to answer many of these questions.

3. Writing Skills. This section tests three areas of English usage: Improving Sentences, Identifying Sentence Errors, and Improving Paragraphs. Look at your answer sheet. Where did you make mistakes? You may need to review some basic rules of grammar: subject–verb agreement, correct use of adjectives and adverbs, correct tense, pronoun usage and reference, and so forth.

Complete Table 6.3 to help you understand your performance on the PSAT. After completing this table, use a highlighter to mark the areas where you need improvement. This can be a guide in your test preparation.

Practice can help you improve your scores, especially if you know which of the three areas was most difficult for you. Go to the College Board's PSAT Web site for more practice questions. You can also visit the College Board's SAT Web site (see Additional Resources) for the SAT Question of the Day.

Other Important Information About the PSAT/NMSQT

So far, we have talked about the PSAT itself. Now let's take a look at those other letters in its name.

Table 6.3   PSAT Performance Exercise

	# of Questions	# of Correct Answers	# of Omitted Answers
Critical Reading			
Sentence Completions			
Reading Comprehension			
Mathematics			
Algebra			
Data			
Geometry			
Number			
Writing Skills			
Improving Sentences			
Sentence Errors			
Improving Paragraphs			

What Is the NMSQT or the National Merit Scholarship Program?

The National Merit Scholarship Program (www.nationalmerit.org/nmsp.php see Additional Resources) is an academic competition for recognition and scholarships that began in 1955. High school students enter the National Merit Scholarship Program by taking the PSAT/NMSQT in their junior year. You must be enrolled full time as a high school student, progressing normally toward graduation or completion of high school, and planning to enroll full time in college no later than the fall following completion of high school. Students must also be citizens of the United States or U.S. lawful permanent residents (or have applied for permanent residence, the application for which has not been denied) and intend to become a U.S. citizen at the earliest opportunity allowed by law.

In your junior year, simply fill in the appropriate boxes in the PSAT Answer Sheet to participate in the competition.

Program Recognition — Of the 1.4 million entrants, some 50,000 with the highest PSAT/NMSQT Selection Index scores (Critical Reading + Mathematics + Writing Skills scores) qualify for recognition in the National Merit Scholarship Program. When you receive your Score Sheet, you will see your Selection Index Score in the upper right-hand side of the sheet. The National Merit Scholarship Program uses a state-by-state *Index Cutoff*, which specifies the score students need to earn on the PSAT. A selection index of 221 would be equivalent to earning a

730 or 740 on each of the three (Critical Reading, Math, and Writing Skills) sub-tests on the SAT Reasoning Test. Since all 50 states must have National Merit semifinalists, the Selection Index Score varies from state to state. More about this in the "Semifinalists" section below. In April following the fall test administration, high-scoring participants from every state are invited to name two colleges or universities to which they would like to be referred by NMSC. In September, these high scorers are notified through their schools that they have qualified as either a commended student or a semifinalist.

Commended Students — In late September, more than two-thirds, or about 34,000, of the approximately 50,000 high scorers on the PSAT/NMSQT receive Letters of Commendation in recognition of their outstanding academic promise. Commended students are named on the basis of a nationally applied Selection Index Score that may vary from year to year and is below the level required for participants to be named semifinalists in their respective states. Although commended students do not continue in the competition for Merit Scholarship awards, some of these students do become candidates for special scholarships sponsored by corporations and businesses.

Semifinalists — In early September, about 16,000 students, or approximately one-third, of the 50,000 high scorers are notified that they have qualified as semifinalists. To ensure that academically able young people from all parts of the United States are included in this talent pool, semifinalists are designated on a state representational basis. They are the top 1% of highest scoring entrants in each state. Consequently, the Selection Index Number varies from state to state. To see a complete listing of the Selection Indexes for 2010 and 2011, visit www.collegeplanningsimplified.com/NationalMerit.html. (See Reference pages) The National Merit Scholarship Corporation also lists the number of students entering the scholarship competition and those receiving recognition by state. See page 9 of the Annual Report for a complete listing at www.nationalmerit.org/nmsp.php. (See Reference pages.)

 NMSC provides scholarship application materials to semifinalists through their high schools. To be considered for a Merit Scholarship Award, semifinalists must advance to finalist standing in the competition by meeting high academic standards and all other requirements explained in the materials provided to each semifinalist.

Finalists — In February, some 15,000 semifinalists are notified by mail at their home addresses that they have advanced to finalist standing. High school principals are notified and provided with a certificate to present to each finalist. A total of 8,200 finalists are notified at their home that they have been awarded a National Merit Scholarship. These awards consist of three types: a one-time $2500

National Merit Scholarship, corporate-sponsored Merit Scholarship awards, and college-sponsored Merit Scholarships.

Two Other Important Awards Granted by the National Merit Program

- The National Achievement Scholarship Program honors approximately 4,600 Black American high school students. A total of 700 finalists are awarded National Achievement $2500 scholarships.
- The National Hispanic Recognition Program honors approximately 3,300 of the highest scoring students taking the PSAT/NMSQT who designated themselves as Hispanic (must be at least one-quarter Hispanic). While there is no monetary award to this recognition, an important component of the program is the CD-ROM distributed to subscribing 4-year postsecondary institutions. This CD-ROM lists the names of all students selected in the program and is mailed in September to these subscribing colleges and universities. Being listed may give students an opportunity to hear from colleges that are particularly interested in communicating with prospective students of Hispanic heritage.

Students may participate in more than one competition but may receive only one monetary award.

Two Other Ways That Taking the PSAT Can Help You: My College QuickStart and MyRoad

My College QuickStart and MyRoad (quickstart.collegeboard.com and myroad. collegeboard.com see Additional Resources) are free personalized college and career-planning programs provided by the College Board. This is a great opportunity for you to begin your college search using the resources of the College Board. We will talk about these programs at greater length in Chapters 7 and 8, but for now we will look at how QuickStart can help you improve your test scores.

To begin, you will need to log on at College Board's PSAT site. Using the access code printed on your PSAT/NMSQT paper Score Report, you will be prompted to create a College Board account if you do not currently have one. It typically takes less than 2 minutes to create your free account.

My College QuickStart includes the following features that can be helpful in understanding your strengths and weaknesses in your test performance:

- My Online Score Report—An enhanced Score Report that allows you to review each test question, your answer, and the correct answer with answer explanations.
- My SAT Study Plan—A customized SAT study plan based on your PSAT/NMSQT test performance, highlighting skills for review and practice.

QuickStart is a great way to prepare for future tests.

Memo to Counselors

After students take the PSAT in mid-October, present the materials about the SAT Reasoning Test, the SAT Subject Tests, and the ACT. This material may be adapted to either 10th or 11th grade counseling sessions.

The two college entrance exams are the SAT and the ACT. In 2010, 1.2 million students took the ACT, and 1.4 million took the SAT (Kaplan, 2010). Most colleges and universities accept both tests, but it is always wise to check the Web sites of the schools to which you may apply. Let's look at the differences between these examinations. This is the first step in deciding which exam is right for you.

The SAT Reasoning Test

The SAT Reasoning Test (see College Board in Additional Resources) is a widely used admissions test among colleges and universities. It tests students' knowledge of subjects that are necessary for college success: reading, writing, and mathematics. The SAT assesses the critical thinking skills students need for academic success in college—skills that students learned in high school. The SAT is typically taken by students in spring of their junior year and then again in fall of their senior year. The test is administered seven times a year in the United States, Puerto Rico, and U.S. territories and six times a year overseas.

You are responsible for registering for the SAT Reasoning Test. This can easily be done online by going to the College Board Web site. You are also responsible for reporting your scores to the colleges and scholarship programs to which you apply. Remember that once you have taken a test, that score becomes part of your record at the College Board and colleges will see your scores for each test administration. However, the College Board has recently modified score-reporting options described below in the New SAT Score-Reporting Policy section.

SAT Question Types and Scoring

The question types are the same as those on the PSAT—just more of them! Remember, the PSAT consists of five sections: two Critical Reading sections, two Mathematics sections, and one Writing skills section. The SAT has 10 sections, including an essay.

The scoring for the multiple-choice sections is accomplished the same way as the PSAT. Each question is worth one point. There is no penalty for blanks—for not answering a question; however, a penalty of one-quarter of a point is taken for each wrong answer, excluding the student-produced answers in the math section. Although there is no penalty for leaving questions blank, you should try to answer as many questions as possible to achieve a better score. Never randomly guess, but if you can eliminate two or three possibilities, you are not guessing and should try to answer the question.

The raw scores for each area—Critical Reading, Mathematics, and Writing Skills—are converted to a scaled score (200–800), which is reported to you on your Score Sheet. In addition, there are two writing subscores for multiple-choice questions and the essay. The essay subscore is determined by adding the scores of the two readers who rated the essay on a scale of 1 (*low*) to 6 (*high*) for a final scale of 2–12.

Test Order

The SAT is composed of 10 testing sections. The first section is always a 25-minute essay, and the last section is a 10-minute multiple-choice Writing Skills section. Sections two through seven are 25-minute sections. Sections eight and nine are 20-minute sections. Test-takers sitting next to each other in the same session may have test books with entirely different content orders for sections two through nine (Mathematics, Critical Reading, and Writing Skills).

The Unscored Section

In addition to the nine scored sections of the SAT, there is one 25-minute section that the SAT uses to try out new questions for future editions of the test. It also ensures that scores on new editions of the SAT are comparable to scores on earlier editions of the test. Don't be worried; this section does not count toward your score. It may be a Critical Reading, Mathematics, or Writing multiple-choice section.

The New SAT Score-Reporting Policy

Score Choice is a new score-reporting feature that gives students the option to choose the SAT scores by test date and SAT Subject Test scores by individual test that they send to colleges, in accordance with each institution's individual score-use practice. Score Choice is optional, and if you choose not to use it, all scores will be sent automatically. Always check the Web sites of the colleges to which you may apply for specific instructions regarding which scores to report when using Score Choice. For example, The State University of New York at Binghamton (2010) gives the following instructions: "Have the testing agency send us your SAT or ACT scores. Binghamton's SAT code is 2535 and its ACT code is 2956. NOTE: Please have the College Board send us your highest SAT section scores by selecting 'Highest Scores Across Test Dates' on the College Board's website. Binghamton currently reviews only critical reading and mathematics scores." Understanding this kind of specific information will help speed your application process.

The SAT Subject Tests

SAT Subject Tests (see Additional Resources; formerly SAT II: Subject Tests) are designed to measure your knowledge and skills in particular subject areas as well as your ability to apply that knowledge. The tests are independent of any particular textbook or method of instruction. The tests' content evolves to reflect current trends in high school curricula, but the types of questions change little from year to year.

Many colleges use the Subject Tests for admission, for course placement, and to advise students about course selection. Some colleges specify the Subject Tests they require for admission or placement; others allow applicants to choose which tests to take. Generally, only the most competitive colleges require the SAT Subject Tests. Most students take Subject Tests at the end of their junior year or at the beginning of their senior year. You should take these tests when you finish a particular course such as biology or U.S. history. Other tests require more cumulative knowledge such as the language and math tests.

Subject Tests fall into five general subject areas:

English
- Literature
- Language

History
- U.S. History (formerly American History and Social Studies)
- World History

Mathematics
- Mathematics Level 1 (formerly Mathematics IC)
- Mathematics Level 2 (formerly Mathematics IIC)

Science
- Biology E/M
- Chemistry
- Physics

Languages
- Chinese with Listening
- French
- French with Listening
- German
- German with Listening
- Spanish
- Spanish with Listening
- Modern Hebrew
- Italian
- Latin
- Japanese with Listening
- Korean with Listening

The ACT

The ACT (see Additional Resources; formerly called the American College Testing Program) assesses high school students' general educational development and their ability to complete college-level work. Every 3 to 5 years, the ACT conducts the ACT National Curriculum Survey initiative to ensure its curriculum-based assessment tools accurately measure the skills high school teachers teach and instructors of entry-level college courses expect. The ACT National Curriculum Survey comprises a comprehensive review of state educational standards documents, survey of educators, and consultation with content area experts across the curriculum.

Again like the SAT, you are responsible for registering for the ACT test. This can easily be done online at the ACT Web site. You are also responsible for reporting your scores to the colleges and scholarship programs to which you apply. Remember that once you have taken a test the score becomes part of your record at ACT. If you have taken the ACT or ACT Plus Writing more than once, the ACT maintains a separate record for each test date. If you ask the ACT to send a report to a college, only the record from the test date you request will be released. You may also request that the ACT report more than one test date record to a college. However, you may not select test scores from different test dates to construct a new record; you must designate an entire test date record as it stands.

Test Format

Through multiple-choice questions, the ACT measures competence in four areas: English, mathematics, reading, and science. The ACT also has an optional writing test that assesses skills in planning and writing a short essay.

- The English test measures skills in two areas: usage/mechanics such as punctuation, grammar, and sentence structure; and rhetorical skills including strategy, organization, and style.
- The mathematics test consists of questions in prealgebra, elementary algebra, intermediate algebra, coordinate geometry, plane geometry, and trigonometry.
- The reading test is divided into four passage areas: prose fiction, humanities, social studies, and natural science.
- The science test assesses knowledge in biology, chemistry, earth/space science, and physics.

The ACT Writing Test (Optional)

The writing test is a 30-minute essay test that measures writing skills, specifically those writing skills emphasized in high school English classes and in entry-level college composition courses. The ACT offers the writing test as an option because colleges and universities make their own decisions about admission requirements. In addition, students are not required to take a test unless a college is requiring it.

The test consists of a writing prompt that defines an issue and describes two points of view on that issue. You are asked to respond to a question about your position on the issue described in the writing prompt. You may adopt one or the other of the perspectives described in the prompt, or you may present a different point of view on the issue. Your score will not be affected by the point of view you take on the issue.

Scoring

Each question is worth one point. There is no penalty for wrong answers or for answers left blank. A raw score is determined by adding the number of correct answers for each subject test, which is then converted into a scaled score based on 1 (*low*) to 36 (*high*). The scale score is what is reported to students and colleges. The writing test is scored by two readers who assess the essay on a 1–6 scale. These ratings are then added together to determine the writing test subscore of 2–12. The ACT also provides percentiles to help students compare their performance with that of other students taking the ACT.

The PLAN

The PLAN® is the ACT's counterpart to the PSAT. As a pre-ACT test, PLAN is a predictor of success on the ACT. Typically, the PLAN is administered in the fall of the sophomore and junior years. The format and scoring of the PLAN is the same as the ACT and includes four multiple-choice tests: English, math, reading, and science. There is no optional writing test. The PLAN is not linked to scholarship-based awards such as the National Merit Scholarships. However, several states, including Michigan, Wisconsin, and Oklahoma, among others, link state-based scholarships to performance on the ACT.

Which Test to Take—The SAT or the ACT or Maybe Both?

Some factors to consider are as follows:

- Which test format is best for you? The SAT and the ACT are different tests—which is the best fit for you?
- Consider the colleges and scholarship programs to which you will apply. Which test is required?
- Is cost a factor? Compare the SAT and the ACT fee waiver/reduction policies.

Your counselor will be able to help you with this.

Table 6.4   Initial Student Plan for Standardized Testing

Name:

Date:

Counselor's Name:

1. Which standardized test do you plan to take?

	Are You Registered? Indicate Yes/No	Date of Test
__ SAT	_____	_____
__ ACT	_____	_____
__ ACT with writing	_____	_____
__ SAT Subject Test	_____	_____
Which Subject Test?	_____	_____
	_____	_____
	_____	_____

2. Method of preparation for SAT/ACT? (Check all that apply)

__ Preparation Class

　　Indicate which _____

__ Online Preparation

__ Private Tutoring

__ Preparing on My Own

How to Prepare—No Matter Which Test You Are Taking

You have a variety of ways to prepare for the SAT and/or the ACT:

■ Take a prep class. Explore the test prep companies as well as look into community-based test prep programs.

■ Use the online test prep programs that both the SAT and the ACT offer. Visit their Web sites for more information.

■ Get the test books published by the SAT and/or the ACT for practice tests.

Good preparation takes time and commitment. Don't take a test without preparation!

Table 6.4 may be helpful to the counselor in overseeing the standardized testing process.

Chapter 7

Assisting Students in Career Exploration

Memo to Counselors

In this chapter we first present recent work on career development theories including Social Cognitive Career Theory (SCCT), which suggests that career choice is influenced by outcome expectancies, career interests, and career self-efficacy. We then provide practical methods to help students explore possible careers by first examining their interests and then expanding their knowledge of what kind of work particular careers entail. Students will use exercises to help them clarify their interests, discover actual work descriptions, and understand the necessary educational requirements for specific careers. We also explain the role of technology in career exploration, using specific Web sites and systems that enhance student research. Most importantly, we emphasize the importance of students maintaining an open mind to the career possibilities that lie ahead of them.

Career Development Theories

Career development is one of the three domains that have been identified by the American School Counselor Association (ASCA) National School Counselor Standards. The goals include acquiring the skills to investigate the world of work; employing the strategies to achieve future career success; and understanding the relationship among personal qualities, education and training, and the world of work (ASCA, 2005). Understanding where students are in their career development is critical to helping them reach these goals. Super (1990) theorized that high school students are in the career exploration stage of career development. They are reviewing occupational preferences as well as making some preliminary decisions about careers as they look into potential college majors. What influences these career choices is important for counselors to know because they can then direct counseling experiences to facilitate and optimize students' decision making and exposure. Social Cognitive Career Theory (SCCT; Lent, Brown, & Hackett, 1994) suggests that career choice is influenced by outcome expectancies, career interests, and career self-efficacy; Bandura (1986) theorized that self-efficacy is determined by persons' judgment about how well they can complete a task. Moreover, career self-efficacy is influenced both by individual variants (e.g., predispositions, gender, race/ethnicity, health status) and by contextual factors such as family background and learning experiences. Tang, Wei, and Newmeyer (2008) studied the factors that impact career choices. They found that learning experiences significantly influence one's self-efficacy, which then influences one's career interests and choices. Another interesting finding of this study is the strong, direct impact of career self-efficacy on career choices in the area of People/Ideas (as measured from Holland's Self-Directed Search, or SDS). It seems that high school students' confidence in occupations involving people's interaction and ideas very possibly leads them to choose such occupations. Learning experiences have a greater influence on the development of *career* self-efficacy for female students than for male students. The common theme for both males and females is the strong role of self-efficacy when they choose occupations that are nontraditional for their gender.

What can we take from this work that can guide career development planning for high school students? School counselors already recognize that self-efficacy and learning experiences impact high school students' career interests and choices. They need to provide learning opportunities that could facilitate career self-efficacy throughout the school. School counseling programs should have career development experiences for students throughout high school. Career Days are one example, of course. Other examples might include mentoring opportunities with corporations. In partnership with a New York City school that has as its theme *technology,* the Microsoft Corporation developed a summer program called the Microsoft Challenge, where student teams were given a common goal and competed against each other to arrive at the goal over a period of several weeks. Included in the experience was an opportunity to be mentored by Microsoft workers and to go to the New York City office of Microsoft to engage in some of the "work" for the project. Other experiences could be developed in partnership with institutions of higher education (IHEs). In Chapter 2, we discussed the importance of such partnerships generally. As part of a New York State grant obtained by Dr. Fitzpatrick and Manhattan College in conjunction with K–12 schools and agencies in the Bronx borough of New York City (2009–2011), we developed two Engineering Career Awareness Days, one given by engineering students for 6–12 students and one given by engineering faculty to counselors.

School counselors should connect with teachers on the important findings described above. If teachers were more aware of the strong link between learning and career self-efficacy, they might be more apt to provide such learning in their curriculum. School counselors themselves can develop activities geared toward understanding oneself in relation to work; some of our suggestions below address this idea. Other activities can include a career inventory (e.g., the Naviance Career Inventory, which is based on the Holland SDS), discussion of student interests, and career self-efficacy. All students should take the SDS (Holland, 1994) early in high school and in their senior year. This measure includes a section asking students to answer yes or no to whether they think they could perform tasks competently.

Finally, as part of the recommendations of the ASCA, school counselors must incorporate career development into their work. ASCA (2005) indicates the need for a counseling curriculum that consists of structured developmental lessons designed to assist students in achieving the desired competencies and to provide all students with the knowledge and skills appropriate for their developmental level.

Exploring Possible Careers

Memo to Counselors

The following curriculum may be adapted to students who have taken the Preliminary Scholastic Aptitude Test (PSAT) or the PLAN® in either their sophomore or their junior year. This curriculum assists students in their initial career exploration and helps them to understand how their strengths and weaknesses, interests, and preferences influence career expectations. Again, this curriculum is presented in the voice of the counselor speaking to students.

Now that you have taken the PSAT (and/or the PLAN) and are thinking about the college process, it is time to explore possible careers. It is never too early to consider the kinds of careers you may want to pursue. Your career should be one that you enjoy and one that uses your strengths—after all, you will be spending much of your life working in your chosen field. Some of you may have a clear career goal now; just remember to keep your options open. Some of you may not have any idea about your future career. That's fine too, but again keep an open mind. The career that you eventually pursue may be one that you have not yet experienced!

This semester we will—

- Complete a personality profile/career interest inventory to see what fields you may want to pursue
- Analyze a skills assessment inventory to help you better understand your strengths and weaknesses

- Learn what majors are important for various careers
- Communicate online with professionals in many career fields
- Begin to research colleges that match your interests
- Achieve a better understanding of how your high school preparation relates to college and career pursuits

Helpful Technological Resources

Some helpful resources we will explore in this section are the College Board's My College QuickStart and MyRoad, the ACT's Educational Planning and Assessment System (EPAS®), and Naviance. (See Chapter 5 for a more extensive explanation of these resources.)

1. My College QuickStart (see College Board in Additional Resources) is a free personalized college and career planning kit based on your test results. To sign in, you'll need the access code printed on your PSAT/NMSQT® (National Merit Scholarship Qualifying Test) paper score report. If you do not already have a College Board account, you'll be prompted to create one. It typically takes less than 2 minutes to create your free account. My College QuickStart provides a personalized list of majors and careers plus access to a personality assessment that suggests other compatible possibilities.

2. MyRoad (see College Board in Additional Resources) is a comprehensive online college and career planning resource that can help you take charge of your future. This program can help you explore college majors to achieve your goals. It will also help you learn about careers from professionals in the real world. Features include:

   a. The ORA Personality Profiler®—an online assessment students take to learn about their personality types and receive major and career suggestions

   b. Sixty-seven profiles of academic fields—from aeronautics to theater—representing 175 instructional programs

   c. Timely articles covering more than 450 occupations—everything from actors and accountants to veterinary technicians and Web designers

   Like My College QuickStart, students who take the PSAT/NMSQT receive free access to MyRoad until they graduate from high school. Students can easily access MyRoad through their College Board account by using their access code printed on their PSAT score report.

3. The ACT's EPAS (see ACT in Additional Resources) was developed in response to the need for all students to be prepared for high school and the transitions they make after graduation. It provides an educational and career planning system in which students can identify career and educational options, establish goals, and determine which courses are necessary

to achieve their objectives. If you have taken the PLAN, you may be able to use EPAS to assist you in career exploration.

4. Naviance (see Naviance in Additional Resources) is the leading provider of planning and advising systems for secondary schools. Nearly 40,000 educators and counselors serving more than 3.5 million students in schools across the United States and in 60 other countries use Naviance products to manage academic and postsecondary advising, communicate with students and families, and analyze data. If your counselors are trained in Naviance, they will use its resources to help you attain a greater understanding of your college and career goals.

By the end of the term, you will have—

■ A *working* list of possible careers
■ A *working* list of possible majors
■ A *working* list of colleges to research
■ A greater understanding of your strengths and weaknesses as a student and how this relates to your choice of a college major and a career

The emphasis is on the word *working* because this is an ongoing process—you are at the very beginning of planning the next stage of your life. Nothing is written in stone!

Understanding your strengths and weaknesses is essential in exploring career possibilities. In the future, you want to find yourself in a career that uses your strengths rather than your weaknesses. The first step in attaining this self-knowledge is to discover your preferred learning style and personality type. The ORA Personality Profiler of the College Board's MyRoad program is an excellent online assessment that students take to learn more about themselves and receive college major and career suggestions. Another wonderful resource is Naviance's personality profile, a Myers-Briggs–style assessment that helps you to understand how you learn best and how that can translate into a rewarding career. You may also refer to Chapter 4 for more information about learning styles. After completing either or both of these assessments, complete the exercise in Table 7.1, using bullet points to describe your personality and preferred learning style.

Table 7.1   Exercise on Personality Type and Learning Style

Personality Characteristics	Preferred Learning Style

Knowing more about who you are as person will help you to understand the kinds of careers that would be the most rewarding for you. Now let's look at how you would start to see a path that may lead you to the career of your choice.

Exercise on Majors and Careers

Think about what interests you most. What do you want to study? What career will you pursue? This is nothing more than the time-honored question, "What do you want to be when you grow up?" It's up to you, but having a plan and clear goals makes life easier. The more you know about what you want to study will make your later college research more effective. (This exercise also appears in Chapter 8 as you begin the college research process.)

Using the College Board's MyRoad described in Chapter 6, list five possible careers that interest you in Table 7.2. Naviance and the ACT's EPAS may also be helpful in researching career interests.

FOLLOW-UP ACTIVITY

Using the College Board's MyRoad, research what kind of specific day-to-day work is entailed in the careers you listed. This Web site provides students with the opportunity to speak online with professionals in various career fields, a great way to understand the day-to-day work involved in any career. Again, Naviance and/or the ACT's EPAS may be used.

It's never too early to research what major and educational background is necessary for a particular career. In Table 7.3, list five careers of interest to you. Then list the appropriate college major and see if a program beyond the college-graduate level is necessary.

Table 7.2   Exercise on Majors and Careers

	Five Areas of Interest to You	Possible Majors	Possible Careers
1.			
2.			
3.			
4.			
5.			

Table 7.3 Exercise on Career Requirements

	Career	Major	Graduate-Level Education Required
1.			
2.			
3.			
4.			
5.			

Now that you have learned more about your personality type and preferred learning style and have begun some career exploration, it is time to begin the college research process. This is presented in detail in Chapter 8. Understanding your aspirations and goals can only enhance your performance as a student. There are so many possibilities in life—keep your options open; you may not have yet encountered the career that you will find most fulfilling.

Chapter 8

Advising Students in College Research (11th Grade)

Memo to Counselors

In this chapter, we explain the essentials of the college search and application process. Students actively engage the terminology of higher education: liberal arts colleges, universities, specialized institutes, community colleges, and the meaning of majors and minors. We also explore relevant factors in college selection such as size, location, on-campus life, and commuting. Students learn how to arrange a college visit and what to look for when on campus. Using the Common Application, students gather the necessary information to complete an actual application. By the end of the academic year, students will compile an initial list of colleges that they believe are good matches for them. We conclude with advice on profitable ways to spend the summer between the junior and senior year.

At the same time, counselors must remind and advise students about standardized testing, which we covered in Chapter 6. While it is the responsibility of students and parents to register for tests, it is imperative that the counselor assists in this process. The main concern is that students are on a course to prepare and take the standardized testing that is necessary for college admission and that they understand relevant information about fee waivers and/or reductions. Table 8.1 may be helpful to counselors in this process.

Engaging in the Language of Higher Education

First of all, you need to learn some new vocabulary.

Table 8.1   Junior-Year Form for Standardized Testing

Name:

Date:

Counselor's Name:

1. Which standardized test do you plan to take?

Test	Are You Registered? Indicate Yes/No	Date of Test
__ SAT	_____	_____
__ ACT	_____	_____
__ ACT With Writing	_____	_____
__ SAT Subject Test	_____	_____
Which Subject Test?	_____	_____
	_____	_____
	_____	_____

2. Method of preparation for SAT/ACT? (Check all that apply)

__ Preparation Class

   Indicate Which _____

__ Online Preparation

__ Private Tutoring

__ Preparing on My Own

Note: See your counselor for information about fee waivers/ reduction forms.

What Is Higher Education?

Higher education is a broad term for various types of education given in postsecondary institutions of learning and usually awarding a degree upon completion of all requirements. To earn a degree, students usually need to have both a major and a minor area of studies.

What Is a Major?

A major is your concentrated area of interest at a college or university. You must complete a majority of your classes in this subject area. Each college or university will specify what courses must be completed to earn a major in a particular field of study. For example, to earn a major in English literature, a normal requirement is 36 credits in this study. However, colleges determine how those credits must be distributed. The college catalog will state the requirements for each major. You will graduate with a degree in your major.

What Is a Minor?

A minor is a set of courses considered sufficient to establish proficiency in a discipline without having to take all of the courses that a major would require. For example, you could major in history and then minor in philosophy, which may require you to take 12 credits in this area. Again, the college catalog will explain the requirements for minors.

Different Kinds of Higher Education

Liberal Arts Colleges

Liberal arts colleges are primarily colleges with an emphasis on undergraduate study in the liberal arts. A liberal arts education allows you to explore any number of career possibilities. Unlike students in professional or vocational programs, students in liberal arts degree programs receive broad exposure to a variety of areas while focusing on a few key specialties that lead to a bachelor's degree.

A liberal arts major offers a broad overview of the arts, sciences, and humanities. Within the context of a liberal arts degree, you can study various disciplines:

- Architecture, fine arts, classics, philosophy
- Language and writing
- English, writing component, foreign language
- Education, early childhood, elementary and secondary
- Social sciences, government, history, anthropology
- Economics, geography, linguistics, sociology, psychology
- Math and sciences such as astronomy, biology, chemistry
- Computer science, geological sciences, marine science
- Nutrition, physical science, physics

Generally speaking, liberal arts colleges have some common characteristics:

- They tend to be smaller institutions.
- They may have some lecture classes, but more emphasis is on classroom teaching.
- They are more likely to have professors rather than graduate assistants teaching undergraduates.
- They are more likely to have greater interaction with faculty.
- Their smaller environment may promote greater social and cultural opportunities.

Top 21 Careers for Liberal Arts Majors

Too often people think that college must prepare them for a specific career. The beauty of a liberal arts degree is that you can find many opportunities to pursue what interests you most.

- Advertising/public relations
- Consulting
- Environment
- Film and television
- Government
- Human resources
- Human services/nonprofit management
- International business
- Investment banking
- Journalism
- Legal/paralegal
- Library and information science
- Marketing and sales
- Museums
- Physical sciences
- Public policy
- Publishing
- Research/health care
- Sports management and recreation
- Teaching
- Technical writing

In a November 30, 2008, interview on *Meet the Press* with Tom Brokaw, Ted Turner, American entrepreneur and businessman, credited his classics education at Brown as a key to his business success (www.msnbc.msn.com). He believes that his liberal arts education has made him the businessman that he is today. So don't think that liberal arts majors are not practical; they translate into many career fields.

Universities

Universities are institutions of higher education, usually comprising a liberal arts and sciences college and graduate and professional schools, that confer degrees in various fields of study. Most universities also have graduate school programs.

For example, a typical university will consist of the following colleges:

- Liberal Arts
- Engineering/Architecture
- Education
- Business

Again, generally speaking, universities share some common characteristics:

- They tend to be medium- to large-sized institutions.
- They have an emphasis on research and scholarly publications.
- They usually have definite name recognition.
- They offer a large range of possible majors.
- They usually have many large lecture classes with smaller discussion groups run by teacher assistants.
- The campus may seem like a city itself.
- They have many diverse social and cultural opportunities.
- Intracampus transportation may be needed to go from class to class.

Remember that a name can be deceiving. Boston College, Dartmouth College, and the College of William and Mary are all universities, but they have chosen to keep their original names for historical purposes.

Some Majors That You Will Find at Universities

Education

Completing an undergraduate degree in education prepares you to teach students in various levels of education from prekindergarten to high school. Further graduate study is required for certification in most states. Students pursuing an education major usually specialize in one of the following areas:

- Childhood (grades pre-K–3/ages 3–8)
- Middle childhood (grades 4–9/ages 8–14)
  - Mathematics
  - Language arts
  - Science
  - Social studies
- Adolescent to young adult (grades 7–12/ages 12–21)
  - Chemistry
  - Dual area science
  - Earth science
  - Integrated language arts
  - Integrated mathematics
  - Integrated science
  - Life science
  - Physical science
  - Integrated social studies
- Multi-age (grades pre-K–12/ages 3–21)
  - Physical education
  - Health education

    – Music education (vocal and/or instrumental)
    – Visual arts
■ Intervention specialist (grades K–12/ages 5–21)

Business

A career in business can involve the obvious functions such as management and marketing, but there is an increasing need for business majors to apply their skills in government, international commerce, health care, arts, and nonprofit organizations. Business principles can serve as the backbone for economic, political, and social systems at all levels. The following is a list of common job titles in the business industry. However, you do not necessarily need a degree in business to pursue these careers; with a liberal arts major you can easily pursue any of the following:

■ Commercial banking
■ Securities
■ Investment banking
■ Corporate finance
■ Accounting
■ Advertising
■ Public relations and business communications
■ Sales and buying
■ Human resource management
■ Management of information systems
■ Marketing
■ Real estate

Technology

Technology majors are designed to give you more than just an overview of the field. You will learn new methods for developing gaming systems. You will learn how to create computer programs that will be able to store data and make it easier to find information. You will be able to stop people from accessing data they should not be seeing. All of these skills can be applied to many different career fields.

    Following are the 10 most popular technology majors:

■ Computer programming
■ Graphics and multimedia
■ Information systems
■ Information systems security
■ Information technology
■ Network management

- Network security
- Organizational leadership
- Technology management
- Web development

As technology changes, so must the people who create it. Whether you work in management, security, or data storage, you will have to stay current and learn the latest information about technology.

Engineering

Most engineering majors concentrate on a chosen specialty, supplemented by courses in both science and mathematics. Depending on the program and the institution, an engineering major could study either industrial practices to prepare for a hands-on job or theoretical principles to lay the groundwork for a research or academic career.

Major Areas of Engineering Degree Programs — The following six areas of engineering have traditionally formed the core of the engineering profession:

- Chemical engineering
- Civil engineering
- Electrical engineering
- Industrial engineering
- Materials science engineering
- Mechanical engineering

Another grouping of engineering programs has emerged more recently and includes only four major areas:

- Chemical engineering
- Civil engineering
- Electrical engineering
- Mechanical engineering

In this scheme, industrial engineering is considered a specialty under civil engineering, and materials is listed under mechanical engineering. This grouping may be seen in Figure 8.1.

Engineering Degree Specializations — More and more, focused engineering specialties are available to the engineering student. Figure 8.1 clusters those specialties under the four major areas in engineering mentioned above, with a smaller fifth section that includes specialties that don't fit into any of the four

Bioengineering and Biomedical Engineering	Chemical
Biological Engineering	Chemical
Ceramic Engineering	Chemical
Environmental Engineering	Chemical
Materials and Metallurgical Engineering	Chemical
Naval Architecture and Marine Engineering	Chemical
Nuclear and Radiological Engineering	Chemical
Ocean Engineering	Chemical
Petroleum Engineering	Chemical
Architectural Engineering	Civil
Civil Engineering	Civil
Construction Engineering	Civil
Environmental Engineering	Civil
General Engineering, Engineering Physics, and Engineering Science	Civil
Geological Engineering	Civil
Industrial Engineering	Civil
Mining Engineering	Civil
Naval Architecture and Marine Engineering	Civil
Surveying Engineering	Civil
Electrical and Computer Engineering	Electrical
Software Engineering	Electrical
Aerospace Engineering	Mechanical
Engineering Mechanics	Mechanical
Materials and Metallurgical Engineering	Mechanical
Manufacturing Engineering	Mechanical
Mechanical Engineering	Mechanical
General Engineering, Engineering Physics, and Engineering Science Engineering Management	

Figure 8.1   Engineering clusters and specialties.

major categories. Often engineering students major in one of these four areas with a specialization within that area. You can pursue either as a specialization or as a college major. Engineering degree specializations include those shown in Figure 8.1.

Technology, Art, and Design Institutes

Institutes specializing in technology and art and design also offer 4-year programs leading to a college degree. These schools usually have few liberal arts requirements and focus on a specific professional goal such as engineering, architecture, art, and design. Many of these schools are the most prestigious in their field and consequently have very high standards for admittance.

Community/Junior Colleges

Community colleges and/or junior colleges are educational institutions that provide 2 years of academic instruction beyond secondary school as well as technical and vocational training to prepare graduates for careers. These institutions award an associate degree upon completion of requirements. Many students find it helpful to attend this kind of school and then transfer to a 4-year college to complete their college degree.

Exercise on Majors and Careers

Think about what interests you most. What do you want study? What career will you pursue? This is nothing more than the time-honored, "What do you want to be when you grow up?" It's up to you, but having a plan and clear goals makes life easier. The more you know about what you want to study will make your college research more effective.

Using the College Board's MyRoad described in Chapter 6, list five possible careers that interest you (Table 8.2). Naviance and the ACT's EPAS® (Educational Planning and Assessment System) may also be helpful in researching career interests.

FOLLOW-UP ACTIVITY

Using the College Board's MyRoad, research what kind of specific day-to-day work these careers entail. The College Board Web site provides students with the opportunity to speak online with professionals in various career fields, a great way to understand the day-to-day work involved in any career. Again, Naviance and/or the ACT's EPAS may be used.

Selecting the Right College for You

Now that you have an understanding of higher education, how do you discover the right college for you? This can be an intimidating experience, but if you look at different aspects of colleges, it can be easier to choose what is best for you. Some factors to consider are discussed in the following sections.

Table 8.2 Exercise on Majors and Careers

	Five Areas of Interest to You	Possible Majors	Possible Careers
1.			
2.			
3.			
4.			
5.			

Size

How do you know the size of a college or university that would be best for you? Chances are, any college or university that you attend will be bigger than your high school, so how do you decide what kind of learning environment is best for you?

Let's first look at some ranges of college/university sizes. (Student numbers are approximate and may vary slightly from year to year.)

1. What is a small to medium-sized college/university? Student bodies at small to medium-sized colleges and universities generally range from 1,000 to 10,000 students.

Boston College	8,770
Carleton College	1,890
Emory University	5,350
Johns Hopkins	2,720
Pomona College	1,400
Reed College	1,260
Rice University	2,600
SUNY Geneseo	5,200

Some common characteristics are as follows:

- May have some lecture classes, but more emphasis on classroom teaching
- More likely to have professors, rather than graduate assistants, teaching undergraduates
- More likely to have greater interaction with faculty
- Smaller environment may promote greater social and cultural opportunities

2. What is a medium- to large-sized university or college setting? This size college or university is approximately 10,000 to 19,000 students.

Boston University	14,560
Cornell University	12,630
University of Montana at Missoula	14,207
University of North Carolina at Chapel Hill	15,690
Ohio University	14,400
University of Southern California	16,090
Syracuse University	13,000
University of Virginia	11,190

3. What is a large university? Generally, the student body ranges from 15,000 to 25,000, and some even have 35,000 and more students.

Florida State University	40,255
Iowa State University	26,000
University of Michigan	25,000

University of Oregon	20,376
Penn State University	31,160
SUNY Buffalo	28,000
University of Texas at Austin	36,000
University of Wisconsin at Madison	29,730

Some common characteristics are as follows:

- Usually have definite name recognition
- Large range of possible majors
- Usually many large lecture classes with smaller discussion groups run by teacher assistants
- Campus may seem like a city itself
- Many diverse social and cultural opportunities
- Intracampus transportation may be needed to go from class to class

Small, medium, large, or somewhere in between—how do you decide? The best way for you to decide what is best for you is to visit colleges. Initially, you may visit colleges because of their size—large, medium, small—visit colleges close to you to get a sense of what kind of collegiate environment is best for you.

Memo to Counselors

While this initial visit of colleges is for the New York City area, it may easily be adapted to any area of the country. What is relevant here are types of colleges: large, urban, sprawling campus, small to medium-sized enclosed campus, and the more suburban campus. Another key factor is to include private and state options.

Look at What Is Around You: Initial Visits of Colleges (Adapted for the New York City Area)

The best way to get a sense of where you might feel most at home is by visiting different types of schools. Even without traveling very far, you can visit local colleges and universities to get a sense of what the "feel" is like. For example:

1. Walk around the New York University campus and see what the large, urban, sprawling campus is like.
2. Walk around Manhattan College or Fordham University and experience the smaller, enclosed campus feel.
3. Get on a train or a bus and visit State University of New York, Purchase, and tour the more suburban campus.

Finding the right college is hard work, and this is a good place to start.

Distance From Home/Commuting or Living on Campus

Following are some issues to consider regarding the distance of your college from your home.

If you live on campus...
- How will you travel to school: public transportation, car, train, bus, plane?
- How frequently would you want to come home: every few weeks, once each semester, vacations only?
- Are you ready to leave home at this point in your life?
- Is it financially possible for you to live on campus?

If you are a commuter...
- How far are you willing to commute each day?
- How much time will it take you to travel each day?
- If you travel by car, is student parking available?
- How accessible is your college by public transportation?

How to Begin Researching Colleges

First of all, familiarize yourself with the resources that you have at your high school. Some typical reference books available in libraries and/or college advising center are

- *Index of Majors*—look up majors that you may be interested in and see what schools have great programs.
- *College Board List of Colleges*—this lists all the colleges and universities in the United States as well as gives the credits that will be given for advanced placement (AP) scores.
- *Fiske Guide to Selected Colleges*—one of the better guides to colleges.
- Financial aid information—this includes basic information as well as possible scholarship information.
- Colleges send in information, including CDs and DVDs that provide virtual tours of campuses. Look at books, catalogs, and bulletins.
- SAT (Scholastic Aptitude Test)/ACT® prep books—you may find these helpful.

Second, use the Internet to make your research more productive. This can literally put you in touch with thousands of colleges. But you need to learn how to use it wisely (see Appendix C, 10 Useful Web Pages for College Research).

As you begin researching specific colleges, keep in mind that you may qualify for some special programs. For example, many states have programs for underrepresented minority groups. Also many colleges are looking for students with special talents in music, art, dance, filmmaking, and athletics. See if you qualify.

Visiting Colleges and Knowing What to Look For

First of all, let's look back to what we have already talked about. Finding the right college is all about discovering the best match for you. Whether or not you live on campus, the college you attend will be your home away from home. Let's find the best place for you.

- In Chapter 4, you completed learning style and personality inventories. Think about what you learned:
  - What are your interests?
  - What do you value?
  - How do you learn best?

  Use what you know about yourself when you are visiting colleges. Ask yourself: Will I grow as a student and a person in this environment? Why or why not?
- Previously, we talked about different sizes and locations of colleges and what may be broad characteristics of these kinds of schools. Remember: Colleges are like people; they have personalities, too. The best way to get a sense of where you might feel most at home is by visiting different types of schools.

Memo to Counselors

Again, this section is for the New York City area but can easily be adapted to other sections of the country. The emphasis is on different kinds of schools that students should visit rather than on naming specific colleges.

College Visits: A Sampling of Different Kinds of Schools in the Area

- Columbia University—a small, private university in an urban area
- Fordham University—a medium-sized, private university with a branch at Lincoln Center
- Manhattan College—a small, private college
- City College—a CUNY (City University of New York) school in Manhattan
- SUNY Purchase—a SUNY (State University of New York) school in the suburbs
- Westchester Community College—a 2-year public college in a suburban area

Some Helpful Tips When Visiting Colleges

- Call ahead and make an appointment for a tour.
- Upon arrival, check in at the Admissions Office.
- Attend a class in a subject that interests you.
- Visit the computer labs, libraries, and gym.

- Eat in the cafeteria and visit the Student Union.
- Talk to students about the pros and cons of campus life.

Questions to Ask, Things to Consider

- How big are the classes?
- Are classes taught by professors or teaching assistants?
- How much of student need is covered by financial aid?
- Is on-campus housing available for all students?
- Do students stay on campus during weekends, or do most go home?
- What kinds of activities are available to students on weekends?
- What grades, test scores, and experiences does this college look for?
- Which tests are required—SAT, ACT, SAT Subject Tests?
- Does the college have core requirements? English, math, science, language?
- How many students graduate on time?
- What percentage of students find jobs or go on to graduate programs upon graduating?
- How diverse and tolerant is the student population? Consider racial, ethnic, sexual orientation, socioeconomic, and geographic diversity and the support systems available for these students.
- What kind of support does the college have for students who face personal or academic challenges or students with learning and/or physical disabilities?

After visiting each college, make sure to fill out the chart provided in Table 8.3. It is easy to forget or to confuse exactly what you liked or disliked about a school, especially if you have visited multiple campuses.

Memo to Counselors

The Common Application Web site is an invaluable tool to students as they apply to colleges. It is important to familiarize them with this site now as a part of filling out an actual application. Once they have done this, they will have gathered the information that is usually required on most applications. You may choose to download the application and have students complete it in hard copy so that you may be assured that students have completed this task and that you have a copy in your files. In the senior year when students are applying to colleges, the Common Application Web site establishes an ongoing list of schools, saves applications and supplements, and provides an online fee payment option. Since online application is increasingly popular, the more experience that students have with this Web site can only benefit them in their senior year.

Table 8.3 Exercise to Evaluate Colleges After Visits

Name of College	Pros— Academics—List at Least Three Specific Aspects of the Academic Program That You Liked.	Cons— Academics— Again be Specific! What Did You Not Like? Why?	Pros—Social/ Extracurricular— List at Least Three Specific Aspects of the Social/ Extracurricular Life That You Liked.	Cons—Social/ Extracurricular—Be Specific About What You Found Negative or Lacking at This College!

Filling Out the Common Application

The Common Application is accepted by 346 institutions of higher learning. By filling out this sample application, you will gather all the significant information that you will need for almost any college application. This will make the college application process much easier for you in your senior year. Counselors should keep a photocopy of this application in the guidance file just in case students should misplace their copies.

Students may download this application by going to www.commonapp.org and registering with the Common App. When you register, you will enter a password of your choice so that you will be able to access your information and files more quickly. This Web site also provides required testing information, application deadlines, and whether or not a supplement is necessary for member colleges.

Section 1: Personal Data

While most of this is self-explanatory, keep in mind that you want to give complete information, including the following:

- Zip codes and area codes
- E-mail and instant messaging addresses (if you choose to share with a college)
- Citizenship information, alien registration number

- Possible career/professional plans (Would you like to study medicine, education, etc.?)
- Whether you will apply for financial aid
- Optional items, which may help colleges see who you are and could work to your advantage

Section 2: Educational Data

This section explains your educational background. Complete information is necessary.

- Zip codes and area codes
- Correct spelling of your counselor's name
- Counselor's title
- Counselor information including phone number and fax number
- Counselor's e-mail address (ask your counselor first)
- CEEB/ACT code (This number should be memorized because you will be using it frequently. Every high school is assigned an identifying number for standardized testing for college entrance. This is how the College Board/SAT Program or the ACT organizations know which high school will receive your test reports.)
- Any other secondary schools attended—list with complete information
- Any courses taken at a college for credit—give all relevant information

Section 3: Test Information

This section is all about standardized testing information. At this time, you should know which tests you are taking. For example, will you take the May SAT? Or the May ACT? Please note that if you have not yet taken the test you should list the date that you will take the exam.

You may be taking an SAT Subject Test. List dates.

The TOEFL is the Test of English as a Foreign Language. You would take this only if English is your second language and you do not believe that your English skills are strong.

Section 4: Family Information

Fill in appropriate circles regarding your parents' marital status and with whom you live. Make sure that all information is complete, including:

- Educational background
- Names and ages of your brothers and sisters

■ The appropriate information for any siblings who have attended or are attending college

Section 5: Academic Honors

List only those academic honors that you have achieved in high school. These include possibilities such as Honor Roll, First Honors, Second Honors, and National Honors such as National Merit Commended Scholar or Semifinalist. Make sure that you list a generic name for an honor society such as the National Honor Society because a college may not recognize a specific name that your school has designated such as the Owls or the Blue Key Society. Be sure to note the year you achieved this honor and the level of recognition. For example, a student would become a National Merit Semifinalist in 12th grade. This would be a national honor.

Section 6: Extracurricular, Personal, and Volunteer Activities (Including Summer)

Colleges want to know more about you: What are your favorite activities and interests? How do you spend your free time?

Fill out this section by listing activities in order of importance to you. Check off the years involved and the approximate time spent, including whether the activity was during the school year and/or the summer. Do you have any positions of responsibility such as president of a club or captain of a team? Any awards or recognition achieved such as a varsity letter or getting a poem published? Use generic names for activities such as school newspaper or yearbook, not the title that your school may use. Remember that someone who is not familiar with your school will be reading this chart.

It is better to have just a few activities that show your serious commitment rather than many activities that don't involve much participation.

You can always attach a resume if you would like, but you must fill out this chart first.

Section 7: Paid Work Experience

Just like your extracurricular activities, work experience tells about who you are and how you spend your time. List the paid jobs that you have had, including summer employment. Again, give complete information:

■ What you did: for example, babysitter, sales person, delivery person
■ Employer's name
■ Approximate dates of employment
■ Approximate number of hours per week

Section 8: Short Answer

The Short Answer is a paragraph of no more than 150 words in which you answer two questions:

- What has been the most important activity or experience for you?
- Why has this activity had an impact on you?

What colleges are seeking to know is why you have devoted time to this particular activity and what this says about who you are as a person. Be conscious of length—this is short, only 150 words. If you are applying online and go over the limit, your answer may be cut off. While it is only 150 words, it must be the right 150 words.

If applying via regular mail, attach your paragraph on a separate sheet of paper. Make sure to put your name on the top of the page.

Section 9: Personal Essay

This is your basic college essay. You will be able to work on this essay in a special Personal Essay Writing Workshop described in Chapter 9.

Section 10: Other Required Information

If you answer yes to either or both of the questions in this section, see your college counselor for further advice.

Make sure that you photocopy this application. Give a copy to your counselor and keep the original in a safe place. You will need it in the fall of your senior year.

Constructing an Initial List of Colleges

Now that you have researched and visited some colleges, it is time to begin to formulate a list of schools that you are considering as good matches for you. Remember that you must be a good match for that college, too.

Some questions to consider as you compile your list:

- Does the college have the majors you want to study?
- Are there any special programs for which you may qualify?
- Does your grade point average (GPA) match the mean/average GPA of the college's last entering class?
- Do your standardized test scores match the mean/average of the college's last entering class?
- Have you considered distance from home? Commuting?
- Have you considered size and type of campus?

Table 8.4   Exercise on Matches

Name of College	Major	Mean GPA	Your GPA	Mean SAT/ACT	Your SAT/ACT

- Have you thought about the social and extracurricular life on campus? Is it right for you?
- Are you interested in a community college?
- What about vocational/technical programs? (Make sure that credits can transfer.)

After carefully considering these questions, complete Table 8.4, an exercise on college matches. You will want to share this with your counselor and your parents. List five to seven colleges that interest you. Now let's see if they are a good match for you.

Special Programs to Think About

As you begin researching specific colleges, keep in mind that you may qualify for some special programs designed to help currently underrepresented groups in higher education. These programs vary from state to state, so it is important that you research what kind of special programs exist within your state. While most states have created scholarships and grants for the most economically disadvantaged students, other special categories exist. For example, North Dakota, South Dakota, and New York have special assistance grants for Native Americans, while Texas has grants for students leaving the foster care system, and New Hampshire provides awards for students who are orphans of veterans. Researching your state's scholarship and grant programs could make a big difference in helping you afford the college that is right for you. Visit College Scholarships.org (see Additional Resources) for a state-by-state listing of special programs.

Two Special Programs in New York State

Higher Education Opportunity Program

The Higher Education Opportunity Program (HEOP; see Cornell University, Office of Minority Educational Affairs, in Additional Resources) is an academic support program established by the State of New York in 1970. It enables motivated students who lack adequate preparation and financial resources for college attendance to pursue a college degree. To meet the specific need of its students, HEOP primarily provides testing, counseling, tutoring, academic advisement, and financial assistance. To assist the student in arranging finances for educational purposes, financial aid is provided through a combination of the following: New York State Tuition Assistance Program (TAP), Pell grants, HEOP grants, HEOP stipends, subsidized Stafford loans, and federal work-study employment.

Educational Opportunity Program

The State University of New York's Educational Opportunity Program (EOP) provides access, academic support, and financial aid to students who show promise for mastering college-level work but who may otherwise not be admitted. Offered primarily to full-time students who are New York state residents, EOP accepts students who qualify, academically and economically, for the program. (See SUNY Binghamton in Additional Resources.)

How to Spend Your Summer

The summer between the junior and senior year is a great opportunity to show colleges who you are.
Let's consider the following:

- Employment
- Internships
- Community service
- Special summer programs
- Combinations of the above

You may want to find employment for the summer. This demonstrates responsibility and maturity and will also provide added income. Think of possibilities in your neighborhood—local stores and summer camp programs are often looking for extra help during the summer. And don't forget, babysitting counts, too. Ask family and friends for tips about who might be looking for extra help during the summer.

An internship is great way to show your responsibility and maturity. Ask your college counselor about businesses, museums, and firms that are offering internships for high school students. This experience may help you decide about a possible career. For example, working for a few weeks at a radio or television station can help you decide if communications is a possible major for you.

Community service is another way to show who you are and what you value. Think about volunteering some of your time in your community in venues such as the following:

- Hospitals
- Nursing homes
- Shelters for the homeless
- Food pantries

This commitment to community service shows your values and your desire to make your neighborhood a better place.

Summer programs can provide opportunities for enrichment. Many colleges, museums, local municipalities, and private groups offer programs for enrichment in the arts, science, computers, and filmmaking among others. Do some research and see if you can find a summer program in an area of special interest to you.

Work, internship, community service, summer program—whatever you choose to pursue helps to paint a fuller picture of who you are. Make the most of it.

Chapter 9

Empowering Students in Their Essay Writing (11th–12th Grades)

Memo to Counselors

In this chapter, we explain why the personal essay is important in the college application process. While some colleges and universities, particularly large institutions, do not require any admissions essays, most do. Students need to understand that this essay is a priority in their application process; indeed it is their way of personalizing their application. Your guidance in writing this essay can impact their success. Using the questions from the Common Application, we provide exercises and activities designed to assist students in focusing on possible topics for their personal essays. We then present a step-by-step process to help students develop their topics as well as provide samples of the personal essay. We also include formats for model Personal Essay Writing Workshops and follow-up activities for counselors and students. In conclusion, we share a sampling of what colleges across the country say about the personal essay.

What Is the Purpose of the Personal Essay?

The purpose of the personal essay is to provide a college admissions committee with the opportunity to know who you are, what your values are, and how you became the person you are. Do not minimize the importance of this essay. The personal essay demands introspection and self-knowledge; it must be both creative and analytical. Your writing and use of language also reveal the way that you think and express yourself. All of these expressions give the admissions committee insight into you as a person. Several revisions of the personal essay are normal. Thoughtful writers plan before they write, think about what they have written, and then evaluate and revise. You want this essay to be the best that you can do.

Keep the following points in mind:

- This is not academic writing—there is no right or wrong answer. You will not be formally graded, but you want this essay to be your best writing: no grammatical errors, punctuation mistakes, or misspelled words.
- No matter what the question is on a college application, the college wants to know about you. What do you value? Why is this important to you? What influences helped make you the unique person that you are?
- While colleges are interested in what you have accomplished, they are more interested in your motivation. Why have you been in forensics for 4 years? Drama? Yearbook, literary magazine, athletics?
- This essay is the main way that you can quite literally speak to the admissions committee, so you want to make the most of it.

Please note that in Table 9.1 numbers 1–5 require two responses: (1) the person, experience, event, fictive or historical figure, and diversity experience that has impacted or influenced you; and (2) how this impact or influence is seen or demonstrated in your life.

Table 9.1   Personal Essay Questions from the Common Application (See Additional Resources)

Personal Essay
Please write an essay (250 words minimum) on a topic of your choice or on one of the options listed below. Please indicate your topic by checking the appropriate box. This personal essay helps us become acquainted with you as a person and student, apart from courses, tests scores, and other objective data. It will also demonstrate your ability to organize your thoughts and express yourself. 1. Evaluate a significant experience, achievement, risk that you have taken, or ethical dilemma you have faced and its impact on you. 2. Discuss some issue of personal, local, national, or international concern and its importance to you. 3. Indicate a person who has had a significant influence on you, and describe that influence. 4. Describe a character in fiction, a historical figure, or a creative work (e.g., in art, music, science) that has had an influence on you, and explain that influence. 5. A range of academic interests, personal perspectives, and life experiences adds much to the educational mix. Given your personal background, describe an experience that illustrates what you would bring to the diversity in a college community or an encounter that demonstrated the importance of diversity to you. 6. Topic of your choice.

Caution: Too often, when discussing a fictional character, a historical figure, or an issue of importance, students fall into writing an analytical paper, much like they would write for an English or social studies class. Remember, this essay is different. This essay must show an influence and how that influence has impacted a student's life. If students choose to answer numbers 2, 4, or 6, they should be careful not to make this essay so analytical that it does not reveal who they are. Be wary of answering number 6, a topic of your choice. Again, the personal essay is about explaining who the student is; a "topic of your choice" may be so vague that it does not reveal the essence of the student.

Memo to Counselors

The following sections describe an approach to helping students write their essays and two models for conducting Personal Essay Writing Workshops. This approach may be adapted for Personal Essay Writing Workshops or for Group Guidance sessions. If possible, this process should begin in the spring of the junior year and be continued in the beginning of the senior year. Frequently, schools involve counselors, English teachers, and sometimes advisors in helping students write personal essays. It is essential that whoever works with students on personal essays understands the nature of this work. You may want to conduct a personal essay seminar for colleagues to ensure they understand that the personal essay is not purely academic writing and to familiarize them with the quality of the response level.

A Step-by-Step Approach to Writing the Personal Essay

Step 1

In the same way that students choose which essay question to answer on a test, they need to look at the options and answer the questions: Which question can I most readily answer? To which question can I most easily bring my own experience? To which question can I write a unique answer?

Have students write out bullet points about at least two of the questions that interest them most. This will help them to narrow their focus to one or two questions.

Step 2

Once students have narrowed their choice of possible questions they might answer, use the exercises in Figures 9.1 and 9.2 as an effective form of prewriting. These exercises use question 1, an event that has impacted a

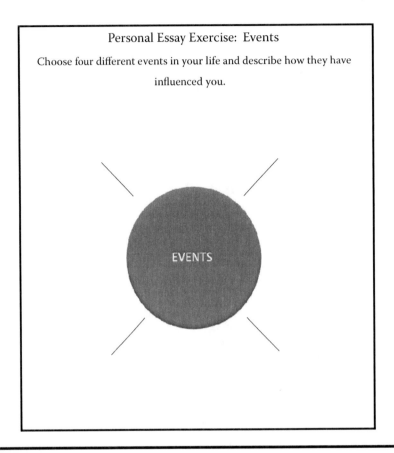

Personal Essay Exercise: Events

Choose four different events in your life and describe how they have influenced you.

EVENTS

Figure 9.1

student's life, and question 3, a person who has influenced a student's life. These exercises can easily be adapted to questions 2, 4, and 5. Students should write out phrases or bullet points above each line of the circle. As students begin to think about the events and the people who are or have been important in their lives, it will become easier to choose the focus of their personal essay.

Step 3

After completing these exercises, students should have a clear idea of not only which question to answer but also which person, event, or experience they wish to discuss. Encourage students to consider which option will best allow them to express the impact or influence of the person or event on their lives.

Once students have narrowed their choices, it is time to write a rough draft (Table 9.2).

Step 4

Students should meet with their counselor and get feedback on the essay. This means revise, revise, revise. It is the only way to perfect an essay.

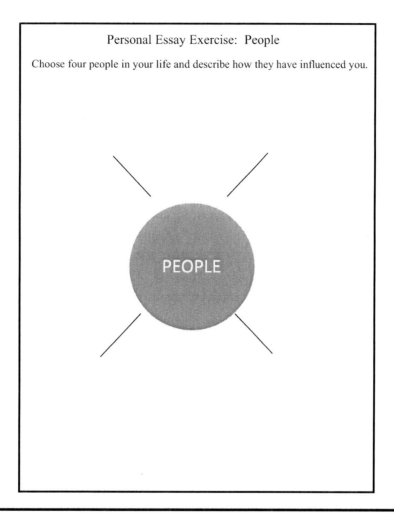

Personal Essay Exercise: People

Choose four people in your life and describe how they have influenced you.

PEOPLE

Figure 9.2

Personal Essay Samples

Following are several examples of personal essays. Although each essay is different, the common denominator is that each personal statement tells the story of an individual in an effective manner. Each student's story rings true: It has an authentic and distinctive voice.

Sample 1

In this essay, Gulus talks about her experience growing up as a Turkish American. She uses the image of a *kilim*, a Turkish carpet, to symbolize the ongoing development of her personality.

Gulus Emre
Harvard University

The way my sister used to tell it, I was left on the doorstep by gypsies. She said I was a gypsy baby born with a defect: my soul was cut in two. The gypsies sensed that they

Table 9.2   Writing a Rough Draft

Some Advice for a Successful Rough Draft

- Begin with a short reminiscence about the person, event, or experience as a way of communicating a memory and setting a framework for the essay.
- Use specific details and sensory images to recreate a scene or recall a person.
- Include a clear thesis in your introduction.
- Show how this person, event, or experience has influenced you. Be specific; do not generalize.
- Assess how this influence may affect your collegiate and future life. Once again be specific.
- Make sure that the majority of the writing develops the impact or influence that the person, event, or experience has had on you.
- Ask yourself if you have developed your thesis; do your paragraphs flow in a logical development?
- Do a line-by-line edit.
- Check that all sentences are complete—no fragments or run-ons.
- Correct spelling and grammatical errors.
- See your counselor for feedback
- Remember, this is a first draft—there is more work ahead!

could not repair the flaw and dropped me on a stoop in Brooklyn to get rid of me and the burden I carried. I was soon rescued by an unsuspecting Turkish woman (AKA Mom) who sensed my cracked core. She took out her medical textbook and special dried herbs and tried to repair the damage. Unfortunately, the herbs she bought were from Stop and Shop, so instead of sewing me up and making me fully Turkish, she accidentally made me half American as well.

Growing up in America, I exhibited peculiar symptoms. My parents found me bopping along to the music of Turkish pop star Sezen Aksu as she warbled out a song about her heavily bearded lover. I told my first "boyfriend," at the age of six, that he would have to meet my parents before he could kiss me. I listened obediently to adults and I helped serve tea to guests who came to visit. By the age of eight, I had learned how to mop the floor, scrub the counter, and beat a carpet. My parents were proud; I seemed to have all the makings of a dutiful Turkish girl.

During my summers in Turkey, my grandparents watched over my behavior more apprehensively than my parents. They were shocked to find me rapping along to Sir-Mix-a-Lot's "Baby Got Back" and horrified when I ran around skinning my hands and knees like a boy. During mealtimes on the porch, I was seated facing the wall so that I wouldn't strike up a conversation with a passerby on the street. By the age of eight and a half, I had hiked on the cliffs surrounding our little country home and boldly swam next to sea urchins and the infamous octopus that lived near our dock. My grandparents were worried; I seemed to have all the makings of a rebellious American girl.

As I got older, I started to knit myself back together, weaving my two half souls together like a *kilim*, a Turkish carpet. Some parts stayed American, some Turkish. I still enjoy serving tea to guests, but I don't wait silently to be addressed anymore because I know how to speak up for myself. I find music about big-bottomed women and large-mustached men equally irresistible. I don't think it's appropriate to write any more about what goes on with boyfriends here, because my religious grandmother would make me pray for forgiveness for my indecency.

My *kilim* is steadily coming together, and I constantly snip off loose or discolored threads and stitch together the rough edges that seem impossible to align. True, it may be uneven and the patterns might seem at odds with each other at times. But that type of patchwork suits me just fine.

Sample 2

This personal essay talks about the impact that a young girl, Laura, had on Brianna when she volunteered in a hospital wing devoted to children with severe illnesses.

Brianna Geary
University of Notre Dame

The first-grade classroom appeared to be a typical one: bright bulletin boards and cheery posters covered the walls, the art supply shelves stood fully stocked, and at the table sat several smiling students. The one difference that separated this classroom from others was that it is located in a children's rehabilitation hospital. The students were attending classes while at the same time being treated for their various illnesses or disabilities. I was their teacher's aide and was assigned to work with a seven-year-old girl named Laura. Sitting down next to her, I smiled at the sweet little girl with curly blonde hair and a friendly grin on her face. She introduced herself to me and began chatting as though we had been friends forever. As we were talking, the teacher handed out cans of Play-Doh. Laura wanted yellow Play-Doh and immediately swapped hers with the boy next to her. As the rest of the class began opening their Play-Doh, I glanced uneasily at Laura. Because of a skeletal-muscular disability Laura's elbows were locked in place, leaving her arms frozen in an almost-crossed position across her chest. As the can of yellow Play-Doh sat on the table in front of her, I hesitated to open it for her, finally asking if she needed help with anything. "No thanks!" she responded with a grin. Sliding off her flip-flops, she propped her feet up on the table, rubbed the soles together to warm them, and deftly peeled the lid off of the can with her feet. Flipping the can upside-down, she shook the Play-Doh loose, then set aside the can and lid and began patting down the yellow Play-Doh, all the while using only her feet. Amazed, I watched as Laura worked with her feet to create perfect Play-Doh "birthday cakes."

For my fifteenth birthday, I asked my surprised parents for a subscription to *National Geographic* magazine. Since then, I have read every issue. To date, my favorite article is about a new machine that can keep a heart pumping outside the body, a useful tool during a heart transplant surgery. The article featured a picture of a human heart hooked up to this device. I found, and still do find, the picture absolutely fascinating. The live, beating heart, its chambers and arteries clearly visible, made what I knew about the heart's function so real and vivid to me. It was possibly this very picture that catalyzed my passion for science into a determination to become a doctor. I became a volunteer because I considered the nationally renowned children's rehabilitation center to be a great place for me to learn about cutting-edge treatment and therapy options available to patients. I was excited to have the opportunity to see firsthand what it was like to work in a hospital.

I loved playing with and teaching the children, and the time I spent with them seemed to melt away all too quickly. I looked forward to working with Laura each week, not because of what I was teaching her, but, somewhat selfishly, because of what she was teaching me: that an illness or disability is not just a list of symptoms, but a part of a person's life. In this case, that person was a remarkable girl named Laura. Quite unconsciously, during my first few moments with her, my thoughts shifted almost immediately from what is "wrong" with Laura to simply who she is.

Meeting Laura completely changed the way I view medicine. Before knowing her, I was interested in science on a factual level; disabilities and illnesses intrigued me, but I lacked any meaningful, personal connection. I've realized that this personal connection is the most important part of practicing medicine. Without a strong and heartfelt desire to do everything in my power to help someone, scientific facts won't help at all. Like a heart without its body, scientific facts are meaningless until they are applied to real people.

Laura did not stop at Play-Doh. One week later, she used her muscular feet skillfully to manipulate a pair of scissors as she helped me cut out bingo cards for the rest of the class. She could also write with her feet, better than most of the other students could write with their hands. Laura's optimism in the face of adversity, her incredible courage and tenacity, and her strong will to live her life to the fullest have inspired me. I used to hope to be a great doctor, surgeon, or researcher who could cure people of their sicknesses. Today, I aspire to be a doctor who can look past a person's illness or disability and see his or her immeasurable potential. When I look at the picture of the heart in that old issue of *National Geographic* magazine, I still experience utter fascination, but now I find myself wondering: whose heart is it?

Sample 3

This personal essay talks about the influence of a person in a student's life. Here, Lindsay describes how her grandmother impacted here life from auditioning for LaGuardia High School of Performing Arts to performing at Carnegie Hall.

Lindsay Harris
Goucher College

My grandmother, my nonna, lives in Penn South, a building complex housing many retired people. Ever since I was a little girl, I remember playing in the little park in front of her building and noticing several older-looking people sitting on benches. One day when we were walking past the benches together, Nonna bent down and whispered that she would never want to sit there. "Once you sit, you're old," she would say. I giggled as I watched her smiling and waving at the old man with the parrot on his shoulder and an old lady feeding the pigeons. My nonna may be retired, but she certainly doesn't live like she is.

It is not as though my nonna never sits on benches. But when she does, it is the bench in an audition room as she flips through *Variety* waiting for her name to be called. Always interested in modeling, Nonna finally took the plunge when she was around 78 (but writing on her resume that she is in her 60s…whoops!). After getting professional headshots and two agents, she has been featured in a few print ads including one for Time Warner Cable. She has even played characters such as Lady Lox (a fussy, old lady) in small movies. At the same time, she has taken acting classes in Penn South. There, she has appeared in roles as big as Eliza Doolittle in *Pygmalion*. She has also performed in their talent shows by joke-telling or singing her favorite song, "I Can't Say No," from *Oklahoma!*

My nonna may be a model for companies, but more importantly, she has been a role model for me. By always getting out there and proving that nothing, not even age, can hold people from achieving their dreams, she has encouraged and inspired me. After all, if my nonna can model, sing, and act at 83, then what can't I do? Her influence has been both subtle and obvious. Looking back to 8th grade when I tried out for LaGuardia High School of Performing Arts, I now realize that I was not alone at the front of the audition room; my nonna's influence was in that room with me as well. Her spirit and strength were there, pushing me to do my best. Later when I auditioned for the most advanced choir at my school, Senior Chorus, her example propelled me to take that chance. This year when I auditioned for my first adult choir, New York City's Collegiate Chorale, I felt that, like nonna, I had achieved a goal that seemed unreachable before.

When the Collegiate Chorale takes the stage at Carnegie Hall for their performance of Verdi's *Requiem* this December, I know where Nonna will be. She won't be on a bench in the park with the man with the parrot. She will be in the audience, comfortably seated in a red, cushioned seat. While I am so enthused about this performance, I am even more excited that she will be there with me one more time. Even though I probably will not be able to see her in the audience, I know that she is with me just as she was in that first audition for LaGuardia.

Sample 4

In this essay, Hans discusses the impact that an event had on him. Visiting his father's family in rural Argentina, he experienced a culture and lifestyle radically different from his life in America.

Hans Orellano
St. Olaf College

I had never seen my mother pack so much hand sanitizer. I didn't have a clue as to why we needed such quantities. The last time I was in Argentina, I was a small boy and could not appreciate the full effect of seeing my Argentine family.

My grandmother lives in an area of Argentina called San Francisco de Solano. The drive to her house would be a nightmare to animal rights activists. Stray, sick, starving, or dead dogs and cats are common like pigeons in New York City. As we got closer, the roads became dirt. In place of a raised sidewalk, a long ditch of sewage bounded the sides of the road.

Arriving at my grandmother's home, I was struck by its decrepit condition. The house consists of brick walls and a tin roof, which shelter two rooms: a kitchen and a bedroom, shared by my grandmother and one of my uncles. Near the front door, there is a tiny outhouse, which I tried not to use, making me feel snooty. The day ended with me realizing how much Spanish I had forgotten from Spanish 1 and why we brought so much hand sanitizer.

Over the next weeks, we visited many family members, and I saw how my other aunts and uncles live. They each have their own children, many of whom cannot go to school because they must work. The last day, I was reluctant to leave and I almost didn't use my hand sanitizer, feeling that it was insulting to my family.

When I got home, I realized how fortunate I really was. Even though I didn't grow up in a luxurious house in a good neighborhood, my childhood was secure and nurturing. I grew up in the South Bronx and lived in a crack house turned parsonage for the church where my mother was the pastor. I didn't think of the people at the church as poor even though many were. I just saw them as members of my church. I never thought about living in what others considered to be a bad neighborhood. It was as normal as visiting my other grandmother who lived in an affluent New Jersey suburb. On the way to school, we would drive by a prison for children from 10 to 14 years old. There was a Burger King next to it and I used to think that it must be tough on them to smell the fries.

What I most remember is that the support from the community for me and my family was tremendous. I didn't fully appreciate our Bronx church until we moved to Manhattan. Even though I went to school in Manhattan and most of my friends lived there, I wanted to stay in the Bronx. Our new parsonage is located between public housing projects and several high-rises with multimillion-dollar apartments. Mexican immigrants live next to the luxury high-rises in rooms without a kitchen or private bath.

When I was growing up in the Bronx, I didn't ask myself about injustices and inequalities. I was more interested in how radios and televisions worked. I liked taking things apart to see how they fit together. I became interested in science, knowing that my maternal grandfather, for whom I am named, was a chemical engineer. Wondering about how things work and how the universe came together led to my desire study physics and to become a physicist.

As I matured, I now question the way people are conscious of injustices and could make a difference, but they don't. So in addition to physics, I am interested in metaphysics. By combining the questions of physics and philosophy, I hope to learn how I can use my talents and education to improve our world. In my Jesuit school, we are taught the Ignatian value—to be "a man for others." I hope to be a physicist for others.

Sample 5

This is the story of Seonghae Jeon, who talks about her experience growing up as the daughter of a hard-working Korean immigrant.

Seonghae Jeon
Hunter College of the City University of New York

When I was much younger, I thought everyone's dad owned a sewing machine and worked every day of the week until midnight. As a kid, I thought my dad was a very rich person because he always had a huge amount of clothes with him but wondered why my family had to live in such a small apartment with no air conditioning. Until my parents decided to immigrate to the United States, mostly because of their financial difficulty, I did not know why my dad stayed up until 12 a.m., repairing clothes with his sewing machine.

For 6 years of my elementary school in Korea, I did not feel confident telling other students what my dad's job was. On the seldom occasion that I gathered the courage to say, "My dad is a tailor," people responded with a face of pity. At a very young age, I learned that my dad's job was not highly valued in society. However, I could never tell my dad that I was not very happy with his job. Instead, I often told him that many of my friends were jealous of me because I could ask him to fix my clothes whenever I wanted without paying money. I could not hurt his feelings because I knew how hard he had been working to support my mother, brother, and me.

Back in Korea, my dad had five different kinds of sewing machines at work and one private sewing machine in his bedroom. Every single day after 9 p.m., I always heard a buzzing sound from my parents' room because my dad worked on the sewing machine repairing his customers' clothes. My brother and I could not sleep until he was done, but we barely complained because it was routine. After he was done working on his customers' clothes, he usually came to our room and asked us if our shirts or gym clothes were fine. He worked hard because he cared for us.

As I became older and grew to his height, I began to view my dad differently. He looked tired and older. It was not that he had more wrinkles or white hairs, but he seemed like he had too much burden on his shoulders. After I entered middle school, my dad and I were not able to communicate as often because I returned home later and he had to work longer and harder to pay for my school uniforms and lunch. I began to hate looking at his back because it looked slightly bent. I felt like I had placed more burdens on him and did not want him to be sad.

He is now 51 years old and still has a sewing machine in his room and still works until midnight. He occasionally comes into my room when I am studying or doing my homework and jokes that 10 years from now, he and I will become "two generations of doctors." He explains that he is a doctor of clothes and that I will hopefully become a "real" doctor. We no longer have time for long conversations with each other. However, without any words delivered, I know how much he loves me and that his love for me has shaped who I am now. Regardless of how other people may view my dad's job, I am proud of being a daughter of a hardworking tailor.

How to Conduct a Personal Essay Writing Workshop—Two Models

Model 1: Conducting a Writing Workshop During the Academic Day

At IN-Tech Academy, a public school in the Bronx, New York, counselors do not have regularly scheduled group guidance sessions. Here the counselors combined an early morning format that extended into first period so that students could attend a Personal Essay Writing Workshop. The IN-Tech model also includes having an admissions counselor from Manhattan College advise students about the importance of this essay. While this workshop was held in the fall of the senior year, students also benefited from attending a similar workshop in the spring of their junior year.

Below is the invitation that seniors received from their college advisor.

The Guidance Department at MS/HS 368 is hosting an intensive noncredit class on the College Application Essay. You have been invited to the second cycle of classes. The dates, times, and topics are as follows:

Monday, September 22	7:45am–8:30am	The College Application Essay: What You Should Know (in the auditorium)
Tuesday, September 23	7:45am–8:30am	How Important Is the College Application Essay? Manhattan College Admissions Office
Monday, September 29	7:45am–8:30am	Sample Essays: The Do's and Don'ts of College Application Essays
Monday, October 6	7:45am–8:30am	Writing Workshop
Tuesday, October 7	7:45am–8:30am	Writing Workshop

Please note that your College Application Essay is an important part of your application process. We strongly recommend that you take advantage of this resource. Should you have a first-period class, you will be given assignments to complete in lieu of your absences. We look forward to seeing you on Monday morning.

Students followed the four-step process for writing the college essays and after the completion of the workshop met with counselors for feedback on their work.

Model 2: Using Regularly Scheduled Group Guidance Sessions to Present the Personal Essay

For counselors who have regularly scheduled group guidance sessions, presenting the how-to of the personal essay can be done in a multiple-week approach. Ideally, this should be done in the spring of the junior year. This could also be combined with a special session with an admissions officer from a local college. Usually, admissions personnel are happy to be involved in these outreach programs, particularly in the spring when their workload is lessened.

Week 1: Explaining the personal essay and its importance. Homework: Choose a question.
Week 2: Using exercises to help students prewrite. Homework: Choose exact topic.
Week 3: Writing a rough draft. Homework: Complete a rough draft.
Follow-up: Make individual appointments to receive feedback on the essay.

If students have made a serious effort to write the personal essay at the end of the junior year, it will make their college application process much easier in the senior year.

HELPFUL HINT

Be conscious of the length of your essay. While the minimum is 250 words, which is quite short, do not make your essay too long. This is not the first chapter in your memoirs. In fact, if you apply online and exceed the maximum number of characters (letters and spaces), your essay may be cut off. Note the approximate length of the sample essays; they are a good indicator of length.

Two Other Suggestions to Incorporate into Either Model

1. Enlist the assistance of the English department. In some schools, the personal essay is a necessary component of the final grade in 11th-grade English and is later revised for credit in 12th-grade English. (Of course, this approach may be used without making the personal essay a graded paper for credit.) In using this method, counselors must convey not only the importance of this essay but also the nature of this particular writing: Neither analytical nor

creative, the personal essay is a combination of both that reveals who the student is. Such an endeavor requires several drafts before a solid personal essay emerges. A counselor/faculty workshop would be helpful in developing an ongoing collaboration between counselors and English teachers. Such a collaboration may have a dramatic impact on both the completion of the personal statement and the quality of the written work. In addition, counselors with heavy caseloads may find much-needed assistance.

2. Seek the help of college admissions officers. If your school has a partnership with an institute of higher education, ask an admissions officer to conduct a personal essay workshop for your students. Usually May and June are opportune times for this to occur since the college admissions workload is lessened. Even if your school does not enjoy a relationship with a particular college, contact the admissions office of a college that knows your school. Usually, colleges want their admissions officers to participate in outreach programs; it is a great public relations vehicle.

What Colleges Say About the Personal Essay

From Boston College (2006):

Writing the "Perfect" Essay

First of all, let us debunk the myth. There is no such thing as a perfect essay. There, we've said it. Now you can clear your mind of the anxiety that typically accompanies students as you sit down to write. Instead, you can focus on using the essay as a tool to let the Committee on Admission learn more about you as an individual.

Many of us feel that in the fall of your senior year, the college essay is the only portion of your application remaining on which you can still have a significant influence. Granted, you will need to continue working hard in your classes, but you have already met people who will speak highly of you in a recommendation, you have already been involved in various extra-curricular activities, and you have likely completed your standardized examinations. The one remaining portion is the college essay. We realize how hectic your senior year is, but take advantage of this opportunity.

The best essays that we read are ones that tell us not only about a specific event, mentor, excursion, or accomplishment, but also tell us how the writer has been affected by their experiences. For example, a typical essay might inform the reader of a trip to France that the student took the previous summer. It might focus on the challenges faced in getting to their destination, the French culture, or even the people that the student met. The better essay, however, takes it to the next level. It makes the experience personal. The student might choose to explain what surprised, frustrated, or inspired them about the trip. The student might choose to focus on how they now view the world a little bit differently after this newfound international perspective.

Another common example is students' essays on a person who influenced their lives. Frequently, we read essays about applicants' grandparents, for example. Many essays simply focus on the attributes that a grandmother has that make her special to the applicant. They may focus on the challenges that a grandmother has overcome or the successes she has enjoyed. They leave the reader knowing that the student loves his grandmother, but not knowing anything more about the student. The better essay, however, might also focus on the way the writer has attempted to emulate these admired qualities. The student might choose to share how learning of his grandmother's life experiences have helped him better understand the world. This allows us to learn more about the student and what makes the student special.

As you can see, in both of these examples, the first essay simply tells us of an experience, but the second essay shows us more about the individual. We walk away from it knowing a bit more about the qualities the applicant possesses and how he or she might fit into our campus community.

We hope that you will not view the college essay as a roadblock between you and your college choice, but as a unique opportunity to be in the driver's seat in the college process. Let your qualities, characteristics, and personality shine through. Best wishes as you begin your journey.

From The State University of New York at Binghamton (Binghamton University, 2010):

4 Tips to Grab the Attention of the Admissions Committee

Choose a Topic	Tell an Interesting Story	Say Something New!	Revise, Revise, Revise
It sounds obvious, but a flaw in many college essays is a lack of focus. Narrow it down to a single point and follow this idea from beginning to end.	Develop your idea with expressive and descriptive words that create a vivid story. Use examples, facts and events to get your point across in your own voice. If the essay guidelines specify a 500-word limit, stay within that limit.	Admissions counselors have your application in front of them; you don't have to list every activity you've been involved in or talk about your grades. Here's your chance to tell them something they can't get from your transcript. Get personal and convince them that you're more than just a GPA and test score!	This is not a case of "for your eyes only." Ask someone whose opinion you respect to review it. Have a helpful guidance counselor or a favorite teacher? Ask them for feedback on content, structure, and word choice. And, make sure there are no spelling mistakes and you use good grammar.

From Carleton College (2009):

Essay Tips

To help you get off to a good start, we've put together the following tips and hints. These are comments from our admissions staff who actually read your essays and evaluate them in the admission process. We can't guarantee results, but this advice might help you get started.

Top 15 Essay Tips From the Readers

1. **View it as an opportunity.** The essay is one of the few things that you've got complete control over in the application process, especially by the time you're in your senior year. You've already earned most of your grades; you've already made most of your impressions on teachers; and chances are, you've already found a set of activities you're interested in continuing. So when you write the essay, view it as something more than just a page to fill up with writing. View it as a chance to tell the admissions committee about who you are as a person.
2. **Be yourself.** If you are funny, write a funny essay; if you are serious, write a serious essay. Don't start reinventing yourself with the essay.
3. **Make it fun.** If you're recounting an amusing and light-hearted anecdote from your childhood, it doesn't have to read like a Congressional Act—make it fun!
4. **Tell us something different** from what we'll read on your list of extracurricular activities or transcript.
5. **Take the time to go beyond the obvious.** Think about what most students might write in response to the question and then try something a little different.
6. **Don't try to take on too much.** Focus on one "most influential person," one event, or one activity. Tackling too much tends to make your essay too watered down or disjointed.
7. **Concentrate on topics of true significance to you.** Don't be afraid to reveal yourself in your writing. We want to know who you are and how you think.
8. **Write thoughtfully and from your heart.** It'll be clear who believes in what they are saying versus those who are simply saying what they think we want to hear.
9. **Essays should have a thesis** that is clear to you and to the reader. Your thesis should indicate where you're going and what you're trying to communicate from the outset.
10. **Don't do a history report.** Some background knowledge is okay, but do not re-hash what other authors have already said or written.

11. **Answer each school's essay individually.** Recycled "utility essays" come across as impersonal and sanitized. The one exception is an essay written for and submitted to Common Application member schools.

12. **Proofread, proofread, proofread.** Nothing says "last-minute essay" like an "are" instead of "our" or a "their" instead of "they're."

13. **Keep it short** and to the point.

14. **Limit the number of people** from whom you request feedback on your essay. Too much input creates an essay that sounds as though it has been written by a committee or results in writing that is absent your own voice.

15. **Appearances count.** Formatting and presentation cannot replace substance, but they can certainly enhance the value of an already well-written essay.

From Colorado College (2010):

Writing

Because strong writing skills are so essential to academic success at CC, we read essays very carefully. You'll write one major essay and a few complementary essays as part of your application process. We believe essays are an important indicator of an applicant's ability to think critically and write clearly and fluidly. The essays are also our chance to get to know you, the applicant, on a more personal level. It is our one chance to hear directly from you. Please take the time to think carefully about what you want us to know about you, and then write your essays in a way that reflects this information. There is nothing inherently better about a funny essay or a serious essay. Please stay true to yourself, write in your own voice, and write about topics that are relevant to you.

From University of Michigan (2010):

Tips for Writing a Great Essay

General

- **Read and *answer* the question asked.** You'd be amazed how many essays we receive that don't relate at all to the question we were asking!

- **There is no "right" answer.** Don't think you know what we want to hear. Whatever you have to say about the topic is of interest to us.

- **Be authentic.** We want to hear your voice in your response—the experiences, opinions and values that have shaped you. Feel free to write on something you are passionate about so we can get to know you better.
- **Be proactive!** Each year, we talk to students who have everything ready but their essays—if they could just get them finished, their application would be complete. Get started on your essays soon, and don't spend months agonizing over whether they're perfect. We don't read through them with a red pen in hand!
- **Avoid re-writing your accomplishments in paragraph form.** You've already given us that information in your application.
- **Re-use essays (or portions of essays) when possible, especially when applying to a lot of schools.** However, make sure to re-read before hitting the submit button or mailing them in! The worst possible way to finish your essay to U-M is to say, "And I just can't wait to be a Spartan!" This happens. Seriously.
- **A research paper is different from an admissions essay.** If you are re-using something you've previously written, make sure it directly answers our question—and not one that a teacher posed to you for an assignment.

From Stanford University (2010):

Essays

In reading all of your writing, we want to hear your individual voice. Write essays that reflect who you are; use specific concrete details and write in a natural style. Begin work on these essays early, and feel free to ask your parents, teachers, and friends to provide constructive feedback. When you ask for feedback on an essay draft, ask if the essay's tone sounds like your voice—it should. If your parents, teachers, and friends do not believe your essay captures who you are or what you believe, surely we will be unable to recognize what is most distinctive about you. While securing feedback is suggested, you should not enlist hired assistance in the writing of your essays.

From the University of Texas at Austin (2010):

Tips on Essay Writing

Plan Ahead

By reviewing requirements for your major choices, scholarships, and programs, you may be able to keep the number of essays you write to a minimum while satisfying admission and other requirements.

Essay Length

If you're writing your essays to fulfill your admission requirements only, you should try to keep them no longer than one page (single-spaced). If you plan to use your essays to fulfill admission and scholarship or honors requirements, follow the length guidelines specified by the individual program.

Take Your Time

Spend plenty of time writing and fine-tuning your essays, and ask for feedback from people you trust before submitting your essays.

Quality Matters

Remember that your goal is to share important things about yourself while skillfully expressing yourself in writing.

Chapter 10

Assisting Students in Constructing the Final List of Colleges (12th Grade)

Memo to Counselors

In this chapter we discuss the tasks that need to be accomplished in the college application process. This includes ongoing college research, developing an activities/résumé sheet, a review of what to look for when visiting colleges, and a presentation of interview tips. We also explain how to build a list of appropriate colleges and then how to narrow that list down to a manageable number of schools. In addition, we provide practical suggestions for counselors to assist students in asking for teacher recommendations, registering for standardized testing, and completing applications.

Counselors must also remind and advise students about standardized testing (Chapter 6). As we stated earlier in Chapter 8, it is the responsibility of students and parents to register for tests. However, it is essential that the counselor assist in this process. The main concern is that students are on a course to prepare for and take the standardized testing that is necessary for college admission and that they understand relevant information about fee waivers and/or reductions. Table 10.1, a modified version of this form from Chapter 8, may be helpful to counselors in this process.

Necessary Tasks in the College Application Process

First of all, make sure that you are preparing for the necessary standardized tests and that you are registered to take them. Your counselor will be

Table 10.1 Senior-Year Standardized Testing Form

Name:

Date:

Counselor's Name:

1. Which standardized test do you plan to take?

	Are You Registered? Indicate Yes/No	Date of Test
__ SAT	_____	_____
__ ACT	_____	_____
__ ACT with writing	_____	_____
__ SAT Subject Test	_____	_____
Which Subject Test?	_____	_____
	_____	_____
	_____	_____

2. Method of preparation for SAT/ACT? (Check all that apply)

__ Preparation Class

Indicate Which _____

__ Online Preparation

__ Private Tutoring

__ Preparing on My Own

asking you to complete a form stating which tests you will be taking and when. Make sure to see your counselor about fee reduction/waiver forms if applicable.

Some helpful reminders are as follows:

1. You can register online, via phone, or via U.S. mail. Make sure that you register early so that you will get the test site that you want.
2. Different kinds of preparation are available such as online tests and prep classes. What help is available in your school and community? Do not take a test without preparation.

Remember, do not send any scores to colleges until you have finished the testing process. If you should take another test, you will have to resend scores. This can become very expensive.

Now it is your senior year and time for serious reflection and action that will help you plan your future. In your junior year (Chapter 8), you created an initial list of colleges that you researched. Hopefully, you visited some of these colleges and thought about what kind of collegiate environment is best for you. Some factors you considered are

■ Size: Are you interested in a large, medium, or small college/university?
■ Does the distance from home matter?
■ Do you want to live on campus or commute?
■ Majors—Refer to Table 8.1, Exercise on Majors and Careers, which you completed in Chapter 8.
■ Does a college have a special program that interests you?
■ Are you interested in a community college leading to an associate's degree?

Using Appendix C, 10 Useful Web Pages for College Research, as well as individual college Web sites, you focused your college research. By the end of the year, you constructed an initial list of colleges that you were considering. Now it is time to move toward finalizing a list of colleges to which you will apply. If you did not accomplish as much in your junior year as you wanted to achieve, it is not too late to restart the college search process. Now is the time to do it!

Here is what *you* need to accomplish:

1. Continue research of colleges that are appropriate for you
2. Construct an activities sheet/résumé (Table 10.3)
3. Visit colleges
4. Interview at colleges
5. Build a list and narrow it down to a reasonable number of schools
6. Meet with your college advisor for advice
7. Seek teacher recommendations
8. Write a strong personal statement
9. Fill out applications
10. Apply for financial aid
11. Extra: Organize your portfolio of special talent accomplishments

No matter where you are in the college application process, there is still time to find the school that is right for you. Whether you are interested in a 2-year program leading to an associate's degree or a 4-year program earning a bachelor's degree, the senior year in high school is filled with much to do. So let's begin, step by step, to make sure that you are doing what you need to do.

Step 1: Researching Colleges and Much More

Have you researched some colleges? If you have done some serious investigation, then you are on your way to building a college list. Are you someone who needs a jump-start to get going? Or maybe you are somewhere in between? No matter where you are in this process, you have time to expand your list and make it a better fit for you.

In addition to Appendix C, 10 Useful Web Pages for College Research, use the additional technology that is available to you to make your college search more effective.

Other Essential Technologies

Memo to Counselors

Refer to Chapter 5 for a more detailed explanation of these programs.

The College Board's QuickStart and MyRoad Programs

My College QuickStart (see College Board in Additional Resources section) is a free personalized college and career planning kit based on your Preliminary Scholastic Aptitude Test (PSAT) results. Using the resources of the College Board is a great way to help in your college search. To sign in, you will need the access code printed on your PSAT/NMSQT® (National Merit Scholarship Qualifying Test) paper score report. If you do not already have a College Board account, you'll be prompted to create one. It typically takes less than 2 minutes to create your free account.

My College QuickStart includes the following features:

■ My College Matches—A starter list of colleges based on your home state and indicated choice of major
■ My Major and Career Matches—Personalized lists of majors and careers plus access to a personality assessment that suggests other compatible possibilities

MyRoad is a comprehensive free online college and career planning resource that can help you:

■ Explore college majors that can help you achieve your goals
■ Build your college list and simplify the college application process

The Common Application

The Common Application online (see Common Application in Additional Resources) is a powerful tool for students. If you are applying to colleges via the Common Application, you may use the online version to research and compare colleges and to prepare and submit actual applications and supplements. In addition, most member colleges accept application fees through this Web site. Simply go to www.commonapp.org to create an account by filling in a user name and creating a password.

Once this account has been established, you can use the search engine to research and compare colleges on the Common Application. A list of MY Colleges is automatically created, and you may then add to or delete schools from your lists. By clicking on a college on this list, you can easily see where you are in the application process. User-friendly symbols enable you to ascertain whether or not applications and/or supplements have been submitted. In addition, the Common App has an information bar that provides deadlines for submission, tests required, supplement forms if necessary, and fee payment information—all of which may be completed online at this one Web site.

Naviance

If your school has the Naviance system, it is an essential resource in helping you to explore colleges that would be a good match for you. Use Family Connection on this system to help you research colleges and keep an ongoing list of possible college choices. Naviance (see Additional Resources) also provides a scattergram that graphically shows how students from your school with similar grades and standardized test scores fared at individual colleges. This can help you decide if you are a good match for a particular school.

ACT

The ACT® (see Additional Resources) Educational Planning and Assessment System (EPAS®) was developed in response to the need for all students to be prepared for college and the transitions they make after high school graduation. This system can help you in researching both colleges and careers.

Step 2: Constructing an Activities Sheet or Résumé

The Activities Sheet/Résumé is a snapshot of your high school interests and achievements. You have already done the initial planning of this in Chapter 8 when you completed the Extracurricular/Work Experience Section of the Common Application. The Activities Sheet/Résumé (Table 10.2) can be helpful in an interview, and you may want to enclose it in your applications as extra information for your file.

Some do's and don'ts for the Activities Sheet/Résumé:

■ Use generic terms for activities and publications; your school may have a specific name for your yearbook or newspaper, but people outside of your community may not know these names. Use *yearbook, school newspaper, literary magazine,* and so forth.

Table 10.2　Sample Activities/Résumé Sheet

Your name	Your school
Your address	School address
Your phone number	School phone number
Your e-mail address	
Academic Honors	
Honor Roll	10, 11, 12
Member of the National Honor Society	11, 12
• President	12
Extracurricular Activities	
Yearbook	9, 10, 11, 12
• Layout Editor	11
• Editor-in-Chief	12
Student Government Representative	9, 10
Athletics	
Varsity Soccer	9, 10, 11, 12
• Soccer Captain	12
• Basketball	9
Community Service	
Hospital Volunteer	9, 10
Coats for the Homeless	11, 12
• Organized school-wide drive for coat collection for the homeless	
Work Experience	
Preschool Camp Counselor	9, 10
Internship at Local Radio Station	11
Summer Activities	
Art Class at Local Museum	9
Creative Writing Class at Local University	10

- List your activities and athletics in order of what is most important to you. Colleges are looking for commitment to an activity or sport rather than a splattering of casual involvement.
- If you do not have a specific category for your résumé such as academic honors, do not list that category on your résumé. Go with your strengths.
- When listing community service and/or work experience, be specific. Name the hospital or the business where you worked.
- Do not put your social security number on your Activities Sheet/Résumé. Unlike your college application, you may use this résumé for multiple purposes such as interviewing for possible employment, and you want to protect your identity.

Step 3: Visiting Colleges—What to Look For

By now you are on your way to formulating your college list. But you need another essential step: visiting schools. In Chapter 8, we looked at specific criteria to look for in a college visit. Let's revisit what we talked about in Chapter 8.

Colleges are like people: they have personalities, too. The best way to get a sense of where you might feel most at home is by visiting the colleges that are on your list. You should definitely visit the colleges that are within an easy commute. Nothing can replace the "sense" of a campus—the feeling that you get when you walk around, see the buildings, interact with people, and envision whether or not this is the right place for you.

So, definitely visit those colleges that are within an easy distance. For those colleges that take more traveling, do not worry. You can still apply and visit later if you are accepted. Colleges have Accepted Students Weekends to help you make the right choice.

Arrange a Visit

- Call the Admissions Office and schedule a tour of the campus.
- If possible, arrange to attend a class and/or meet with a professor in an area of your academic interest.
- If you have a special talent—music, drama, athletics—arrange to meet an instructor or coach.
- Eat in the cafeteria; this may be replacing your usual diet. Sometimes the Admissions Office will give you a free meal.

What to Look For

Remember that a tour of campus is a public relations tool—they want to show what makes the college look good. That's fine, but look beyond that; for example—

■ How large are the typical classrooms? The college may say that it has a small teacher–student ratio, but if you see many large lecture halls, you may want to question it.

■ You will see the latest labs and computer centers, but are they typical?

■ The dorm room looks great, but you may find out that only upperclassmen are allowed to live there.

■ That athletic center looks great, but can nonteam members use it? How often?

■ Watch how students interact. Is it a friendly environment?

■ What is the social life like: clubs, activities, sports?

■ If you have a special interest—politics, debate, community service—explore what this college has to offer.

A Few Final Tips

If visiting with friends, try not to be influenced by their reactions to a particular college. This is a very individual process, and what is good for one person may not be for another. Chances are, you will not be attending college with your closest friends.

Using the chart provided in Table 10.3, write down your impressions of the college; this can help you to understand what you are looking for in a college. Finally, even if you have not scheduled an appointment for a tour with the Admissions Office, stop in and let them know who you are and that you are visiting. They want to know who is interested in their campus.

Note: It is important use the chart in Table 10.3 to write down your impressions after visiting a campus. Do this immediately after a visit. All too often, students confuse colleges if they do not record their reactions to a college visit.

Table 10.3 Exercise on Evaluating College Visits

Name of College/ University	What I Liked About the Academics	What I Did Not Like About the Academics	What I Liked About Social/ Extracurricular Life	What I Did Not Like About Social/ Extracurricular Life

Step 4: Interviewing—Another Way to Learn More About Colleges and Let Them Know More About You

Many colleges interview prospective students. Interviewing is not mandatory, and, in fact, many large colleges and universities do not have the staff to do any interviewing. If you choose to interview, make the most of it. This is a two-way opportunity: Admissions staff can talk to you in person, and you have the chance to present yourself in a positive light and ask pertinent questions about the college.

Interviews may be on-campus with an admissions officer, or they may off campus with an alumnus of the school. No matter which interview method, be prepared to discuss your academic interests and extracurricular involvement.

■ Do your homework: You do not know what an interviewer will ask, but be prepared to show your knowledge of the college. Be ready to ask at least two intelligent questions—one about academics and one about quality of life on campus.

■ Any special programs that interest you? For example, don't ask about whether or not there is a major in astronomy—you should know that from your research. Ask about internships or possible research in the area of astronomy.

■ Are there any extracurricular groups that especially attract you? Be prepared to discuss why you are interested in a particular activity and any past involvement.

■ Regarding social life, ask about cultural events on campus or collegiate connections with the local cultural activities.

■ Bring a copy of your Activities Sheet. It gives the interviewer a thumbnail sketch of your interests and helps to generate a dialogue.

■ Think of body language: Be dressed appropriately, make eye contact, and speak clearly.

■ Practice interviewing with an adult—a teacher, counselor, parent, family friend. This can help you feel more relaxed in an actual interview.

■ A postinterview thank-you note or e-mail is a polite way of letting the interviewer know of your interest in the school.

Step 5: Constructing a Final List of Colleges—Building and Narrowing Your List

As you research colleges, ask yourself: What do I want to study? Liberal arts, business, engineering, architecture, education? (See Chapter 8 for greater detail.)
First of all, here are some terms you need to review:

■ What is a major? A major will be your concentrated area of interest at the college or university. You will graduate with a degree in your major.

■ What is a minor? A minor is a set of courses that is sufficient to establish proficiency in a discipline without having to take all of the courses that a major would require.

Liberal Arts Major

A liberal arts education allows you to explore any number of career possibilities. Unlike students in professional or vocational programs, students in liberal arts degree programs receive broad exposure to a variety of areas while focusing on a few key specialties that lead to an associate's, bachelor's, or master's degree. A liberal arts major offers a broad overview of the arts, sciences, and humanities.

Education Major

Completing an undergraduate degree in K–12 education prepares you to teach students in kindergarten through high school, while a graduate degree in this field provides continuing education for the classroom teacher in his or her primary subject area or grade level. Your graduate degree, along with experience as a classroom teacher, opens the door to a career in administration and teacher education. You can earn a teaching license in your choice of more than 20 specialties.

Business Major

A career in business can involve the obvious functions such as management and marketing, but there is an increasing need for business majors to apply their skills in government, international commerce, health care, arts, and nonprofit organizations. Business principles can serve as the backbone for economic, political, and social systems at all levels.

Technology Major

Technology majors are designed to give you more than just an overview of the field. You will learn new methods for developing gaming systems. You will learn how to create computer programs that will be able to store data and make it easier to find information. You will be able to stop people from accessing data they should not be seeing. All of these skills can be applied to many different career fields.

Engineering Major

Most engineering majors concentrate on a chosen specialty, supplemented by courses in both science and mathematics. Depending on the program and the institution, an engineering major could study either industrial practices to prepare for a hands-on job or theoretical principles to lay the groundwork for a research or academic career.

Remember, it is perfectly fine to be unsure about what your major will be. In fact, most students change their major several times over the course of their college career. If you do not know what you want to study, you are better off attending a liberal arts college where you can experience a broad range of courses.

Don't forget to consult the Majors Web page at A2ZColleges.com (see Additional Resources) on the 10 Useful Web Pages chart (Appendix C). This offers a list of college majors and leads to colleges in the United States that offer programs in that major. Students can choose from subjects they are interested in by clicking on, for example, biology or veterinary science. It does not, however, give career choices under each. Another helpful Web page is the College Board's College Search page (see Additional References) to find schools that offer majors of interest to you.

Now that you have considered what to study and researched possible colleges and universities, how do you decide which schools are good matches for you? All colleges publish the average grade point average and median standardized test scores of their entering freshman classes.

■ Compare your school grade point average and your SAT or ACT scores with those of students who are attending a particular college you are considering as a possible choice. Is this a good academic match for you? Do you have a reasonable chance of being accepted? Remember, the grades and score that colleges report are usually averages, which means that there are some students above and some students below those numbers. Use it as a general guideline, not a litmus test.

■ Another factor is diversity: Will you be happy in this environment? Colleges also publish the ethnic, racial, and religious compositions of their student bodies. This is an important factor to consider because this will be your home away from home.

■ Another consideration is whether this school offers any special programs that pertain to you. These programs could be special academic programs or opportunities for underrepresented groups in the student body.

Coming up with your final list of colleges is hard work but well worth the effort. A year from now you will be starting a new stage of your life, and you want to be happy with it. Use Table 10.4 to list 5–10 colleges or universities to which you are considering applying. How do you match up? Do you have the credentials that the college is seeking? Does the college have what you want? By completing this chart, you should be able to narrow your initial list of colleges and decide which schools are the best matches for you.

A Cautionary Note: If you are interested in a vocational/technical school, make sure that the credits you will earn can be transferred to an institution of higher learning.

Table 10.4   Exercise on College Matches

Name of College	Major/ Special Programs	Mean GPA	Your GPA	Mean SAT/ ACT	Your SAT/ ACT

Step 6: Meeting With Your College Advisor

Memo to Counselors

Inform students about policies regarding scheduling appointments, correct procedure for transcript requests, the Secondary School Report, and other pertinent information.

Your college advisor is your advocate: Schedule a meeting with your college advisor as soon as possible. Your college advisor can do the following:

■ Help you to establish a realistic college list.
■ Assess your chances of acceptance at specific colleges based upon the school record of past acceptances.
■ Advise you about any special programs. This includes academic as well as opportunities for minority students. Most states have established programs for groups that are underrepresented in colleges and universities. Your college advisor will know if you qualify.
■ Review your Activities Sheet, Short Answer Essay, and Personal Statement.
■ Assist you in selecting teachers to ask for recommendations.
■ Speak with representatives of colleges and special programs on your behalf.

Most importantly, your college advisor is the person who will write the Secondary School Report. This is the main school recommendation that colleges depend upon to know who you are as a person and as a student. Stay in frequent touch with your college advisor. This can only help you.

Step 7: Seeking Teacher Recommendations

What Are Teacher Recommendations?

A teacher recommendation is an academic appraisal of your performance and ability in a particular class. Teachers evaluate students on their class participation, projects, papers, presentations, labs, and test performance. Teachers may also reflect upon a student's improvement, academic commitment, initiative, and potential for growth. While these letters are primarily academic, teachers will also comment on you as a person. For example, they may evaluate leadership traits, ability to work with others, and approach to challenges. If teachers also know you through activities, sports, community service, or other activities, they will usually discuss your performance in the appropriate area.

Not all colleges require teacher recommendations, but many do—and these are important! Usually colleges want two teacher recommendations.

Why Are Teacher Recommendations Important?

Teacher recommendations are important because they give colleges further information about you as a student. Your grade point average on a transcript is just that—a number. But a letter written by one of your teachers can make that number say much more. In selecting students, college admissions counselors want to make sure that you are a good match for their school. Knowing more about you helps them in their decision making.

Whom Should You Ask?

Keep in mind that these recommendations are about your academic performance. They are not about which teacher you like most or which teacher you think likes you. Teachers who have given you good grades will find it easier to write a recommendation for you.

When selecting teachers for recommendations, follow these guidelines:

- Your junior-year grades are the most significant because they show your most recent and most mature performance. What are your best grades? Can you ask these teachers?
- You may also look at your grades from an earlier year if you have that teacher for a course in your senior year. This way that teacher can comment on your growth.
- It does not look good if the only teacher you can ask for a recommendation is from 9th grade.
- Usually, it is best to ask teachers from major subjects rather than minor subjects unless you are applying to a special program that is in the teacher's area of expertise such as music or art.

■ Finally, there is no magic formula: Recommendations do not have to be written by an English teacher and a math teacher—just two teachers from two different academic disciplines. Always check what the college is requiring. For example, an engineering program may want a recommendation from a math or science teacher.

When approaching teachers, politely ask for their help. Most teachers will not agree to write a recommendation unless they are able to write good comments about you.

Memo to Counselors

Advise students that these are confidential letters and, consequently, more effective if students waive their right to see the recommendation.

What About Other Recommendations?

Colleges vary on this, so check with the college admissions office. If a person knows you well—a coach, an employer, a community service director—you may want to ask him or her to send a letter on your behalf. Recommendations from people who really do not know you carry very little weight. You do not want to antagonize the admissions office with a lot of paper that means nothing.

Step 8: Writing the Personal Essay

This is presented in detail in Chapter 9.

Step 9: Filling Out Those Applications

As you begin to fill out applications, make sure that you understand the kind of admission policy each college has. Different types of admission plans are presented below (Common Data Set Definitions, 2010–2011):

■ *Regular admission* is the most common admission plan. This simply means that if the due date is January 1, all of the materials that you are responsible for submitting must be received by that date. The admissions staff begins to consider applicants after the posted deadline.
■ *The early action plan* allows students to apply and be notified of an admission decision well in advance of the regular notification dates. If admitted, the candidate is not committed to enroll; the student may reply to the offer under the college's regular reply policy.

- *The early decision plan* permits students to apply and be notified of an admission decision (and financial aid offer if applicable) well in advance of the regular notification date. Applicants agree to accept an offer of admission and, if admitted, to withdraw their applications from other colleges. There are three possible decisions for early decision applicants: admitted, denied, or not admitted but forwarded for consideration with the regular applicant pool, without prejudice (commonly referred to as *deferred*).
- *Rolling admission* is an admissions plan in which the college considers each student's application once all of the required credentials are received. There is usually a date when colleges will begin to accept materials. Colleges usually notify students of their status relatively quickly. This plan is in effect at some of the most selective universities, including the University of Michigan and the University of Wisconsin. Applicants should submit as early as possible. Many colleges use the rolling decision procedure throughout the year. You may apply to some schools right up until August.

Memo to Counselors

Review "Filling Out the Common Application" in Chapter 8 for more details.

Now about that application: If you filled out a sample Common Application in your junior year (Chapter 8), you have already gathered the necessary information you will need. If you haven't, don't worry; now is the time to do this. Whether you are using the Common Application or a state university or private college application, all of these institutions ask for basically the same information.

Today, many colleges prefer online applications. Use technology to make the application process easier. Hopefully, you are familiar with the Common Application and Naviance from your college research. You may also have visited individual college Web sites. Now let's use this technology in the application process.

Commonapp.org

The Common Application online is a powerful tool for students. If you are applying to colleges using the Common Application, you may use the online version to prepare and submit actual applications and supplements. In addition, most member colleges accept application fees through this Web site. If you do not have an account, simply go to www.commonapp.org to create an account by filling in a user name and creating a password.

Once this account has been established, you can use the Search Engine to research colleges. A list of MY Colleges is automatically created, and you may then add or delete schools to your list. By clicking on a school on MY Colleges, you can easily see where you are in the application process. User-friendly symbols enable you to ascertain whether or not applications and/or supplements have been submitted. In addition, the Common App has an information bar that provides deadlines for submission, tests required, supplement forms if necessary, and fee payment information—all of which may be completed online at this one Web site.

Naviance

If your school has this system, you may have used it to research colleges. Use Family Connection on this system to help you keep an ongoing list of possible college choices. You may also use this system to submit applications and fees to many colleges.

Individual College/University Web Sites

Most colleges and universities provide an online application and fee payment method on their Web sites. Some practical suggestions follow:

- Fill out applications online and then print them for editing and proofreading before submitting.
- Be conscious of word counts for both the Short Answer section and the Personal Essay on the Common Application. You will be cut off if you exceed the word limit. This may also be true for essays on individual college applications. Again, print, edit, and proofread before submitting.
- You are responsible for sending your standardized test scores from the College Board and/or the ACT. You may do this by phone, regular mail, or e-mail.
- Make sure that your application folder is complete by checking with the admissions office. This means that all of your supporting materials are on file: application, scores, teacher recommendations, transcript, and Secondary School Report. If any part of your file is missing, follow up with the appropriate person. Be your own advocate.

If you choose to send hard-copy applications rather than online applications, make sure the envelopes are properly addressed and have the correct amount of postage.

Step 10: Applying for Financial Aid

Paying for college is an intimidating prospect. However, both federal and state governments as well as colleges grant financial aid for qualifying students. Most likely, your school will conduct a financial aid night where a college financial aid officer will help your parents/guardians complete the Free Application for Federal Student Aid (FASFA). This document is submitted to a central agency that assesses the financial aid needs of students. This information is then sent to the colleges that you listed on the FASFA. If you are admitted to a college, you will also receive financial aid information that will help you to determine which college to attend.

Financial aid has many shapes and sizes from outright grants to loans to work-study. Work with your parents/guardians, people at your school, and advisors from prospective colleges to make it possible for you to attend the college that is right for you.

For more detail, refer to Chapter 15.

Step 11: What About Extras?

Do you have special talents? Music, art, creative writing, film, dance, sports—the list goes on. Colleges are looking for students who have pursued and developed their talents. So you want to let a college know more about you. Send a portfolio of your artwork and/or creative writing. How about films you have made or musical/dance performances that you have recorded? Colleges do want to know about what you have accomplished. Usually, this information may be sent online as supplementary materials or via regular mail. Generally, when an admissions office receives portfolios, recordings, or videos, they send them to the appropriate academic department for review. This may help you. Coaches want to know about you, too. Send statistics, videos—whatever will present you in a favorable light. If you are a serious athlete, ask your high school coach to contact possible college coaches.

When visiting a college, make an appointment to speak to the coach or to the art or music teacher. Let them know about your interest and what you have accomplished.

Remember, this is all about finding the right college for you.

A Final Word: It Is Never Too Late!

If you get behind in the college process, for whatever reason, keep in mind that many colleges have rolling admissions policies where you can apply even after you graduate from high school. There is always a way to move on to the next stage of your life.

Chapter 11

Helping Seniors Make the Transition to College (12th Grade)

Memo to Counselors

In this chapter, we examine the separation issues, both affective and cognitive, that many seniors may be experiencing as they face the transition from high school to college. We also focus on issues that seem to be particularly problematic for urban adolescents. For example, students from families of low socioeconomic status who often help with younger siblings find it difficult to think they can leave their families or consider assuming loans for college. Some urban students become very comfortable in their high schools, which can become second homes. Some thinking suggests that these students may sabotage graduating and moving on. Thus, this critical chapter focuses on how counselors can help students complete the necessary tasks for graduation. We will also provide examples of leave-taking exercises to help students make this transition.

The Counselor's Role in the Transition to College

It is the senior year, and the student talk is all about college, majors, meeting new friends, going away, starting the next phase of a person's life. Counselors are happy and sad at the same time as they know that students, some of whom they have known for 4 years, will soon be gone. It is that time when we all hear and speak the words and language of *transition*. Students will make huge academic and affective leaps from high school to college. How best can counselors serve them during this last crucial time in their adolescent lives, to enable them to arrive in college with optimal chances for success? The answer is through small group and individual counseling sessions devoted to transition. In developing an approach of optimal areas to explore in these sessions, counselors need to consider both academic and affective adjustments that students will have in completing high school and starting college. Some thinking related to both of these areas, academic (cognitive) and psychosocial (affective), follows.

Consider these statistics regarding academic performance. In a research report on college readiness changes from 1991 to 2002 (Greene & Winters, 2005), it was determined that only 71% of students who entered high school in the United States in 2002 graduated with a regular diploma. The rate in 1991 was also 71%. Even fewer students have the skills and qualifications to go to a 4-year college. Only 34% of all students who entered high school in 2002 had the credentials to apply to college when they left. The good news is that in 1991, only 25% of students were qualified. That is an improvement of 9%, which is very significant. The authors suggest that the accountability movement of the 1990s forced schools to increase the standards students need to graduate, that standardized test scores improved, and that more students became qualified for college work. Yet, of the students who do apply and were accepted into 4-year colleges, only 59% of them earned their degrees in a 6-year time frame (Kelly, Schneider, & Carey, 2010). In 2003, only 16% of Hispanics earned a college degree by the age of 29 compared with Caucasians (37%) and African Americans (21%). While much discussion could be had over all these numbers, for purposes of the topic of this chapter, the most compelling statistic is the one that says that while our students graduate from high school, many of them do not complete college. Indeed, professors indicate that 50% of the students are not prepared (Hart & Associates, 2005).

Can counselors help *academically* during the senior year to further enable students to go to college academically stronger? In other words, can you help the academic transition? Yes, you can! While some might suggest that such aid is really the purview of teachers, counselors are often the ones who have the most impact on what seniors do in their courses and with their time—certainly during the last semester.

One way to help students transition academically is to challenge them to expend effort on something new, for example, an elective course, a project, something that both bolsters their confidence in learning about something new (e.g., a science course, a new language) and increases their self-awareness about their capacity to learn new and novel topics. Why? Because college students drop courses, change majors, and change colleges in large numbers during their first year, often because they are not confident in their choices and/or face new, novel kinds of work. So, transitioning them with exposure to something new while they are in their comfort zone of the high school senior year can aid them in being more confident and more persevering. How, when, and where can you help direct such a feat? How often have you had a senior who took all the traditionally mapped out courses and who was ready to take the minimal number of classes in the second term? How many of you have seniors who were burned out as a result of their junior or senior year, were accepted in an early decision in their senior year, and then wanted to do nothing? Sometimes information is the best way to sell an idea. If students really thought about how they would be adjusting to new course material along with all the other new elements of college, they might be more willing to consider the "try something new" idea, described above.

A second academic focus for counselors in group sessions could revolve around how well students can gain and evaluate information critically. Carr and Rockman (2003) cite the finding of a government report predicting that 50% of the students who would go to college in 2004 would not graduate at all. They further state that one of the main contributing factors is the inability of these students to find and use information effectively. College students must read and evaluate texts, and they must learn how to use academic resources in the library. In an article entitled "A Transition Checklist for High School Seniors," Owen (2010), a librarian, described survey responses from professors about what students cannot do and what college freshmen say they cannot do with regard to information literacy. The responses were categorized into five themes:

General Knowledge

One general problem nearly all high school seniors and college freshmen have is that they don't know what they don't know! Before teaching students information literacy skills, school librarians often need to demonstrate to students that they have skill deficiencies, and that is not always an easy task. Students have two other general research problem areas: they don't know who to ask for help when (and if) they recognize that they need it (Pandora 2004), and they don't understand basic library jargon (Daniel 1997) such as "OPAC," "scholarly journal," and "primary sources."

Research Process and Questions

Students have difficulty articulating research questions and topics. They often choose research questions and topics that college faculty consider shallow or "pop" (Daniel 1997; Fitzgerald 2004). College freshmen do not follow the steps of research processes they are taught (Daniel 1997), such as the Big6, DIALOGUE model, or Kuhlthau's Information Seeking Process. As a consequence, they do not accurately estimate the time required for research (Daniel 1997), cannot take advantage of the full range of library services such as interlibrary loan, and experience stress that sometimes leads to acts of plagiarism.

Searching for Information

College students are deficient in the area of searching for information. Students tend to rely on Web search engines as their main information search strategy. They do not realize that most college-level research resources are not available on the free Web and are not formatted as

Web sites. Because of their reliance on free Web sources, they do not find the other formats of information their professors expect (Daniel 1997). Those students who attempt to use college library Web sites do not distinguish between OPACs and on-line databases (Islam & Murno 2006); many equate them with Web search engines like Google. Consequently, they use Google-type search strategies rather than the more sophisticated terms required for effective searching of library resources (Daniel 1997) such as keywords, alternate search terms, Boolean terms, controlled vocabulary, subject headings, and field searching. When they retrieve search results, they do not know how to parse and interpret them. As a result, they have difficulty finding the full text of articles on-line or in print and using Library of Congress (LC) call numbers to put their hands on books (Daniel 1997). Perhaps their difficulties with LC call numbers are in part responsible for their tendency to ignore reference resources (Quarton 2003). Additionally, most students do not regroup when their first attempts to find resources are unsuccessful; they are more likely to decide that there are no resources on their topic (Daniel 1997).

Evaluating Information

When students do locate information, they are not sufficiently critical of it (Daniel 1997). They often use the first resources they encounter rather than wade through search results to find relevant, adequate, and accurate information using standard evaluation criteria. They do not distinguish between popular and scholarly articles (Matorana et al. 2001). Students frequently dismiss useful print resources and accept inadequate or inaccurate information (Matorana 2001), especially in the form of data and statistics.

Using Information

Students also need to improve the way they use the information they locate. Students do not synthesize, communicate, and argue theses using evidence effectively (Fitzgerald 2004). They have difficulty representing, analyzing, and critiquing the ideas of others ethically. They find it challenging to write without plagiarizing (accidentally or otherwise) and lack facility in using multiple citation styles. (Owen, 2010, p.21)

While Owen recommends that high school librarians and teachers address these gaps, counselors can play a role here as well. Owen and Oakleaf (2008) have developed a Checklist of Student Skills around these themes, which is shown in Table 11.1 for your use along with a description of the areas described above.

Table 11.1   Checklist of Student Skills

General
• Know what they don't know
• Know who to ask for research help
• Understand library jargon, e.g., "peer-reviewed"

Research Process and Questions
• Follow research process steps, e.g., info lit model
• Estimate time required for research, e.g., Interlibrary loan
• Define a research question or topic that's not shallow or "pop"

Searching for Information
• Find different formats of information
• Understand that Web search engines rarely locate college-appropriate information
• Distinguish between OPACs and online databases
• Conduct effective searches using
• Keywords, alternate search terms
• Boolean terms, e.g., AND, OR
• Controlled vocabulary, subject headings
• Field searching, e.g., author, title
• Interpret search results, e.g., book chapters vs. article
• Find full text of articles
• Find books using Library of Congress (LC) classification, not Dewey
• Use reference books in the library
• Regroup when first attempts to find resources don't work, e.g., try a different database

Evaluating Information
• Weed through search results to find adequate and accurate information
• Evaluate information using standard evaluation criteria
• Distinguish between popular and scholarly articles
• Disregard inadequate or inaccurate information

Using Information
• Synthesize, communicate, and argue a thesis using evidence
• Analyze data and statistics
• Represent, analyze, and critique the words and ideas of others ethically
• Write without plagiarizing (accidentally or otherwise), e.g., use in-text citations
• Cite sources properly using multiple citation styles, e.g., KnightCite

Source: P. Owen. (2010). A transition checklist for high school seniors. *School Library Monthly*, V, XXVI, 8, April, 2010. Retrieved from http://www.infowen.info/checklist.pdf

A transition group meeting could well focus on this topic with students first taking the survey, followed by discussion of the previously described sections, followed by providing the data from the survey to the faculty.

So much of the early collegiate educational experience is related to learning to write better and develop grade-worthy papers. The information above can easily become the focus of a few transition group meetings. Extending this academic issue out of the classroom and into the counseling department may enable students to deal with it independently from getting a grade in one of their courses. Academic counseling must be a part of the transition to college.

Knowing that an individual student has the skills to survive the first-year collegiate experience academically can have a ripple effect on the psychological transition, which may well be the more difficult of the two processes. In Chapter 4, we spoke of the enormous changes that occur during the move from middle school to high school, including changes in parent involvement, peers, teachers, and learning. Overriding and interacting with all those changes is the transition from child to adolescent, which has both clear physical and psychological characteristics. While the physical change from the senior year in high school to college is nowhere near that change from middle school to high school years, several of the other changes are evident and in some cases more pronounced.

Smith and Zhang (2009) studied students' perceptions and experiences with key factors during the transition from high school to college. Some of their findings are particularly relevant to counselors in their roles in the high school to college transition process. They found that parents, friends, high school teachers and counselors, college professors and academic advisors, college orientation programs, and first-year seminars all play a role in a student's transition. More importantly, they noted that mothers are the most helpful resource in the transition process, followed by high school counselors, fathers, friends, and teachers. College and academic advisors provide the least number of helping behaviors.

In the study, extensive gender and racial differences were found in the students' perceptions of helpfulness and the reported number of times students received help. Female students tended to report a greater number of helping behaviors as well as a greater degree of helpfulness from the factors. Female students were also more likely than male students to report that mothers, friends, and high school counselors were helpful. Black students were more likely than White students to report high school counselors as more helpful, whereas White students were more likely than Black students to report receiving help from their fathers. There were no significant differences among students concerning the amount of help received from high school teachers, college academic advisors, and professors.

Students' perceptions of high school counselors' discussion of preparing for and gaining access to college and helping with school-related problems was positively related to their freshman grade point average (GPA). This was in contrast to the role played by high school teachers. None of the high school teachers' behaviors showed a significant positive impact on college GPA (Smith & Zhang, 2009). How helpful high school counselors are as perceived by students might be more important than even the number of times high school counselors provide assistance to them.

High schools should pay more attention to the needs of college-bound students, particularly Black students, since they rely more on the services of counselors than do White students. The authors conclude by stating: "If school districts are serious in their quest to increase the number of college bound minorities, then they should provide more resources for guidance counseling and information about preparing for and gaining access to college. Eighty-four percent of the students in our study received some form of help from their high school guidance counselors regarding preparation for college." (Smith & Zhang, 2009, p. 654)

Finally, the authors suggest that high schools and colleges should work together to ensure that college-bound students, particularly those who are disadvantaged, receive the academic assistance that they need to make a smooth transition to college (Smith & Zhang, 2009).

It is quite clear that counselors, in engaging in the work of college advising, have a serious impact on students' psychological well-being during this transition phase. Including transitional groups focused on the tasks of transitioning including both academic and personal should be developed.

Other research has examined the transitioning of "risky" behaviors. Fromme, Corbin, and Kruse (2008) studied the behavioral risks during the transition from high school to college. Results indicated that those individuals who were most likely to engage in behavioral risks during their senior year in high school continued to engage more frequently in behavioral risks during their first year of college. Evident behaviors were increases in the number of sexual partners and the frequency of alcohol and marijuana use in college. At the same time, decreases in aggression, driving after drinking, and property crimes were observed during the transition from high school to college. Few gender differences were found, with men reporting only a higher prevalence of property crimes and greater marijuana use. No effects were found for socioeconomic status, but Caucasian students reported greater involvement in all behavioral risks except multiple sexual partners.

The authors suggested that decreased adult supervision, overall greater personal freedom, and increased availability and opportunity were likely contributors to the increases observed in drinking, marijuana use, and sexual behaviors. Likewise, the increased privacy afforded by living at a college away from home provides greater opportunity for sexual behavior. Furthermore, they suggest once again a role for high school counselors during this transition:

> Whereas many colleges and universities offer universal prevention programs to all incoming students (often in conjunction with freshmen orientation), a more effective approach may be to offer targeted programs to college-bound high school seniors, especially men, Caucasian

students, students from rural high schools, and those electing to live in private dormitories. (Fromme et al., 2008, p. 7)

The difficulty and importance of support in navigating developmental tasks, including not only cognitive and behavior adjustments but also interpersonal relationships and emotional adjustment during the latter part of the senior year in high school cannot be underestimated. The impact on the first-year collegiate experience cannot be denied. Counselors must recognize their important role and make the development of transitional group counseling activities a required part of the senior-year transition.

How Can the Counselor Help?

Memo to Counselors

So how can you help your seniors develop the necessary maturity for a successful transition to college? Remember that often it is the counselor who has the greatest impact on the student. What follows is a twofold approach to this transition. First of all, the curriculum focuses on self-evaluation in which students reflect upon their high school experience and analyze their strengths and weaknesses. Secondly, we present a suggested model for a senior project that would require students to use and to understand a more sophisticated methodology of research, a key element in a successful transition to college. Whether or not your high school has a special project for seniors, this is a worthy program to advocate because it not only develops a more mature study skills approach to learning but also enhances the sense of responsibility that is inherent in higher education. Again, the curriculum portion of this chapter is written in the voice of the counselor and is particularly appropriate for second-semester seniors who have completed the college application process.

Now, as seniors, you may well feel that you have one foot still in high school and the other already in college. That's natural, but this is also the time to evaluate and to reflect upon your high school experience. By doing this, you will gain valuable insight that can assist you in the transition to college.

Student Self-Evaluation

First of all, let's review your high school experience from three perspectives: academics, social, and involvement in extracurricular/athletic life. In Table 11.2, list your strengths and weaknesses in these areas and assess what you would change in the future. This is not about what you want to major in or what you think might be the right career for you. Rather, this exercise is designed for you to reflect on what you did that worked for you and what did not. There are no right or wrong answers, only some pointers for the future.

After completing this chart, analyze what you feel needs change. For example, as you look back, did you develop and use solid study skills and time management methods? What could you have done differently that might have enhanced your success as a student? In Table 11.3, list *specific* examples that could improve your success.

After evaluating your high school experience, now it is time to anticipate your life as a college student. Some of the early work that you did as a 9th grader still applies here. Remember the Goals Exercise in Chapter 4—it applies here as well. Think about what you want to accomplish and how you will achieve your goals. Table 11.4, reprinted below, is a modified version of the chart from Chapter 4. The model of establishing goals and the anticipating a method of accomplishing these goals is a life lesson that will serve you well.

Table 11.2   Exercise on Reflection on High School—Part 1

Area	Strengths	Weaknesses	What to Change in College
Academics			
Social			
Extracurricular/ Athletics			

Table 11.3   Exercise on Reflection on High School—Part 2

Area	Strengths	Weaknesses	What You Can Do to Improve in College
Academics			
Social			
Extracurricular/ Athletics			

Table 11.4   Exercise on Establishing Goals for Your First Semester of College

Goals	How to Achieve
Academics	
Extracurricular Activities	
Sports	
Other	

Table 11.5   One Final Exercise as You Leave High School

What did you like most about high school?	
What did you dislike most about high school?	
If you could, what would you change about high school?	

As you leave high school, take with you the tools that will help in your future life: study skills, time management and articulation of clear goals and a methodology to attain them. In Table 11.5 is a final exercise as you prepare to leave high school.

Memo to Counselors

What follows below is a format/calendar, or a model timeline, for a Senior Project that helps to develop the higher-level research skills that students need in college. Many schools use this model as a way of dealing with the proverbial "senioritis" in May, but it is also be an effective way of strengthening study skills and research techniques that will aid students in a more successful transition to college.

Senior Project Model

The Senior Project begins in mid-May and culminates in mid-June.

> March: Students attend an assembly in which they learn about the Senior Project and its requirements. The Senior Project usually requires a written paper with a bibliography and footnote page as well as an oral presentation to the student body.
> March: Students select a topic of interest to them. Topics may be as diverse as the Mayan Calendar to the exploration of Mars.
> March: Students select an advisor who approves their project.
> April: Students present initial research to their advisors.

What is essential here is the kind of research that students do. Normally two scholarly journals and at least two scholarly books are a minimum. In this way, students begin to discriminate among the immense information available to them on the Internet and learn to discern the difference between juried material and what is simply posted on the Web.

> May: Students present a thesis that they will explore to their advisors.
> Follow-up meetings are held with advisors to ascertain student progress.

Mid-May: Seniors are no longer in regular classes so that they can focus on the Senior Project.

June: Seniors present their Senior Project to younger students as well as hand their papers to their advisors.

In this model, students do receive a grade per se, but it is the method of research that is important—something that will serve them well in the transition to college.

THE COUNSELOR AS
CREATOR AND MANAGER

Chapter 12

The Advising Office: More Than Just Good Organization

Memo to Counselors

In this chapter, we provide a framework for the successful running of a college advising office; that framework relies on the American School Counselor Association (ASCA) National Model for school counseling programs that has been mentioned several times in the book. In particular, we discuss a variety of goals based on the ASCA standards and on our suggestions in prior chapters. We then present an example of an institution of higher education (IHE)/K–12 partnership development of a college advising office family room.

We then move to the day-to-day work of the office, including developing forms for student requests, scheduling meetings, and sending out transcripts. We will also present a model of a school profile and discuss the information that is essential to present a snapshot of the senior class. In addition, we discuss interaction with colleges, including scheduling visits of representatives, organizing college fairs, planning college visits, and contacting admissions officers regarding applicants. But, first, we want to provide a mind-set for the college advisor.

Best Characteristics of a College Advising Office

Throughout this book we have suggested some new ideas for college advisors beyond what has been traditionally considered appropriate. For example, while counselors have always been concerned about and helpful in enhancing student academic performance, we have offered some very specific academic/cognitive approaches that might seem more like roles that are limited to teachers (e.g., academic information literacy skills). Helping students academically is so critical; we—educators, counselors, and principals—must all become versed in best practices. As we move through the first quarter of the 21st century with all the global changes that are now part of the fabric of life, we must continue to define where we are going as college admissions counselors.

ASCA National Model

We want to advocate that the ASCA National Model: A Framework for School Counseling Programs should become the basis for the development of the college advising office too. Knowing that good college advising offices are already very well organized, we want to focus on some themes about professionalism that should also become the hallmark of our advisement work. In this chapter, we want to inform you of the ASCA framework, how it should help further shape your office, and how business is conducted in that office. Please refer to the ASCA National Model for more details (ASCA, 2005).

The ASCA model consists of four themes and four elements that make up the model. These components are considered critical to the optimal functioning of counseling programs. We want to emphasize the inclusion of college advising work. First, the model's emblem is reproduced in Figure 12.1.

Figure 12.1 ASCA emblem. (© American School Counselor Association. With permission.)

The Four Themes

The four themes relate to how we proceed professionally in our work. They include leadership, advocacy, collaboration, and systemic change. We believe these themes should also drive our work as college advisors. Let's look at how they might relate to college advising.

- Leadership
  - College advisors serve as leaders in ensuring student success.
  - College advisors are effective leaders by working with others to influence change.
  - College advisors work with administrators to further the identity of the school.
- Advocacy
  - College advisors believe, support, and promote student goals to achieve in school and be successful in college.
  - College advisors work proactively to remove barriers to learning including cognitive and psychosocial.
- Collaboration and Teaming
  - College advisors work with all stakeholders.
  - College advisors work with IHEs and communities on programs (as suggested in Chapter 2 on partnerships).
  - College advisors work with IHEs in transitioning and data collection about retention rates of students in college.
- Systemic Change
  - College advisors are in a special position to be heard about needed systemic change due to their role in helping students gain entrance to college.
  - College advisors have the ability to use data such as admissions history and graduation rates from colleges to engender needed changes for academic success.
  - College advisors should be leaders of change or renewal of successful policies when new data indicate a particular course of direction.

Those four themes are first and foremost at the heart of our work. They are the strongest way in which we can connect to and provide our most professional expertise to our students and our schools. We must be strong leaders to truly advocate for our students. Strong leadership includes knowing how and when to collaborate. Lastly, being involved with systemic change—in fact, leading it—is a challenge to all those in education, but it is crucial for anyone who hopes to make an impact on 21st century educational systems in the United States. We can do this—that is, college advisors can and should be in the lead for examination of programmatic changes.

Integrally related to those four themes are the four elements of the ASCA National Model as described below. While the four themes rule our professional hearts, the four elements rule our organizational schema for delivery of best counseling services.

The Four Elements

The four elements are the underpinnings in providing a counseling program. Included are foundation, delivery system, management systems, and accountability. Let's look at how they might relate to college advising.

- Foundation
  - College advisors understand and encourage the infusion of the mission of the school and the counseling department.
  - College advisors help facilitate development in three domains: academic, career, and personal/social, including transitions.
- Delivery System
  - College advisors use a developed counseling curriculum in their work such as the curriculum we have devised in this book.
  - College advisors engage in individual planning.
- Management Systems
  - College advisors have certain responsibilities that are clarified with administrators so that counselors can be most effective.
  - College advisors use data to inform their work.
  - College advisors develop master schedules and calendars to inform others of important milestones.
- Accountability
  - College advisors ask themselves if their students are different as a result of their college advising program.
  - College advisors track postgraduation data and other academic and psychosocial indicators about successful transition into college.

These four elements are the guides to our office organization. Of particular note to us in this book are two of the elements, the delivery system and the management system. In this book we have focused primarily on academic lesson plans throughout the curriculum, while recognizing the important psychosocial and physical development that is naturally going on. Looking at just the three domains of academic, career, and personal/social that the ASCA National Model focuses on (see Foundation, above), we believe the curriculum directly offers lessons for you to facilitate development in those areas.

Academically, we have developed plans for critically learning better study habits, focusing on learning styles that work, and using inventories (e.g., Naviance's learning style inventory) that provide external validation to students about their learning skills. The careers domain has also been addressed through lesson and through exposure to inventories (e.g., College Board, Naviance). Personal/social, which is often done traditionally by school counselors (it is our nature), has also been addressed in ideas about transitioning and in developing advisories through group counseling classes.

The Management Systems in the ASCA model "addresses the *when* (calendar and action plan), *why* (use of data) and *on what authority* (management agreement and advisory panel) the program will be implemented" (ASCA, 2005, p. 22). For purposes of college advising, we first strongly urge you to develop an advisory council to review the college advising program. The group might include your IHE partner, teachers, parents, and community and business members. Fewer meetings and some online blogs might prove very effective in gaining feedback on your programs.

Next, we want to call your attention to the *management agreement* idea, which is urging us to develop agreements with administrators (e.g., principals) to understand specifically counselor responsibilities. In a recent study commissioned by the Bill and Melinda Gates Foundation, results indicated that high schools students believe their counselors provided little meaningful advice on colleges and careers (Johnson, Rochkind, Ott, & DuPont, 2009; Steinberg, 2010). The report, *With Their Whole Lives Ahead of Them*, examined the myths and realities about why so many students fail to finish college. A small part of the study focused on high school counselors. Approximately 600 people were surveyed. Among the questions asked were two questions about their counselors. Those two questions and the responses are in Table 12.1.

In an interview with Jacques Steinberg of *The New York Times*, Jim Jump, the current president of National Association for College Admission Counseling (NACAC), echoed the report's findings in expressing his concern that "so many other things are tossed on counselors' plates that actual counseling takes up a very small part of the time" (Steinberg, 2010, p. A20). Counselors generally, as well as college advisors in particular, need to start to lead the way in determining how we can best serve our constituencies.

The management agreement is an idea whose time has come. Through leadership and collaborative skills, we must press to specify what is important to a school's mission and to our work. Clearly, we can't do it all. We suggest that you review another document designed for the ASCA National Model, one that truly would benefit anyone in the counseling office, let alone the college advising counselors: the "Secondary School Counselor Management Agreement" (Figure 12.2 and also on the CD). This is an agreement between the principal and the school counselor about the responsibilities of a school counselor. It could be tweaked and adapted for use for the counseling department as a whole and for the college advisors. The form's contents are rather thorough in addressing many of the responsibilities of counselors and needs of the counseling office. Certainly, such a form could be modified to conform to a college advisor's role or to include the college advisor function in a department one. You might want to focus less on items such as work after school and support staff and more on exactly what is expected that you are doing—academic, career, and college advising. While many schools have a separate college advisor, other schools distribute the college advising across counselors. Most importantly, meeting and discussing the elements of something like this form with the principal is highly recommended; you need to take the lead in this endeavor.

Table 12.1   With Their Whole Lives Ahead of Them Report Questions
Q40. Which of these comes closer to describing your own experiences with the counselors in your high school? • The counselors usually made an effort to really get to know me and to treat me as an individual, 47% • I usually felt I was just another face in the crowd, 48% • I never had any experiences with counselors in high school (VOL), 2% • Don't know, 1%
Q41. How would you rate your high school counselors in the following areas? [Base: Those who had experiences with counselors.] Helping you think about different kinds of careers you might want to pursue • Excellent, 14% • Good, 22% • Fair, 33% • Poor, 29% • Don't know, 2%
Helping you decide what school was right for you • Excellent, 13% • Good, 17% • Fair, 32% • Poor, 35% • Don't know, 2%
Explaining and helping you with the application process • Excellent, 18% • Good, 25% • Fair, 25% • Poor, 29% • Don't know, 2%
Helping you find ways to pay for college, like financial aid or scholarship programs • Excellent, 15% • Good, 22% • Fair, 26% • Poor, 33% • Don't know, 4%

Source: Johnson, J., Rochkind, J., Ott, A., & DuPont, S. (2009). With their whole lives ahead of them. A study for the Bill and Linda Gates Foundation by Public Agenda. Retrieved from http://www.publicagenda.org/files/pdf/theirwholelivesaheadofthem.pdf

 **AMERICAN SCHOOL COUNSELOR ASSOCIATION**

Secondary School Counselor Management Agreement

(Counselor/Principal Agreement)

School year _____ School _____ Date _____

STUDENT ACCESS:

Students will access the school counselor by:

_____ Grade level   _____ Domain   _____ By academy/pathway

_____ Alpha listing   _____ No caseload (See any counselor)   _____ Other please specify _____

COUNSELOR OF THE DAY:

Our counseling program will _____ will not _____ implement counselor of the day.

DOMAIN RESPONSIBILITIES

Looking at your site needs/strengths, counselors will be identified as the domain counselors for the following areas:

Academic domain: _____

Career domain: _____

Personal/social domain: _____

Rationale for decision: _____

PROGRAMMATIC DELIVERY

The school counseling teams will spend approximately the following time in each component area to ensure the delivery of the school counseling program?

_____ % of time delivering guidance curriculum

_____ % of time with individual student planning

_____ % of time with responsive services

_____ % of time with system support

SCHOOL COUNSELOR AVAILABILITY:

The school counseling department be open for student/parent/teacher access from _____ to _____

The department will manage the division of hours by: _____

The career center will be open from _____ to _____

The department will manage the division of hours by: _____

Programs and services presented and available to parents include:

Example: guidance newsletter, parenting classes, parent information night

Secondary School Counselor Program Management Agreement

Programs and services presented and available to staff include:

Example: department liaison, topical information workshops (child abuse, ADD, etc.)

Community liaisons, programs and services will include:

Figure 12.2   Secondary School Counselor Management Agreement form. (© American School Counselor Association. With permission.)

THE SCHOOL COUNSELORS WILL BE COMPENSATED FOR EXTRA WORK HOURS (BEYOND WORK DAY) BY?

_____ Extra duty pay (fund?)   _____ Comp time   _____ By principal/counselor negotiation

_____ Flex schedule   _____ Per union regulations _____ No option for this

MATERIALS AND SUPPLIES

What materials and supplies are necessary for the implementation of the school counseling program:

The following funding resources support the school counseling program:

PROFESSIONAL DEVELOPMENT

The school counseling team will participate in the following professional development:

PROFESSIONAL COLLABORATION

The school counseling department will meet weekly/monthly:

_____ As a counseling department team   _____ With administration

_____ With the school staff (faculty)   _____ With subject area departments

_____ With the advisory council

OFFICE ORGANIZATION

Responsibilities for the support services provided the counseling team will be divided among the support services staff :

The school counseling assistant will: _____

The clerk will: _____

Volunteers will: _____

The registrar will: _____

The receptionist will: _____

Others will: _____

_____   _____

Lead Counselor signature & date   Principal signature & date

Figure 12.2   (Continued) Secondary School Counselor Management Agreement form. (© American School Counselor Association. With permission.)

All stakeholders want the college advising office to operate effectively. In many ways that office mirrors the success of the school to the outside world. The most important components for allowing that to happen are those previously listed. Empowered counselors empower students. Counselors who can lead, collaborate, advocate for students, and press for critical data-driven systemic changes will undoubtedly develop an office where students feel wanted and well served. So, remember these characteristics. On the CD is the emblem for the ASCA National Model. Make a copy for the office to remind you of its vision.

A Grant-Developed College Advising Room: Making Use of an IHE Connection

Through the Optimal College Readiness grant described in Chapter 2, we were fortunate to be able to help a K–12 school develop a set of offices that were student and parent friendly. One of our goals in this grant was to help the parents and the students of urban schools focus on academic needs and on understanding the financial aid process. We had noticed that while many of the students wanted to go to college and had the needed academic profiles, their parents did not understand the financial aid aspects and, due to language barriers, were less comfortable with coming in to see the counselors. We developed one room through grants funds, a small room but with a table and a flat-screen monitor that flashed information for students, was able to show Naviance or the Free Application for Federal Student Aid (FAFSA) to parents in a small setting, and provided a comfortable place for parents to meet individually with counselors. We trained counselors-in-training from Manhattan College to help, and college personnel in the admissions office and the financial aid office gave support.

A second room was developed where the counselors-in-training would also work. A financial aid advisor from the college was fluent in Spanish, as were a number of the counselors-in-training. Parent–student workshops were part of the grant as well. At the end of this academic year (2010), 100% of the students in the senior year had filed their FAFSA accurately and had applied to college. What is most important in this story for future college advising efforts is not the 100% figure but, rather, how a college and a school worked together in identifying what was needed to help families who want their children to go to college. We were fortunate to have the State of New York's Higher Educational Services Corporation recognize the need to support these ideas through the grant. The college was very generous in time and effort, including providing outreach funding, and the school's principal and counseling department head saw the value of using counselors-in-training for some of the work. Partnerships can be powerful.

Components of a Well-Organized and Effective Counseling Office

Much has been written about some of the most fundamental components that make an office function well on the inside and demonstrate a professional approach on the outside. Many sources are available to find them, including the NACAC Web site (see Additional Resources) and book (NACAC, 2008). Here are some components that we think are especially important. Some of them are described in detail below, and others are simply listed:

College Handbook—developed by your counseling office, this manual should contain everything every student and parent should know about the entire college application process. It should be organized by year, be parent and student friendly, and include, among other things, the following:

■ A calendar starting with the sophomore year that includes important testing dates, planned parent–family meetings, and college application deadlines

- A section on courses needed to graduate, needed for entrance generally to 2-year colleges and 4-year colleges.
- A description of the various standardized tests
- A description of financial aid and scholarship searching
- A short but thorough set of suggestions on teacher recommendations and development of the college essay
- Tips on college visits, interviews, and filing applications
- A description of how to use an online system such as Naviance, College Board, or whatever the school uses, including scattergrams
- Prepping for the Preliminary Scholastic Aptitude Test (PSAT) and the SAT and/or ACT®—pros and cons

Learning to Study Better—The Role of Private Tutors
- The SAT vs. the ACT
- Calculating the real grade point average (GPA)
- Early decision vs. regular decision
- Division I vs. Division II or III athletics
- Higher GPA vs. harder courses

Office Policies (should be in the handbook)
- Organization of applications
- Meeting college deadlines
- Disclosure of confidential information

Data-Gathering System
- Historical data on admits, rejections, wait lists
- Comparisons on GPA, SATs, and so forth
- Exit surveys on quality of school and college office experience
- Should be organized over a period of years

The School Profile

Creating and/or updating your school's profile is an all-important task because it gives college admissions staff a snapshot of both your school and the current senior class. This document should convey a sense of the school mission and how it is threaded throughout the curriculum and the overall character of the school. By analyzing pertinent academic information, colleges can understand the level of academic rigor and competition within a school community.

What to Include

1. The basics
   a. Name and address of school, telephone, fax, and specific e-mail if appropriate

b. Type of school (public, private, boarding)

c. Grade levels

d. Total enrollment

e. Number of teaching faculty

f. Size of senior class

g. Accredited or approved by

h. Name of principal

i. Name of director of college advising

j. Names of other college advisors

k. Include contact information if appropriate

2. What defines your school

a. A brief mission statement (or excerpt)

b. A brief description of the community facts that help to describe students served

3. Grading policies

a. The marking system, including passing grade and weighted grades

b. Method of computing GPA and ranking (if computed)

c. Policy regarding GPA and rank reports to colleges

d. If your school does not compute GPA, a distribution chart of junior-year grades (For each course, state the number of students receiving specific grades. Colleges can then easily see that, for example, only 3 students received an A+, while 16 received a B and 2 earned a C− in a particular class. This can help them to assess student performance more fairly.)

e. Graduation requirements

4. Curriculum

a. Honors, Advanced Placement offerings, college study, and so forth

b. Special features of the curriculum (e.g., Does your school emphasize technology, science, history?)

5. College attendance of graduates

a. A table showing postsecondary enrollment for the last 3 to 5 years

b. Specific names of the colleges students are attending

6. Recent standardized tests scores (presented according to test content, e.g., Critical Reading, Mathematics, and Writing Skills for the SAT)

a. The range of junior SAT and/or ACT scores for the middle 50% of the class

b. A list of all Advanced Placement courses and the number of students taking the test and the number of students receiving 3 or higher. This may be done over a 2–3 year period.

7. Number of students receiving National Merit Recognition

8. Any other pertinent information that would be helpful in interpreting a student's application (e.g., Does your school require community service or work study? If so, list required hours.)

School Description

IN-Tech Academy is an urban public school in the borough of the Bronx in New York City. We educate students in middle and high school, grades 6 through 12. Our first high school graduating class was in June 2007. We are a young, developing high school. Our focus is to develop self-reliant learners who are prepared through technology and academic rigor to become productive and responsible citizens of their local and global communities. We are committed to fostering a college preparatory culture for our middle and high school students, the majority of whom will be first-generation college graduates. We presently have four GEAR UP (Gaining Early Awareness and Readiness for Undergraduate Programs) cohorts, in the 8th, 9th, 10th, and 11th grades. GEAR UP is a federally funded grant program designed to increase the number of low-income students who are prepared to enter and succeed in postsecondary education. GEAR UP provides students with academic support, early awareness, and readiness for college study. GEAR UP grantees serve an entire grade of students beginning no later than the 7th grade and follow the students through high school. Our GEAR UP students collaborate with the City University of New York at Lehman College.

Grading and Class Rank

Our grading system is numerical, ranging from 55 to 100. The passing grade is 65. We have honors classes and advanced placement classes. The honors classes and advanced placement classes are weighted. IN-Tech does compute GPA but does not rank.

The Curriculum

Subject Requirement	Graduation	Honors and Advanced Placement Courses	
English	8 Semesters	*Offered to the Class of 2010*	
History	8 Semesters	Science and Math	
Global	4 Semesters	Advanced Trigonometry	2 Semesters
American History	2 Semesters	Physics	2 Semesters
Economics	1 Semester	Advanced Placement	
Participation in Government	1Semester	Calculus AB	2 Semesters
Science	6 Semesters	Environmental Science	2 Semesters
Living Environment	2 Semesters	English Language and Composition	2 Semesters
Earth Science	2 Semesters	English Literature	2 Semesters
Chemistry	2 Semesters	Technology Courses	
Mathematics	6 Semesters	CISCO Programming	4 Semesters
Art, Music, Dance, and/or Drama	2 Semesters	A+ Computer Programming	2 Semesters
Foreign Language	2 Semesters	Virtual Enterprise	2 Semesters
Health	1 Semester		
Physical Education	7 Semesters		
Electives	7 Semesters		

Enrollment	2009–2010
Freshmen	163 (92 Boys, 71 Girls)
Sophomores	172 (85 Boys, 87 Girls)
Juniors	95 (40 Girls, 40 Boys)
Seniors	103 (60 Boys, 43 Girls)
Total	533

Figure 12.3 **IN-Tech Academy school profile. (From IN-Tech Academy. With permission.)**

Faculty		
Administrators	**Teachers**	**Counselors**
5	72	5

Diplomas Awarded

Diploma	*Requirements*
Local	1 English, 1 Global History, 1 U.S. History, 1 Math, and 1 Science with a passing score of 65 on 3 regents exams and a passing score of 55 on 2 regents exams
Regents	5 required regents, with a passing score of 65 on all 5 regents exams
Advanced Regents Diploma	5 required regents, plus 1 language regents, an additional math and science regents with a passing score of 65 on a total of 8 regents exams
Advanced Regents Diploma w/Merit	Passing score of 85 on all 8 regents exams required
Advanced Regents Diploma w/Honors	Passing score of 90 on all 8 regents exams required

Dual Enrollment College Courses

Qualified students may take introductory college-level courses offered only to high school students at City University of New York at Lehman College and/or Monroe College. Minimum requirements to enroll for English, psychology, philosophy, and business courses at Lehman College are a score of 75 on the New York State English regents and/or 55 on the Critical Reading section of the PSAT. A score of 85 on the Math B regents is required for math courses. Students may take up to two courses per semester with a recommendation from their guidance counselor. Students must be enrolled in the Virtual Enterprise program to enroll at Monroe College. Students are permitted to take one course per semester.

Student Test Performance

The range of SAT scores for the middle 50% of the class of 2009:

Critical Reading: 410	Math: 443	Writing: 424

College Matriculation 2007–2009

Art Institute of New York	Mercy College
Berkeley College	Monroe College
Boston College	Pace University
College of Mount Saint Vincent	Penn State University
Columbia University	Pikes Peak Community College
City University of New York (CUNY) Baruch College	Pontifica Universidad Catolica Madre y Maestra
CUNY Borough of Manhattan Community College	State University of New York (SUNY) Albany
CUNY Bronx Community College	SUNY Binghamton University
CUNY City College	SUNY Buffalo State
CUNY Hostos Community College	SUNY Delhi
CUNY Hunter College	SUNY Geneseo

Figure 12.3   (Continued) IN-Tech Academy school profile. (From IN-Tech Academy. With permission.)

CUNY John Jay College of Criminal Justice	SUNY Herkimer Community College
CUNY Kingsborough Community College.	SUNY Institute of Technology
CUNY LaGuardia Community College	SUNY New Paltz
CUNY Lehman College	SUNY Old Westbury
CUNY New York City College of Technology	SUNY Oneonta
CUNY Queensborough Community College	SUNY Oswego
DeVry University	SUNY Purchase
Dowling College	SUNY Ulster Community College
Finger Lakes Community College	SUNY Westchester Community College
Illinois Institute of Technology	Syracuse University
Ithaca University	University of Central Florida
Manhattan College	University of Chicago
Manhattanville College	Wood-Tobe Coburn

Figure 12.3 **(Continued) IN-Tech Academy school profile. (From IN-Tech Academy. With permission.)**

Figure 12.3 is an example of the IN-Tech Academy School Profile, which was developed through the partnership between the high school and Manhattan College. As a recently developed public school in the Bronx borough of New York City, IN-Tech faced the challenge of creating a counseling program and writing its first School Profile.

Interaction With Colleges

Scheduling Visits From College Representatives

Generally, college admissions representatives will contact college advisors to arrange a visit where they can meet with interested students. This is a wonderful opportunity for students to meet in a small group setting and ask pertinent questions about a particular college. Counselors should be proactive in scheduling these visits; if you have not heard from a college that would be a good match for your students, do not hesitate to contact them. Make sure to establish a contact list of all representatives for future use.

To keep all of this running smoothly:

■ Create a calendar listing the colleges visiting and the time of the meeting. A sample from IN-Tech Academy appears in Table 12.2.
■ Post the calendar in the counseling office and any other appropriate spaces. Also post the calendar electronically if possible.

Table 12.2   Sample of College Representative Visit Calendar

College	Date	Time
University of Pennsylvania	October 4, 2007	11:30 a.m.
Colby College	October 5, 2007	11:45 a.m.
Brown University	October 5, 2007	11:45 a.m.
Hamilton—Diversity Overnight Program	October 6, 2007	
Amherst College	October 9, 2007	11:45 a.m.
Massachusetts Institute of Technology	October 9, 2007	11:45 a.m.
SUNY College Night	October 9, 2007	4:30 p.m.
Harvey Mudd College	October 10, 2007	11:45 a.m.
University of Southern California	October 10, 2007	11:45 a.m.
Spirit Day—Do Not Schedule	October 11, 2007	11:45 a.m.
Haverford College	October 12, 2007	11:45 a.m.
Yale University	October 12, 2007	11:45 a.m.
University of Chicago Students of Color Open House	October 12, 2007	
McGill University	October 15, 2007	10:30 a.m.
Davidson College	October 15, 2007	11:45 a.m.
University of Chicago	October 16, 2007	11:45 a.m.
Williams College	October 16, 2007	11:45 a.m.
Clark University	October 16, 2007	12:20 p.m.
Stevens Institute of Technology	October 17, 2007	11:45 a.m.
Harvard University	October 17, 2007	11:55 a.m.
Bryn Mawr College	October 18, 2007	11:45 a.m.
Georgetown University	October 18, 2007	11:55 a.m.
Northeastern	October 19, 2007	9:00 a.m.
California Institute of Technology	October 19, 2007	11:45 a.m.
State University of New York at Albany	October 19, 2007	11:45 a.m.
Bard College	October 19, 2007	11:55 a.m.
Oberlin College	October 22, 2007	11:45 a.m.
SUNY Geneseo	October 22, 2007	11:45 a.m.
Hobart and William Smith Colleges	October 23, 2007	11:45 a.m.
Bates College	October 23, 2007	11:50 a.m.

(Continued)

Table 12.2 Sample of College Representative Visit Calendar (Continued)

College	Date	Time
Rice University	October 24, 2007	11:45 a.m.
University of Vermont	October 25, 2007	11:45 a.m.
Duke University	October 25, 2007	11:55 a.m.
Smith Women of Distinction 3-Day Program for HS Seniors	October 26, 2007	
Brandeis University	October 26, 2007	11:45 a.m.
Pennsylvania State University	October 29, 2007	11:55 a.m.
University of Pittsburgh	November 1, 2007	11:45 a.m.
Wesleyan University	November 1, 2007	11:55 a.m.
University of Maryland, Baltimore County	November 2, 2007	11:45 a.m.
Trinity College—Preview Weekend	November 3, 2007	
Middlebury College	November 8, 2007	11:45 a.m.
Smith College	November 12, 2007	8:30 a.m.

■ Since it is not always possible to have representatives visit when students are free, counselors need to create a system of knowing which students want to attend a particular session. One method is to have students register with the counselor, who then gives the student a pass to leave class for the meeting. Counselors then must follow up to make sure that students have attended and returned to class promptly. A sample of a model pass is shown in Figure 12.4.

■ If your school uses the Naviance system, college visits and passes are done electronically.

■ Discuss the attendance policy with administration officials and faculty. Too often, teachers may be frustrated by students missing their class for a college session. Some schools require that students demonstrate a significant interest in a college in order to miss a class. Create your policy.

Visits with college representatives are important. For some students, it may be the only significant contact that they have with a college. Counselors should insist that students have done their homework about specific colleges so that this important interaction is not spent on questions that can be easily answered by reading the course catalog. Encourage students to ask about internship or special programs rather than inquiring about whether or not the college has a particular major.

College Fairs

College fairs are a wonderful opportunity for students to see a range of colleges and gather information about them. However, colleges are interested in using

IN-Tech Academy

INFORMATION NETWORK & TECHNOLOGY

MS/HS 368X

The Magnet School for Applied Global Technology

2975 TIBBETT AVENUE

BRONX, NEW YORK 10463

College Fair Pass

Student Name: _____

Class: _____

Date:_____   Time: _____

To: Auditorium

Reason: To Attend College Fair

Staff Signature:_____

From: _____

Time: _____

Staff Signature:_____

IN-Tech Academy

INFORMATION NETWORK & TECHNOLOGY

MS/HS 368X

The Magnet School for Applied Global Technology

2975 TIBBETT AVENUE

BRONX, NEW YORK 10463

Pass to Guidance

Student Name: _____

Class: _____

Date:_____   Time: _____

To: Guidance Room 127

Reason: Meeting with College Representative

Staff Signature:_____

From: _____

Time: _____

Staff Signature:_____

IN-Tech Academy

INFORMATION NETWORK & TECHNOLOGY

MS/HS 368X

The Magnet School for Applied Global Technology

2975 TIBBETT AVENUE

BRONX, NEW YORK 10463

College Fair Pass

Student Name: _____

Class: _____

Date:_____   Time: _____

To: Auditorium

Reason: To Attend College Fair

Staff Signature:_____

From: _____

Time: _____

Staff Signature:_____

IN-Tech Academy

INFORMATION NETWORK & TECHNOLOGY

MS/HS 368X

The Magnet School for Applied Global Technology

2975 TIBBETT AVENUE

BRONX, NEW YORK 10463

Pass to Guidance

Student Name: _____

Class: _____

Date:_____   Time: _____

To: Guidance Room 127

Reason: Meeting with College Representative

Staff Signature:_____

From: _____

Time: _____

Staff Signature:_____

Figure 12.4   Sample passes for college representative visits and college fairs. (From IN-Tech Academy. With permission.)

their time and money productively; they want to reach as many students as possible. Depending upon the size of your junior and senior classes, the preferred method of organizing a college fair would be to join with a number of other schools in your area for your fair. In this way, colleges are happy about the number of students they will impact, and high school students benefit from exposure to multiple colleges. Some tips for organizing college fairs are as follows:

■ Utilize existing partnerships with other schools.
■ Divide responsibility among counselors for contacting colleges.
■ Choose a setting that can accommodate appropriate numbers.
■ Advertise the college fair.
■ Depending upon the number of students, include sophomores if possible.
■ Include parents if possible.
■ Add some new colleges each year; it helps to broaden students' outlook.

Advising Students About Interviews

Counselors should remind students that interviews are rarely mandatory; in fact, many schools, particularly large universities, simply do not have the people power to engage in the interview process. However, if students chose to interview, they should be prepared. Some counselors do engage in mock interviews with students; however, given heavy caseloads, this may not be possible. In Chapter 10, we presented interview tips to students, which are reprinted below.

Interviewing—Another Way to Learn More About Colleges and Let Them Know More About You

Many colleges interview prospective students. Interviewing is not mandatory, and, in fact, many large colleges and universities do not have the staff to do any interviewing. If you choose to interview, make the most of it. This is a two-way opportunity: Admissions staff can talk to you in person, and you have the chance to present yourself in a positive light and ask pertinent questions about the college.

Interviews may be on campus with an admissions officer, or they may off campus with an alumnus of the school. No matter which interview method, be prepared to discuss your academic interests and extracurricular involvement.

■ Do your homework: You do not know what an interviewer will ask, but be prepared to show your knowledge of the college. Be ready to ask at least two intelligent questions—one about academics and one about quality of life on campus.
■ Any special programs that interest you? For example, don't ask about whether or not there is a major in astronomy—you should know that from

your research. Ask about internships or possible research in the area of astronomy.

■ Are there any extracurricular groups that especially attract you? Be prepared to discuss why you are interested in a particular activity and any past involvement.

■ Regarding social life, ask about cultural events on campus or collegiate connections with the local cultural activities.

■ Bring a copy of your Activities Sheet. It gives the interviewer a thumbnail sketch of your interests and helps to generate a dialogue.

■ Think of body language: Be dressed appropriately, make eye contact, and speak clearly.

■ Practice interviewing with an adult—a teacher, counselor, parent, family friend. This can help you feel more relaxed in an actual interview.

■ A postinterview thank-you note or e-mail is a polite way of letting the interviewer know of your interest in the school.

Planning College Visits

For many students, the organized school college visit may be the only way they can tour a college campus. Consequently, many schools include this as part of the college advising program. Some suggestions for a successful trip:

■ Counsel students that while they are with friends on this trip they should try to make it their own experience. Chances are they will not attend college with their high school friends, but it is all too easy for them to be influenced by peer reaction and not to experience the college campus for themselves.

■ Attempt to include, if distance allows, different kinds of colleges: the urban, sprawling campus; the suburban campus; the small enclosed campus; and a large state university.

■ Contact the colleges to arrange for tours and information sessions. Don't be shy about asking for food vouchers for the cafeteria!

■ Ask students to complete the Exercise on Evaluating College Visits (Table 10.3) available on the CD and in Chapter 10.

■ Make appropriate travel arrangements and collect any fees if necessary.

■ Have students complete a posttrip evaluation for future planning.

Contacting Colleges About Student Applications

As the counselor, you are the student's advocate, and you want to help your advisees find the best possible match for themselves. What is appropriate contact with college admission officers? First of all, it is appropriate, given your caseload, that you follow up with individual colleges to see if they have any questions regarding your school or the student. Do avoid comparing students: it is not the job of the counselor to recommend one student over another. Given the large numbers of applications and budgetary cuts, large state universities might not have contact with counselors. However, do pursue any opportunity to place a student's application in a more favorable light by explaining school policy, grading, and any other relevant information.

Chapter 13

Writing the Secondary School Report

Writing the Secondary School Report (SSR) or the counselor letter is one of the most important challenges that the college advisor encounters. As the advocate for the student, the counselor should present the student's high school record in the best possible manner. This letter not only highlights a student's achievements but also places these accomplishments in a context that makes the reader understand their importance. Additionally, the SSR addresses any unusual family or personal circumstances that may affect a student's performance. In effect, this letter makes the student come alive to an admissions committee.

Most importantly, the SSR presents the student as a whole person. While a teacher recommendation addresses the academic ability of a student in a particular discipline, the SSR reveals a student in a more comprehensive fashion: a student, a member of the school community and perhaps the broader community, and as an individual who interacts with others. This letter interprets what a student has achieved in high school and suggests future potential.

Gathering Information

In this section are some suggestions that can help counselors no matter what the caseload—from light to moderate to heavy.

Ideally, the counselor should have individual meetings with the student. This provides a way of getting to know the student and understanding his or her goals and aspirations. Prior to meeting, the counselor should review the *official school file/record* for a student, paying particular attention to the student's transcript. Some schools also require the counselor to have individual meetings with the parents to discuss college prospects for their child. The counselor should take notes during these meetings or write a brief summary immediately after a session. If the counselor is in a school with a very heavy caseload, these meetings may not be possible. Whether or not the counselor meets with the student and/or parents individually, the following suggestions are a way of gathering useful information for writing the SSR.

In addition to official school records, use *counselor files* to amplify background material about students. If these are not in existence, advocate for them. Counselor files for students are separate from the school's official files or records. By having a separate file, extra information regarding student achievement, extracurricular activities, community service, and employment can be readily available to the college advisor.

Some Specific Suggestions to Enhance the Counselor Files

- Create a system in which students ask two teachers yearly to write a few sentences about their academic performance in class.
- Suggest that students request two moderators/coaches write a few sentences about their participation in a school activity.
- Request that students ask employers or community service supervisors to describe their work ethic and/or contributions to their program.
- Remind students to give counselors copies of any awards or achievements that they may have earned, especially outside of the school context.

Some schools require that parents to fill out questionnaires about their child. While this may be helpful, the counselor must also ascertain the accuracy of responses.

Use the sample request forms provided in Tables 13.1–13.3 as follows: Table 13.1 for teachers, Table 13.2 for moderators and coaches, and Table 13.3 for community service and employment supervisors.

Now that the counselor has gathered initial information about a student, what next? The SSR is an essay, and like all good essay writing, it involves three stages: *prewriting*, *writing*, and *revising*.

Table 13.1 Teacher Request Form

Student Name _____   Date _____
Teacher's Name _____   Subject_____
Please write two to three sentences describing the student's performance in your class. If possible, use specific examples.
_____
_____
_____
Please return to _____ (name of counselor) by _____.

Table 13.2 Moderators and Coaches Request Form

Student Name _____   Date _____
Name of Moderator/Coach _____   Activity/Sport _____
Please write two to three sentences describing the student's performance and/or contribution to your activity or sport. If possible, use specific examples.
_____
_____
_____
Please return to _____ (name of counselor) by _____.

Table 13.3 Community Service and Work Supervisor Request Form

Student Name _____   Date _____
Name of Community Service/Employment Supervisor _____
Community Service Project/Employment _____
Please write two to three sentences describing the student's performance in community service/employment. If possible, use specific examples.
_____
_____
_____
Please return to _____ (name of counselor) by _____.

Prewriting

In the prewriting stage, the operative word is *analysis*.

First, examine the transcript. What does it reveal about the student? Look for patterns: Is there an upward progression? A downward progression in a particular subject? Any unusual grades—something that seems out of character with the other grades? These need to be investigated. Ask: Why did this occur? Are there any extenuating circumstances to explain this low grade?

What level of classes has the student opted for: more difficult courses or extra courses? Difficult classes that may have resulted in a lower grade than a regular class in the same subject? What academic characteristics might this suggest: genuine interest in learning, creative thinking, desire to encounter greater challenges?

Does the transcript indicate specific academic strengths of a student? Has the student pursued studies in these areas? Does the student demonstrate any academic weaknesses, and, if so, are there any extenuating circumstances to explain these? For example, a low English grade may result from another language spoken at home.

ACTIVITIES

Extracurricular Please list your principal extracurricular, community, volunteer and family activities and hobbies in the order of their interest to you. Include specific events and/or major accomplishments such as musical instrument played, varsity letters earned, etc. **To allow us to focus on the highlights of your activities, please complete this section even if you plan to attach a résumé.**

Grade level or post-graduate (PG)	Approximate time spent	When did you participate in the activity?	Positions held, honors won, or letters earned	If applicable, do you plan to participate in college?
9 10 11 12 PG	Hours per week / Weeks per year	School year / Summer		

○ ○ ○ ○ ○ _____ _____ ○ ○   ○
Activity

○ ○ ○ ○ ○ _____ _____ ○ ○ _____ ○
Activity _____

○ ○ ○ ○ ○ _____ _____ ○ ○   ○
Activity

○ ○ ○ ○ ○ _____ _____ ○ ○ _____ ○
Activity _____

○ ○ ○ ○ ○ _____ _____ ○ ○   ○
Activity

○ ○ ○ ○ ○ _____ _____ ○ ○ _____ ○
Activity _____

○ ○ ○ ○ ○ _____ _____ ○ ○   ○
Activity

Work Experience Please list **paid** jobs you have held during the past three years (including summer employment).

Specific nature of work	Employer	School year	Summer	Approximate dates (mm/yyyy - mm/yyyy)	Hours per week
_____	_____	○	○	_____	____
_____	_____	○	○	_____	____
_____	_____	○	○	_____	____
_____	_____	○	○	_____	____

Figure 13.1   Activities and work experience sheet. (From Common Application, www.commonapp.org)

Next, study the Activities Sheet. What does it say about the student as a person? In Chapter 8, students filled in the Common Application's Activities and Work Experience Sections. Students were asked to submit a copy of these forms (Figure 13.1) to their counselor for the counselor files.

Again, look for patterns: Is there a commitment to a particular activity or sport? Remember that some activities are extensions of the classroom, such as debate, mock trial, literary magazine, yearbook, school newspaper, and Model United Nations.

Has the student contributed to the school community or participated in activities that represent the school in competitive events such as sports, chess, debate, and Model UN? Is the student involved in schoolwide activities such as student government and student community service projects?

Consider the following:

- Evidence of leadership—Has the student held any leadership positions?
- Work-related activity—Has the student demonstrated responsibility and commitment?
- Community service—Has the student participated in school- and/or community-based activities that show commitment?
- Family responsibilities—Is the student responsible for younger siblings or contributing to the family income in some way?

Think about what these commitments mean: Do they suggest positive traits such as leadership, responsibility, maturity, and time management skills?

Synthesize the information gathered from the counselor file and the analysis of the transcript and activities sheet. What kind of portrait emerges of this student?

Writing

The SSR or the counselor letter, like any other good essay, requires a beginning, a middle, and an end. This means an introduction, middle paragraphs that develop essential ideas, and a conclusion. In this stage of writing, you will work on your *first draft*.

Introduction

How a counselor begins this essay is crucial: In the opening sentences, the counselor can present both the student and the context of the school environment. Try to begin with a story or short description of the student, one that provides a succinct picture of that person and catches the reader's interest. Remember, admissions counselors are human, too; make your beginning catch their interest so that they say, "I want to know more about this student." This not only reveals the student's personality, but it also demonstrates the counselor's knowledge of the student. In essence, the introduction provides an overview of what the essay will develop more fully. Below is a sample introduction paragraph that accomplishes this.

Sample Introductory Paragraph

In many ways, Luis is one of the real success stories at Academy X. With a cumulative GPA of 3.75 and a National Hispanic Scholar Semifinalist Award, he has certainly achieved a great deal. As a leader in the Heritage Club and the Retreat Program, Luis models the ideal of community service and commitment. However, when his achievements are viewed within the context of Luis's family history as well as the competitive nature of a scholarship school such as Academy X, his accomplishments are even more pronounced.

Body

In the body or the middle of the essay, talk about the culture of your school—who makes up the student body and what the values and traditions are that make this school unique. Below is an excerpt from Luis's recommendation that addresses the culture of the school.

Sample Body Paragraph—Describes School Culture

Students from almost every ethnic, social, and economic background are represented at Academy X, allowing students to encounter this wealth of diversity at a formative age. For many students, the scholarship that this school awards enables them to have an extraordinary education—one that, in many cases, they might not otherwise be able to experience. Once here, the competition is legendary; to listen to the students speak, teachers and classes take on mythic proportions. All courses are honors and accelerated, and the passing grade is 2.5. It is within this context that Luis has not only thrived as a student but also grown as a person.

- Highlight a student's place and performance in the community in both academics and extracurricular activities.
- At the same time, the counselor cannot ignore low points in a student's high school career. Here, the aim is to present any explanation or extenuating circumstances that may explain a low grade or aberration on the transcript.
- Do not recite the transcript or activities sheet. Refer to both as needed. Remember that the admissions committee has this information.
- It can be helpful to know the overall performance of the junior and senior classes in their academic subjects. For example, a student may have a relatively low grade in a subject, but, upon analysis, that particular grade may be high for a specific teacher.
- Do use quotes from teachers that highlight a student's performance, such as, "Matt's paper on the Mayan calendar displayed his careful research and analysis. In addition, his paper was well written and organized—one of the best I have seen."
- Do talk about family or personal experiences that will help to put your student's high school overall performance in context.

Sample Body Paragraph—Describes Family/Personal History

Luis was 7 years old when his parents immigrated to the United States from Ecuador. His first language is Spanish, and he often acts as an interpreter for his parents. It is interesting to listen to his views on life in Ecuador, which he has visited several times. After living in Astoria, Queens, the attitudes and mindsets that he encounters in many of his relatives in South America seem confining. For instance, he is quite struck by gender roles and the traditional lifestyles that he has experienced in Ecuador. At the same time, he has a deep appreciation of what his parents' immigrant experience has been and views his trips as a way of knowing his parents' culture.

Conclusion

Conclude with a recommendation that suggests how this student will thrive in a collegiate environment. For example, "I enthusiastically recommend" or "I am confident that" suggests that the counselor believes that this student is an excellent candidate for higher learning.

Revising

As in any writing, it is essential that the college advisor revise the SSR. Check for content. Does this letter give a genuine picture of the student? Is it well written? Does it contain any grammatical errors? A counselor does not receive a grade for this letter, but poor or careless writing reflects negatively on the school, the counselor, and the student.

What Not to Include

The counselor is often privy to sensitive information regarding the student. From drugs and alcohol to family problems and school disciplinary issues, counselors are frequently placed in the position of deciding what to include in the SSR. This also involves the disclosure of information regarding emotional and physical health issues as well as learning disabilities and attention deficit disorders. The operative word here is *caution*. Federal law—the Family Educational Rights and Privacy Act—protects students; violation of student privacy only invites a lawsuit. Fortunately, some federal guidelines do exist. The Department of Education's Family Policy Compliance Office (FPCO) has a Web site with useful information on this subject (see Additional Resources).

Most schools have also defined their school policy regarding the disclosure of sensitive information to comply with federal guidelines. Never discuss sensitive information in the SSR without first consulting the principal. While some schools have developed release forms for parents to sign allowing counselors to address sensitive issues such as learning disabilities and attention deficit disorders, this is tricky ground. Again, if a student has had disciplinary issues, consult your principal regarding school policy. This question is on most applications and must be answered honestly. Proceed with all due caution.

A final word about the SSR: Write it on school letterhead and try to limit it to 1½ pages if possible.

Chapter 14

Working With Parents

This chapter presents a framework for interacting and working with parents. We first focus on recent research about parental involvement. Then we offer some practical advice about beginning the college process early and including parents in the discussion of college planning. We also discuss how to conduct a College Information Night for parents and give suggestions about using guest speakers from local colleges. Included is a sample agenda for a junior-year College Information Night. In addition, we present a sample parent questionnaire and then provide helpful suggestions for individual meetings with parents.

Parental Involvement

We can all recall the example of the parents who were not at all involved in their child's college advising process. We can also all recall parents who became too involved in the process. Somewhere in the middle may be the best place to be.

Parents can clearly play a valuable role. The power of parents has been well documented in many studies. Parental support and encouragement has been shown to be one of the most if not the most important factor in their child's educational aspirations (Auerbach, 2002; Hossler, Schmidt, & Vesper, 1998; Stage & Hossler, 1989). Students who are strongly encouraged by their parents to attend college are much more likely to attend 4-year institutions than students who do not receive that support from their families (Hossler et al., 1999). Students take their cues from their parents about what is reasonable to expect for their educational goals, and they plan their future accordingly (Auerbach, 2002; Ceja, 2004; Tierney & Auerbach, 2005). More specifically, parental involvement has been positively associated with better academic success, quality of the parent–student relationship, and aspirations for higher education (Jeynes, 2007). When do they think they should be in this process? When do we see them as involved?

While most parents become involved, they are generally involved in the later stages of the process. You might recall from Chapter 4 that once children transition into high school, generally parents are less involved and are more likely to expect their children to be more independent in school and in their daily activities. Thus, parents step back in the first 2 years of high school and then start to become more involved during the junior year. We also know that a parent's level of education plays a significant role in helping their children to go through the college process as well as to persist in their academic performance to gain acceptance for college. In the United States, many minority parents have not had the opportunity to go to college, and some from immigrant groups may not have finished high school. Yet they want college for their children. The Pew Hispanic Center/Kaiser Family Foundation (2004) noted that 95% of Latino parents believed it was "very important" that their children go to college. Lack of knowledge about college, poor communication due to language issues, and unfamiliarity with the U.S. education system have been cited as issues for Latino parents in not being able to help their children in the college advising process (Auerbach, 2002; Tierney & Auerbach, 2005; Torrez, 2004). It seems clear that parents want to be involved, but the involvement comes later in the process or does not actually happen due to other issues as noted above.

When thinking about how and when to involve them in the college advising process, we can envision a wide range of active involvement and involvement over several years. We want parents to have general discussions about the importance of college and its role in their child's future, about important personal growth as a result of going to college, and about how college will be financed; some of these discussions should start in the 9th grade, not in the junior year. As counselors, we also want parents to continue to support their children throughout the adolescent developmental stage with its enormous changes cognitively, physically, and psychosocially—in other words, throughout high school. These normal developmental changes also strongly impact their aspirations. We would advocate that parents be attentive and supportive as their children move through high school—about their academic work and about their development personally into strong, confident young adults. With the infusion of technology and the Internet into the schooling process, parents and guardians should be integrally involved in the growth of the child's academic skills for college. *The Wall Street Journal* articles "Does the Internet Make You Smarter?" (Shirky, 2010) and "Does the Internet Make You Dumber?" (Carr, 2010) presents the two sides of the influence of the Internet on intelligence and learning. "Amid the silly videos and spam are the roots of a new reading and writing culture," says Shirky. "The cognitive effects are measurable: We're turning into shallow thinkers," says Carr in the same article. Clearly debatable, it is important for parents and guardians to actively foster the development of strong and deep learning habits. Fitzpatrick (2008) reviewed a series of studies related to best predictors of college grade point average (GPA) in the college freshman year, including high school GPA, intelligence quotient (IQ), and the Scholastic Aptitude Test (SAT). Self-discipline in studying was the best predictor. She concluded that all of us—parents, counselors, teachers—must continually help students to be self-disciplined learners. Thus, parents are really integral supporters in a variety of areas. Of course, the focus here for the most part is on the college process, but before parents can support their children in this they must attend to their role in enhancing academic and psychosocial development. Without that support, the college advising process cannot proceed effectively.

Before we move on to some specific ideas and plans for parent involvement in the college process, we want to share with you two elements of the ethical standard B.1 for school counselors as specified in the American School Counselor Association's National Model (ASCA 2005). Standard B.1 addresses parent/guardian rights and responsibilities. Under that standard, Section A indicates that the professional school counselor "respects the rights and responsibilities of parents/guardians for their children and endeavors to establish, as appropriate, a collaborative relationship with parents/guardians to facilitate the student's maximum development." (p. 146). Section D indicates that the professional counselor "is sensitive to diversity among families and recognizes that all parents/guardians, custodial and noncustodial, are vested with certain rights and responsibilities for the welfare of their children by virtue of their role and according to law." (p. 147). What is of most relevance to our discussion of parental involvement throughout high school and not just in college advising is that we counselors have an obligation ethically to develop a strong collaborative relationship with parents. Furthermore, we need to be certain that our ethical obligation of sensitivity to diversity enables us to have the vision to make sure that the families have optimal opportunities to understand the college advising process.

Beginning the College Planning Process Early

We now turn to some specific ideas that we have found successful for early planning in the college advising process.

Parent Small Group Meetings—Freshman Year

Parent group meetings related to college advising are generally started during the junior year. We suggest that if you do not have general parent meetings during the freshman year, you should start them. These do not specifically relate to college advising, but rather they should deal with different topics related to 9th grade (e.g., transitioning, increased academic rigor, study skills). These meetings serve a broader function besides the content of the meeting: they help parents/guardians meet each other, meet you and your staff, and become otherwise more engaged in the institution.

A sample meeting could be one on study skills, which are so critical in the academic transition. Start the meeting with a little set of questions about how parents think their children should study. How much time should your children spend at night? Where should they study? Should you help them? Small groupings make it easier for parents to participate. Food, of course, helps too, as well as short meeting lengths and, most of all, letting parents walk out with some guidelines on paper.

Another meeting could focus on the school program Web site. Most schools have some type of Web site that parents need to review, and some schools have more sophisticated, interactive sites where parents can see what the homework is for a class, when standardized tests are administered, and so forth. Naviance also has a career planner and a study skills inventory that parents may view.

Plan four meetings for the year as a start, two each semester. Balance academic topics with psychosocial. These meetings could be connected to report card night. Remember Chapter 2 on partnerships, and try to recruit counselor interns to help out in these meetings.

Other Sample Event Ideas Across Years

1. Parent–student PLAN/PSAT workshop (sophomore and junior years)—students receive their scores and a presentation on alternative ways to improve so that they can work on their performance.
2. Free Application for Federal Student Aid (FAFSA) workshops (junior and senior years)—try to get your college partner's financial aid staff to help you present the first workshop to sophomores and their families; also include someone who speaks the language of your students' parents if needed. Our experience in doing this work (through a grant devoted to college advising, Optimal College Readiness) is that parents need early exposure and multiple exposures to this process, including individual help in some cases.
3. How to read your report card and understand high school graduation requirements (freshman and sophomore years).
4. College visits with other students and their parents (junior year)—this structure enables parents to continue to gain support from other parents, strengthens that connection, and enables them to see how others view the colleges. Through the OCR grant in spring 2010, we were able to fund 23 students and their families in New York City to see local colleges. In this particular case, most of the families were Hispanic, and even though they lived in New York City they had not seen most of these schools. Figure 14.1 is an event report showing the success of the event.

Sample Workshop Framework for Diverse Populations

The workshop outline presented here was developed for a school–college collaboration and described in detail in a study exploring the parental involvement

Event Report: Manhattan College/IN-Tech Academy

Event Name: NYC College Familiarization Tour
Location
City/Borough: Bronx   Facility: N/A
Event Date: June 11, 2010   Time(s): 9:45 a.m.–3:30 p.m.
Actual Attendance: 24 parents/23 students
Attendees Certified CACG-Eligible:* ☑ Yes   ☐ No
Evaluations Completed: ☐ Yes   ☑ No
Overall Evaluation Rating: ☐ Poor**   ☐ As Planned   ☑ Excellent**

Summary of Program Activity

Parents and students were provided the opportunity to take a tour around New York City identifying key colleges located in New York City.

Summary of Program Outcomes

Parents and students had the opportunity to familiarize themselves with historical landmarks and colleges/universities in the city of New York. Parents and students became familiar with New York University, Barnard College, Columbia University, Borough of Manhattan Community College, Pace University, Cooper Union, City College, Fordham University, Hunter College and John Jay College of Criminal Justice. Twenty-four (24) parents and twenty-three (23) students attended the trip.

Comments for Future Events

This event/tour/trip was a success. The parents and students enjoyed it. We should aim for more tours for next year. This will enable students and parents to become more aware of the college options available to them in the city of New York.
Form completed by (please print): Name: Rose Fairweather-Clunie

Title: Principal

Figure 14.1   Event report.

of a group of Hispanic parents in a number of schools in the western part of the United States (Fann, McCafferty, Jarsky, & McDonough, 2009). It is important to read this study as it presents an innovative approach to working with Hispanic families and a truly detailed and thorough plan for including these families in the college advising process. It is described briefly here.

In the study, the authors developed four workshops for schools from poor districts in California. They focused on middle schools, not high schools, but the workshop themes are adaptable. The workshops focused on two elements: (1) providing parents with information on college-related topics (similar to our suggestions above); and (2) in-depth research into Hispanic parents and their college needs that would help drive the workshops. The workshops were given in Spanish. The workshops were as follows:

■ Night 1: An overview of the college choice process, an exploration of parent knowledge about college, and suggestions for parents on how to actively participate in their children's college-planning process.
■ Night 2: Knowing the system, or "system smarts." Parents were given step-by-step instructions to help their children prepare for and apply to college.

- Night 3: Financial aid, specifically designed to relieve parental fears about being able to afford to send their children to college.
- Night 4: Review of the topics, a reemphasizing of strategies parents could use to support their children's college plans. Parents were given a take-home "Family Action Plan" to complete.

The researchers found that some workshops led to specific issues, such as Hispanic families worrying about their female children leaving home for college and about their children going out after high school to work. Their results confirm our suggestions in this chapter about how counselors should approach parents and projects. That is, they strongly urge the development of college–school partnerships because these provide more specific expertise in certain areas (e.g., financial advice); that workshops be given regularly due to the critical need for information about this process and the need for parents to be empowered; and, as we have stated before, that the workshops offer parents opportunities for stronger connections with the schools.

College Information Nights

Ideally, schools conduct multiple College Information Nights starting as early as the sophomore year. Usually, two information nights occur in the junior year and one in the beginning of the senior year. Figure 14.2 is a sample agenda of a typical College Information Night for second-semester juniors. Note that financial aid is addressed in a separate information night. This model works well for schools where counselors have at least two formal, individual meetings with parents: one in the second-semester junior year, in which an initial list of colleges is established, and another one in the first-semester senior year. In conducting this junior-year College Information Night, counselors should prepare a packet of helpful, general information about the college application process.

Understandably, information about college research and the admission process can be overwhelming, especially for parents who are engaging in it for the first time. The point of this initial meeting is to give an overview, not a detailed description of how to file applications or send test scores. That kind of detailed information can be given in a written packet in which the counselor explains methodology and provides forms to which both students and parents can refer for school policy. Most schools have a senior-year College Information Night for parents and students, an ideal time to distribute the more detailed information. This junior-year College Information Night also provides an opportunity for the counselors and parents to interact more personally, thereby laying the groundwork for a strong family–counselor relationship in this ongoing process.

A follow-up College Information Night at the end of the junior year helps to build upon the momentum established. College admissions officers are happy to speak to parent–student groups about the process. This is an especially good

Junior-Year College Information Night Agenda

1. Welcome.
2. Introduction.
   - Explain that parents and students are in a *process*.
   - Briefly discuss the success of the current senior class.
   - Assure them that they will leave with a packet of material to help them in this process; they don't have to memorize it all that night.
   - Provide an overview of the information to be presented.
3. Use an ice breaker for students and their parents/guardians to generate a brief discussion. One successful method is to have parents and students separately fill out brief questionnaires about college. Include questions about preferred distance from home, dorm life—coed vs. single sex—and frequency of home visits. It never fails to make people laugh at the different responses and ease the tense anxiety in the room.
4. Now, the essentials of the college admissions process; give a brief synopsis of the following:
   - What colleges are looking for in candidates
   - The quality of the high school transcript
   - Standardized test scores
   - Extracurricular activities/sports/work experience/community service
   - What others say about the candidate—the counselor letter and teacher recommendations
5. How to get started in the process:
   - Initial list of schools that may be good matches at first individual meeting with parents and student
   - Importance of research and use of technology
   - College visits
   - Interviewing
   - Preparation and taking of SAT and/or ACT
   - Asking teachers for recommendations
   - Explain the role of Naviance and the commonapp.org Web site
   - Announce the Financial Aid Workshop date
6. Spend the summer productively
   - Community service
   - Work experience
   - Special enrichment programs

Figure 14.2   Junior-year college information night agenda.

time for admissions officers to make these presentations because the crunch time for their work has passed. If you have partnered with a college or university, use this connection to find speakers. If not, contact colleges that know your school and ask for a guest speaker to visit. At this evening, present some brief information, but let the majority of the evening belong to your guest speaker.

Parent Questionnaire

Many counselors use a parent questionnaire (Figure 14.3) as a means of gaining insight from parents about their son or daughter. This questionnaire becomes a vehicle for the parent to share viewpoints, expectations, and experiences that may help the counselor better understand the student. This is especially true for those counselors with heavy caseloads. Ideally, this questionnaire should be given to parents in the beginning of the second-semester junior year and returned preferably prior to the first parent–student–counselor meeting or by the end of the semester. Added to the information in the student's file, this questionnaire can be useful both in advising the student and parents and in writing the Secondary School Report.

Both the junior-year College Information Night agenda and the parent questionnaire may be accessed on the CD.

Dear Parents,

No one knows your son or daughter quite the way you do. We are asking for you to share your insight, experiences and expectations with us as we experience the college research and application process. Please return this questionnaire to your child's college advisor by [date].

Name:

Student Name:

College Advisor:

1. What do you regard as your child's greatest strength?
2. What do you regard as your child's greatest weakness?
3. What do you consider to be your child's most important achievement in high school? Why?
4. What kind of learning environment do you want for your child's collegiate experience? Explain why.
5. How does your child react to setbacks? Please give an example.
6. How do you feel about your child living on campus? Is he or she ready for this experience?
7. Does your child have a significant experience/achievement outside of school? If so, what is it?
8. What are the first three adjectives that come mind that describe your child?
9. What are your expectations for future college and career success?
10. Is there any extra information that you would like to share?

Figure 14.3 Parent questionnaire.

Individual Meetings With Parents and Students

For counselors with heavy caseloads, individual meetings with parents may not be possible. Some techniques that may be useful in working with parents in this case are to develop a *detailed* college handbook that outlines college advising procedures and policies and contains sample forms for requesting transcripts, secondary school reports, teacher recommendations, and any other pertinent information. Many large schools have increasingly used e-mail as an effective way of communicating with parents.

For schools that do have individual meetings with parents and students, counselors should be familiar with the student counseling and school files. This includes the student's GPA and/or grades, standardized testing, extracurricular involvement, community service, sports, and other related information as well as any relevant family circumstances. If possible, ask parents to submit the parent questionnaire prior to this first meeting so that the counselor has time to read their answers. Be sure to pay close attention to both the parents' views on college as well as the student's. In this initial meeting, it is still early: Junior grades are not yet complete, and for the most part SAT and/or ACT® scores may not have been posted. However, it is possible to suggest a list of 8–10 colleges based on student and parent interest in conjunction with your knowledge of the student. Also, take this opportunity to explain the Naviance scattergram if the school has this service. This can be very helpful in allowing parents and students to see possible chances of admission. If not, ask the student to work on the Exercise on College Matches in Chapter 8 (Table 8.4). Immediately after the visit, write a summary of the discussion for future reference.

Chapter 15

Financial Aid and Merit-Based Scholarships

This chapter is a discussion of the all-important role that financial aid and merit-based scholarships play in the college process. Our emphasis is on providing an overview while at the same time encouraging counselors to be proactive in this process. Thus, the chapter does not review all the intricacies of financial aid. Rather, we want to highlight once again the important role of counselors as leaders and advocates. We present a framework for conducting a sample Parents' Financial Aid Workshop and explain the effectiveness of having a college financial aid officer as a guest speaker. Also included in this chapter is a discussion of the various federal financial aid programs involved in need-based financial aid as well as a discussion of merit scholarships. We conclude with suggestions about how counselors can develop a multitiered approach to educating parents and students about the financial aid process.

As students research colleges and compare academic programs, campus life, and varied opportunities such as study abroad and internships, the essential affordability factor looms large. For most students and parents this is an over-reaching issue: how to pay for this collegiate experience. Added to the normal anxiety of the college application process is the fear that, if accepted, students may not be able to attend the college of their choice due to financial reasons. Frequently, this fear is exacerbated in low-income parents and first-time college parents who are unlikely to be familiar with the financial aid process and all that it entails. For non-English-speaking parents, the process may seem overwhelming, and at times they may require an interpreter to help them navigate the process. Even to the fairly seasoned parents who have previously experienced this process, changes in forms and procedures occur that they must learn and master.

As counselors, our proactive role is essential in the financial aid process. In previous years, conducting a Financial Aid Night led by a local college financial aid officer in the senior year might have sufficed; however, in these increasingly complex social and financial times, a much more sophisticated approach is needed. If our students are to receive as much financial aid as possible, a multi-tiered approach is needed. This includes multiple Financial Aid Nights, work-shops where parents may receive help in filling out forms, bilingual mentors to assist people still learning English, and a hotline form of communication where parents can contact experts for answers to questions. Counselors must have a hands-on approach in ascertaining that essential forms such as the Free Application for Federal Student Aid (FAFSA) have been filed. Naturally, this does not mean that counselors are privy to personal income facts but only that they are assured that the form has indeed been filed.

First of all, what is financial aid? Essentially, financial aid is any financial assis-tance that helps students attend a postsecondary institution; this includes 4-year and 2-year colleges and vocational/trade and technical schools. Financial aid falls into two broad categories: need-based financial aid and merit-based scholarships. Each type of assistance has its own definitions, application procedures, sources of revenue, and deadlines. To achieve optimum results, counselors should be consistently attentive in helping both students and parents understand these dif-ferences. (See Appendix B for financial definitions.)

Need-Based Financial Aid: An Overview

Need-based financial aid can come from the federal government, state govern-ments, colleges and universities, and private sources. To be eligible for need-based financial aid, parents must complete the FAFSA. This form uses a federal methodology to measure the family's ability to pay for college expenses and determines the expected family contribution (EFC) toward the cost of college. This numeric figure results from a complex calculation based on taxable and nontaxable incomes of parents and student as well as assets and any other ben-efits they may receive. In order to determine whether or not a student qualifies for need-based financial aid, parents must file the FAFSA in the second semester of the senior year and each year that the student attends college.

Filing the FAFSA

One of the most important and first steps in receiving financial aid is filing the FAFSA. The counselor can take a leadership role in this process without being an expert in financial aid. Here is a model of this process that we helped develop at an urban school. In 2009–2010 at IN-Tech Academy in the Bronx borough, New York City, where we have piloted much of our college and career curriculum, 100% of the senior parents filed FAFSA forms, giving their children a much better chance of attending the college of their choice. Parents had previously attended Financial Aid Information Nights in the junior year, where they learned about the terminology and process of financial aid. The following agenda/directional program, How to Apply for Need-Based Financial Aid, was successfully used at a Financial Aid Workshop for senior parents. This particular workshop was held in a computer room so that parents could actually work on the FAFSA form. Since IN-Tech Academy has a partnership with Manhattan College, financial aid officers and counselors-in-training assisted the school counselors in helping parents to complete the FAFSA. Especially important in this setting was the inclusion of bilingual mentors for parents for whom English is a second language.

How to Apply for Need-Based Financial Aid

Table 15.1 presents an overview for a workshop on the FAFSA. Ideally, the Financial Aid Workshops should begin in the sophomore year so that parents may become familiar with the financial aid process. As suggested in Chapter 14, counselors should ask financial aid staff from their school's institution of higher education (IHE) partner to help in presenting the first workshop to sophomores and their families; also include someone who speaks the language of your students' parents if needed. If your school does not have a partnership with an IHE, seek help from colleges that know your school. The authors' experience in doing this work (through a grant devoted to college advising, Optimal College Readiness) suggests that parents need early exposure to this process and multiple exposures, including individual help in many cases.

Table 15.1 Completing the FAFSA Workshop

How to Apply for Need-Based Financial Aid
Go to www.fafsa.ed.gov. • Click on the current year and start the application. • The FAFSA Web site has become very user friendly. • Use the Help bars to find answers to many questions while completing the application.
Documentation needed: • W-2/1040/schedules/alimony/child support/dividends/other income • Social Security income • Disability income • Any document that shows that you or parent/guardian has received money throughout the year.
Monies need to be declared. • Danger/penalty of fraud: It is a legal matter. • Be prepared to be verified. • The government randomly selects a percentage of applicants to send in their financial documents so the institutions can verify the information is correct.
Mistakes on the FAFSA are red flags that will result in being asked to verify the information on the application.

Understanding the Student Aid Report

After the FAFSA has been analyzed, parents receive a Student Aid Report (SAR). This is the official summary of the FAFSA and states the all-important EFC. This is the figure that is deducted from the cost of attendance at a particular college. The remaining amount indicates your financial need or eligibility for financial aid which will vary from college to college simply because aid eligibility at a particular college depends on both the cost of attendance and the EFC. The SAR also provides a listing of all of the answers submitted on the FAFSA. These should be reviewed carefully, and if any changes are necessary they should be made and resubmitted. These changes could affect the EFC.

Types of Federal Financial Aid Programs

Federal student aid is financial assistance that is available through the U.S. Department of Education's Office of Federal Student Aid (see FAFSA in Additional Resources). Federal student aid covers school expenses such as tuition and fees, room and board, books and supplies, and transportation. This aid can also help students pay for a computer and dependent child-care expenses.

Federal student aid falls into three categories: grants, work-study, and loans.

1. Grants are, in effect, a gift; they do not have to be repaid.
   a. The Pell grant is designed for low-income students.
   b. The Federal Supplemental Educational Grants is for students with extreme financial need.
   c. The Academic Competitiveness Grant (ACG) is for students who have a Pell grant and have graduated from a rigorous secondary school, are enrolled at least half-time in a degree program, and have achieved a 3.0 grade point average (GPA).
   d. The National Science and Mathematics Access to Retain Talent Grant (National SMART Grant) is for students who have a Pell grant; are in the third or fourth year of a degree program majoring in the sciences, math, technology, engineering, or certain needed languages; and have a 3.0 GPA.
2. Federal work-study assistance provides jobs to undergraduate and graduate students, allowing them to earn money to pay education expenses.
   a. Generally, work-study is administered on-campus by the college or university.
   b. Wages are usually minimum-wage level.
   c. Hours worked are determined by student need, when they apply, and funding level of the college.
3. Loans are a type of financial aid that must be repaid with interest.
   a. Federal Stafford loans are student loans that must be repaid and are available to both undergraduate and graduate students under the Federal Direct

Loan Program. If it is a subsidized Stafford loan (demonstrated need for the loan), students are not responsible for interest while attending at least half-time and the principal is deferred. If it is an unsubsidized Stafford loan (financial need was not demonstrated), the principal is still deferred, but students are responsible for paying interest on the loan.

b. Federal PLUS loans are available to parents of dependent undergraduate students who are enrolled at least half-time. The PLUS loan is also available to graduate and professional-degree students. Financial need is not a requirement.

c. Federal Perkins loans are low-interest (5%) loans that must be repaid; the maximum annual loan amount is $4,000 for undergraduate students and $6,000 for graduate students.

State Need-Based Financial Aid

Nearly all states have some form of need-based financial aid. States use the FAFSA's assessment of need and the EFC to determine the amount of assistance. States may also require parents to submit additional forms. Usually, state financial aid is in the form of a grant and may only be used within the state, although some states have developed reciprocal agreements. This financial aid may be combined with federal financial aid. The National Association of State Student Grant and Aid Programs (see Additional Resources) maintains a Web site that links to each state's financial assistance commission (NACAC, 2008).

Need-Based Financial Aid From Colleges and Universities

The amount of aid that a college or university may offer to a student varies greatly. The National Center for College Costs (see Additional Resources) http://www.collegecosts.com) is a detailed Web site about financial aid and includes opportunities for parents and students to better understand the process. It suggests that students find out if the college funds 100% of demonstrated need, if the college makes any adjustments to the federal formula, and what the specific breakdown is of the need-based financial aid award package from the college.

Merit Scholarships: An Overview

Merit-based scholarships are another form of financial assistance for students who qualify. Merit scholarships are not tied to demonstrated financial need but are a recognition of achievement in academic performance and special talent areas such as dance, music, art, and sports. The most prestigious of the merit scholarships is the National Merit Scholarship Awards (see Chapter 6 for detailed information). In addition, a variety of civic, corporate, special interest, and similar groups award merit scholarships to qualifying students. Many of these scholarships demand a particular GPA, usually a 3.0 for renewal of the scholarship.

Recently, many colleges have been awarding merit scholarships to incoming students who do not qualify for any financial assistance for a variety of reasons. This could be a marketing tool designed to make parents who are paying the full burden of college feel that they are getting some aid. In other cases, colleges want to attract students who have been identified as strong in academic talent. For the most part, these scholarships are contingent on achieving and maintaining a high GPA, such as 3.0 or higher, and can be easily lost in freshman year.

Suggestions for Building a Multitiered Financial Aid Advising Program

First and foremost, in developing a multitiered financial aid advising system, it is essential to think about beginning this process no later than the sophomore year. As noted above, many parents need frequent exposure to the financial aid process. This is particularly true for first-time college parents, low-income parents, and parents for whom English is a second language. A multitiered approach includes the following:

- Several information nights for parents in the sophomore, junior, and senior years
- Interactive workshops, which ideally can be conducted in a computer room where parents can engage in the FAFSA process
- Personal counseling—again with the assistance of an IHE partner so that counselors will be able to give personal attention to many parents
- Inclusion of bilingual counselors, depending upon the needs of the parent group
- Establishment of a hotline communication format so that parents can call with questions

The model of the single Financial Information Night is certainly obsolete in most schools. If counselors are to be proactive on behalf of their students, they must be leaders in developing new models that will better serve the needs of their students. This multitiered approach can be adapted to the needs of various schools.

Chapter 16

Advising Students With Learning Disabilities About College

This chapter first focuses generally on important background knowledge, planning, and strategies that counselors might want to consider in working with students with learning disabilities. We then present a more specific discussion on evaluating the qualifications for extended time in standardized testing and on ascertaining whether students should attend mainstream colleges or more specialized college programs. Finally, we suggest when counselors should advise students to have reevaluations and why and when to send the testing evaluation to colleges.

Wow—it is May and you have succeeded in gaining acceptance into a fairly competitive college for one of your learning disabled students. Congratulations. Everyone is so pleased about it all: student, family, friends, and high school faculty. But you have this lingering thought: How will the student do? Will he or she thrive or just survive? If you have helped this student not only in choosing the right college after engaging in good, solid research about colleges but also psychologically in becoming a strong personal advocate, then the student will be fine.

Important Knowledge and Planning Ideas

First, let's look at some statistics about students with disabilities and college. According to the 1995–1996 National Postsecondary Student Aid Study (NPSAS, 1996), as reviewed by Horn and Berktold (1999), roughly 6% of all undergraduates reported having a disability, with approximately 29% of those reporting that they had a learning disability and 21% reporting another health-related disability or impairment that presumably included mental illness or depression. By 2004, the population of college students with disabilities had increased, with the latest data showing that approximately 11% of college students reported having some type of disability (Horn & Nevill, 2006). Approximately 18.3% of these college students reported that they had a learning disability or attention deficit/hyperactivity disorder (ADHD), while 21.9% reported having mental illness (Horn & Nevill, 2006). Furthermore, findings from the Beginning Postsecondary Students Longitudinal Study indicate that only 16% of college students with disabilities earned a bachelor's degree compared with 27% of those without a disability. Thus, the landscape of who goes to college with disabilities continues to change, and students with disabilities seem to have more difficulty completing their degrees.

By the time they are ready to graduate, learning disabled students should have a good idea of how they best learn, how they prioritize their time, and how they can succeed in getting good grades. They have enjoyed a level of support and accommodation that is brought to the student through high school mandated services. What should we, the college advisors, be addressing specifically to help these students get the best match in their college and succeed there? The application process and the counselor's role in this kind of advising starts months, even years, prior to the time the actual application is made as it does for all students. Just as student athletes might receive some differential advising that focuses on their specific priorities for college, so too will your students with learning disabilities. "Remember that they are always students first—they are not LD [learning disabled] students, but students with learning disabilities" (Kravets & Wax, 2008, p. 122).

Of course, college life will be different. It is clear that today, more so than ever, higher educational institutions are addressing the needs of learning disabled students. However, there is much variation in the levels of service offered by colleges and the kinds of learning environments that are available for these students. Most importantly, the colleges do not seek out learning disabled students; students must be their own advocates. They must be ready to identify themselves and seek out support services and accommodations while developing into adult learners. Counselors need to engage in appropriate steps with these students to help them choose the best collegiate environment academically.

When to Have a Psychoeducational Reassessment

The initial psychoeducational assessment should be done as early as possible if parents suspect or know that the child has a potential learning disability or ADHD. Such assessments should be done again in high school. To receive accommodations in entry testing or in college, the assessment must be recent. A psychoeducational evaluation is valid for approximately 3 to 5 years from the completion of testing. Most learning disabled high school students have had previous testing demonstrating a discrepancy between their intellectual ability and their achievement. The evaluation also highlights areas of strengths and weaknesses. Ideally, these students have received the accommodations that help them to address gaps in their particular learning weaknesses. The federal government has established guidelines for classification of learning disabilities and appropriate accommodations. Most states have also developed similar guidelines that follow federal standards. These accommodations may be essential in gaining acceptance into college and later academic success. Given the calendar of standardized testing, which for many students begins in the sophomore year for the PSAT and/or the PLAN®, students who qualify for extended time need updated evaluations. This is, of course, even more essential as they enter the junior and senior years when they are taking the SAT and/or the ACT for college admission. Consequently, depending upon the initial assessment, many students are reevaluated before or at the beginning of the junior year or during the summer between the junior and senior years.

Most high school students will understand the information in the psychoeducational assessment report. That information is critical in making changes, getting help, and setting goals. Students who are able to articulate their personal learning style, whether in the classroom, in setting up a course of study, in personal tutorials, or even in determining a living and study environment, are much further along in becoming their own advocates and succeeding in the college of their choice. Most if not all of these steps have occurred early in the student's schooling but should be reevaluated after later testing. Strengths and weaknesses should be reevaluated in the latest testing, study habits should be modified, and the student should take ownership in evaluating the postsecondary educational options available.

Academic Strategies

The following are suggestions for counselors to help students focus on their academic profile:

- Help students early on in their high school years to understand their academic strengths and weaknesses.
- Help students understand their disability including their Individual Education Plan (IEPs).
- Help students understand the link between the two.
- Empower students to be active in developing strategies to deal with the impact of their disability on their school performance.
- Plan group counseling opportunities that revolve around their needs, including strong attention to study skills.
- Help them to focus on academic transition during their senior year in high school.

Confidence-Building Strategies

Equally as important as the academic focus is attention to helping these students gain confidence in their own ability to advocate for their needs. This may even be more critical due to the very different environment in college. Many lists of the differences between college and high school can be found. Table 16.1, a

Table 16.1 What Are the Differences Between High School and College?

In High School	*In College*
High school is *mandatory* and usually *free*.	College is *voluntary* and *expensive*.
Your time is structured by others.	You manage your own time.
You need permission to participate in extracurricular activities	You must decide whether to participate in co-curricular activities.
You can count on parents and teachers to remind you of your responsibilities and to guide you in setting priorities.	*You* must balance your responsibilities and set priorities. You will face moral and ethical decisions you have never faced before.
Each day you proceed from one class directly to another, spending 6 hours each day—30 hours a week—in class.	You often have hours between classes; class times vary throughout the day and evening and you spend only 12 to 16 hours each week in class
Most of your classes are arranged for you.	You arrange your own schedule in consultation with your adviser. Schedules tend to look lighter than they really are.
You are not responsible for knowing what it takes to graduate.	Graduation requirements are complex, and differ from year to year. You are expected to know those that apply to you.
Guiding principle: You will usually be told what to do and corrected if your behavior is out of line.	Guiding principle: You're expected to take responsibility for what you do and don't do, as well as for the consequences of your decisions.
High School Classes	*College Classes*
The school year is 36 weeks long; some classes extend over both semesters and some don't.	The academic year is divided into two separate 15-week semesters, plus a week after each semester for exams.
Classes generally have no more than 35 students.	Classes may number 100 students or more.
You may study outside class as little as 0 to 2 hours a week, and this may be mostly last-minute test preparation.	You need to study at least 2 to 3 hours outside of class for each hour in class.
You seldom need to read anything more than once, and sometimes listening in class is enough.	You need to review class notes and text material regularly.
You are expected to read short assignments that are then discussed, and often re-taught, in class.	You are assigned substantial amounts of reading and writing which may not be directly addressed in class.
Guiding principle: You will usually be told in class what you need to learn from assigned readings.	Guiding principle: It's up to you to read and understand the assigned material; lectures and assignments proceed from the assumption that you've already done so.

Table 16.1   What Are the Differences Between High School and College? (Continued)

High School Teachers	College Professors
Teachers check your completed homework.	Professors may not always check completed homework, but they will assume you can perform the same tasks on tests.
Teachers remind you of your incomplete work.	Professors may not remind you of incomplete work.
Teachers approach you if they believe you need assistance.	Professors are usually open and helpful, but most expect you to initiate contact if you need assistance.
Teachers are often available for conversation before, during, or after class.	Professors expect and want you to attend their scheduled office hours.
Teachers have been trained in teaching methods to assist in imparting knowledge to students.	Professors have been trained as experts in their particular areas of research.
Teachers provide you with information you missed when you were absent.	Professors expect you to get from classmates any notes from classes you missed.
Teachers present material to help you understand the material in the textbook.	Professors may not follow the textbook. Instead, to amplify the text, they may give illustrations, provide background information, or discuss research about the topic you are studying. Or they may expect *you* to relate the classes to the textbook readings.
Teachers often write information on the board to be copied in your notes.	Professors may lecture nonstop, expecting you to identify the important points in your notes. When professors write on the board, it may be to amplify the lecture, not to summarize it. Good notes are a must.
Teachers impart knowledge and facts, sometimes drawing direct connections and leading you through the thinking process.	Professors expect you to think about and synthesize seemingly unrelated topics.
Teachers often take time to remind you of assignments and due dates.	Professors expect you to read, save, and consult the course syllabus (outline); the syllabus spells out exactly what is expected of you, when it is due, and how you will be graded.

(Continued)

Table 16.1   What Are the Differences Between High School and College? (Continued)

High School Teachers	College Professors
Teachers carefully monitor class attendance.	Professors may not formally take roll, but they are still likely to know whether or not you attended.
Guiding principle: High school is a teaching environment in which you acquire facts and skills.	Guiding principle: College is a learning environment in which you take responsibility for thinking through and applying what you have learned.
Tests in High School	*Tests in College*
Testing is frequent and covers small amounts of material.	Testing is usually infrequent and may be cumulative, covering large amounts of material. You, not the professor, need to organize the material to prepare for the test. A particular course may have only two or three tests in a semester.
Makeup tests are often available.	Makeup tests are seldom an option; if they are, you need to request them.
Teachers frequently rearrange test dates to avoid conflict with school events.	Professors in different courses usually schedule tests without regard to the demands of other courses or outside activities.
Teachers frequently conduct review sessions, pointing out the most important concepts.	Professors rarely offer review sessions, and when they do, they expect you to be an active participant, one who comes prepared with questions.
Guiding principle: Mastery is usually seen as the ability to reproduce what you were taught in the form in which it was presented to you, or to solve the kinds of problems you were shown how to solve.	Guiding principle: Mastery is often seen as the ability to apply what you've learned to new situations or to solve new kinds of problems.
Grades in High School	*Grades in College*
Grades are given for most assigned work.	Grades may not be provided for all assigned work.
Consistently good homework grades may raise your overall grade when test grades are low.	Grades on tests and major papers usually provide most of the course grade.
Extra credit projects are often available to help you raise your grade.	Extra credit projects cannot, generally speaking, be used to raise a grade in a college course.

Table 16.1   What Are the Differences Between High School and College? (Continued)

Grades in High School	Grades in College
Initial test grades, especially when they are low, may not have an adverse effect on your final grade.	Watch out for your *first* tests. These are usually "wake-up calls" to let you know what is expected—but they also may account for a substantial part of your course grade. You may be shocked when you get your grades.
You may graduate as long as you have passed all required courses with a grade of D or higher.	You may graduate only if your average in classes meets the departmental standard—Check your catalog for your major's standard.
Guiding principle: "Effort counts." Courses are usually structured to reward a "good-faith effort."	**Guiding principle: "Results count." Though "good-faith effort" is important in regard to the professor's willingness to help you *achieve* good results, it will not *substitute* for results in the grading process.**

Source: Southern Methodist University, Altshuler Learning Enhancement Center. http://smu.edu/alec/transition.asp. With permission.

list of differences from a community college, is fairly representative and can be used as the basis of a serious discussion with all students, including those with learning disabilities, about being their own advocates. This table captures how profoundly different college is from high school in so many ways. The chart is applicable to all students, not just those with learning disabilities. It is quite clear, however, that all students will have to advocate for their needs. One might ask what the psychological predictors of success in college are for students with disabilities, and can we develop ways to foster them on the high school level? Some research has indicated that the development of self-determination has been associated with positive outcomes in students with disabilities, including enhanced physical and psychological health, higher self-esteem, and improved general well-being (Deci & Ryan, 1985; Field & Hoffman, 1994; Wehmeyer & Schwartz, 1997).

In a recent study examining the characteristics of successful college students with disabilities, the authors found support for a model of academic identity development for college students with learning disabilities, including the integrative self-determination themes of persistence, competence, career decision making, and self-realization (Anctil, Ishikawa, & Scott, 2008). They found that these students had a high level of self-knowledge about their disabilities, their abilities, their goals, and their interests. The National Center on Secondary Education and Transition has noted that successful college students with disabilities are initiators, advocates, and active participants, which the National Center contends is often the opposite expectation of high school special education recipients and special educators (Stodden & Conway, 2002). The students in the study mentioned how their parents helped them become their own best advocates and learn how to be persistent in asking for needed services. In college, students will have to gather all these resources to gain the needed accommodations.

The following are suggestions for counselors to help students focus on developing their confidence and academic identity:

- Help them practice self-advocacy skills.
- Help them use their understanding of their disability (noted under previous suggestions) to gain confidence in their abilities and work ethic.
- Help them believe that persistence influences competence.
- Help students to reflect on the supportive role of parents, teachers, and others during high school.
- Help them think about developing social support networks in college.

For your seniors, find the Anctil, Ishikawa, and Scott (2008) study and reprint the portions that were direct clinical interviews with these successful college students with disabilities. Use them as the basis for some group guidance discussions with your students.

Now for very specific advice for your students with learning disabilities:

- Advise students to research the academic services that a college offers. This can vary greatly from school to school.
- Do not send your student's psychoeducational evaluation or Individual Learning Plan (ILP) with the application or the Secondary School Report. Most college admissions staff are not trained in reading and evaluating them. Let a student's record speak for itself. Depending upon your school's confidentiality policy, you may or may not have alluded to a student's learning issues. (This is addressed in Chapter 13, "Writing the Secondary School Report.")
- Once a student is accepted and has made a deposit, the parents or student should send the psychoeducational evaluation and/or ILP to the appropriate academic committee that evaluates special needs. This committee can be found by simply contacting the college.
- Parents and students should follow up to make sure that all accommodations are being met.
- Many colleges also offer specialized tutoring services at an extra cost. Before entering into an agreement with a college, make sure that the student wants to be involved in this process. Frequently, students develop strategic skills that serve a similar purpose such as finding study groups for a particular class or an editing partner for papers. Extra programs may not be necessary.
- Remember: Students need to learn to advocate for themselves—after all, who knows better what they need to succeed?

In advising students with learning disabilities, counselors understand the issues that they face and the difficulties that they encounter. At the same time, it is the counselor who also appreciates the strides these students have made and the success they have achieved. As they prepare to transition to the demands of college, counselors need to encourage students with learning disabilities to continue to be advocates for themselves and to be resourceful in finding strategies to compensate for areas of weakness. What they have learned in high school will serve them well in their college and future careers.

Chapter 17

Future Directions

In this chapter, we address some of the forces that will continue to impact our work in college advising. Again, data are informative, so we want to report important findings from recent studies. We also know that the way in which we learn is changing, as will the ways in which students go to college and gain financial aid. Ultimately, we will return to one of the primary foci of this book: the role of the college advisor.

In Chapter 12, we discussed one part of the study *With Their Whole Lives Ahead of Them*, commissioned by the Bill and Melinda Gates Foundation (Johnson, Rochkind, Ott, & DuPont, 2009; Steinberg, 2010), specifically the few questions that related to high school counselors. We now want to call your attention to the main focus of the study, which was on the myths and realities about why so many students fail to finish college. They note the following statistics about the real collegiate population according to the U.S. Department of Education:

- Only 20% of young people who begin their higher education at 2-year institutions graduate within 3 years.
- In 4-year institutions, about 4 in 10 students receive a degree within 6 years.
- Most college students work while at college.
  - Among students in 4-year schools, 45% work more than 20 hours a week.
  - Among those attending community colleges, 6 in 10 work more than 20 hours a week, and more than a quarter work more than 35 hours a week.
- Only 25% of students attend the sort of residential college we traditionally think about when we think of college.
- And 23% of college students have dependent children.

The fact is that our students are struggling once they get to college to stay in college. Many have to work and go to school; they cannot keep up with their academic responsibilities. Unfortunately, those statistics are getting worse. According to the article "Once a Leader, U.S. Lags in College Degrees," the United States used to lead the world in the number of 25- to 34-year-olds with college degrees. Now it ranks 12th among 36 developed nations (Lewin, 2010). Canada now leads the world in educational attainment, with about 56% of its young adults having earned at least associate's degrees in 2007 compared with only 40% of those in the United States.

These are compelling numbers for all those whose professional expertise revolves around college-going students including, importantly, counselors. Grantmakers for Education, an organization for those who make gifts to educational programs, convened a group of philanthropists and policy experts to talk about how to bolster college-completion rates. The problem begins long before college; indeed, it starts in K–12, according to the host of the event (Lewin, 2010).

The group's first five recommendations all concern K–12 education, including calling for more state-financed preschool programs, better high school and middle school college counseling, dropout prevention programs, an alignment with international curricular standards, and improved teacher quality—in that order.

College costs were also implicated with recommendations for more need-based financial aid and further efforts to keep college affordable (Grantmakers for Education, 2010).

Once again, we are brought into the discussion about how best to address these issues. In looking toward future directions for us, as stated earlier in Chapter 2 on partnerships, we must not only be brought into the work of the future here (i.e., better middle school and high school college advising), but also we must be more than just players. We must be leaders in directing and in participating in these endeavors that have clearly been identified as important goals for the future.

Concurrent to the developments described above is a raging debate about how learning in the 21st century is changing, including as we noted in Chapter 14 whether the Internet makes people smarter or dumber (Shirky, 2010; Carr, 2010). David Brooks of *The New York Times* recently compared books and the Internet in an article aptly titled "The Medium Is the Medium." You might recall from Chapter 1 how he coined the term "the cognitive age" as indicating that our students just have to be smarter and have better learning skills due to the complexity of learning in the 21st century. In "The Medium Is the Medium," he profoundly contrasts the Internet-versus-books debate in stating that what really matters is how people are engaged in these two different activities: "These two cultures foster different types of learning" (Brooks, 2010, Op. Ed.). He believes, and we agree, that the kind of learning he discusses as coming from the deeper analysis of reading will be more significantly needed in the 21st century cognitive age. For us, a focus on the various academic and cognitive approaches in our college advising curriculum, including among others an emphasis on study skills and being a proactive reader, places you, our reader, at the forefront of what may be asked of students, their teachers, and their counselors in the very near future.

All of these concerns about the future and our role in fostering optimal academic, career, and personal development in our work as college advisors only further compel us to embrace the four themes of the American School Counselor Association (ASCA) National Model: Leadership, Advocacy, Collaboration, and Systemic Change. We must do so if we are to truly recognize the serious nature of tasks ahead as defined in this final chapter for us all and if we want to be players in future developments.

Of them all, we believe the most powerful change agent for school counselors generally, and for college advisors in particular in view of our direct connection to postsecondary education, is in developing our skills as leaders for all the reasons already mentioned in this book. We offer you a vision of leadership crafted by Baker and O'Malley (2008) in their book titled *Leading With Kindness: How Good People Consistently Get Superior Results*. The book, really focusing on business rather than on counseling or education, describes six ingredients of leading with kindness: compassion, integrity, gratitude, authenticity, humility, and humor. These characteristics are all part of our makeup as counselors and should be embedded in any department or counseling office. We suspect they are since they are probably inherent in most of our natures. But take this with you: being kind while leading, according to Baker and O'Malley, is one of the most crucial attributes of some of the world's most successful business leaders. Let's apply it to our world of school counseling and college advising.

We hope we have empowered you in your future work by providing a truly enriched curriculum in college advising. We hope we have empowered you to be leaders in all your efforts as you work with our most important resource—our children and their future. Finally, we hope we have inspired you to lead with kindness and feel its power!

Appendix A: Gaining Admission to U.S. Military Academies

U.S. Military Academy at West Point, NY: www.usma.edu/
U.S. Naval Academy at Annapolis, MD: www.usna.edu/
U.S. Air Force Academy at Colorado Springs, CO: www.usafa.af.mil/
U.S. Coast Guard Academy at New London, CT: www.cga.edu/
U.S. Merchant Marine Academy at Kings Point, NY: www.usmma.edu/

While each of the military academies is a unique institution, they share some common requirements and procedures. It is essential to visit the individual academy Web site to understand the requirements, procedures, and deadlines that candidates must meet. Acceptance at the military academies is highly selective.

General Requirements
(Adapted From the Academy Web Sites)

A candidate must be a U.S. citizen, at least 17 and not yet 23 years of age on July 1 of your year of admission. Candidates must not be married, pregnant, or have a legal obligation to support a child or children. If a candidate is a naturalized citizen, documentation must be provided.

Precandidate Questionnaire

Most academies require candidates to file a Precandidate Questionnaire/ Application, which is a screening tool to determine whether or not a candidate will be competitive for admission. At this point, the admissions office is evaluating a candidate's academic credentials: high school transcript and standardized test scores. If candidates are determined to be competitive, they will receive additional forms to complete and may move on to the next step.

Obtaining a Congressional Nomination

A candidate cannot be offered admission without a congressional nomination. (Of the five academies, only the U.S. Coast Guard Academy does not require a congressional nomination.) Candidates should write a letter to their congressional representative and/or senators requesting a nomination. Members of Congress determine their own application deadlines, so candidates should apply early. The majority of the members of Congress use a competitive nomination process, in which 10 candidates are named to compete for a single vacancy. A minority of the members of Congress names a single candidate as their primary nomination, and some choose to number or rank the alternates. Candidates who have an excellent academic and extracurricular activity record have a good chance of gaining admission with an alternate nomination.

Taking the SAT and/or the ACT

Again, entrance to the military academies is highly selective, and performance on standardized tests is an important factor in the admissions process. If taking the ACT, check the military academy Web site to see if the Writing Test is required.

Medical Examination

All candidates are required to undergo a thorough medical examination since graduates will be commissioned in a wide variety of career fields with strict medical standards.

The Candidate Fitness Assessment

The purpose of the test is to evaluate coordination, strength, speed, agility, and endurance. Generally, the test consists of a one-mile run, a "shuttle" run, a kneeling basketball throw, abdominal crunches, push-ups, and pull-ups or a flexed-arm hang for women (when pull-ups cannot be accomplished). The test can be administered by anyone with a physical education degree, an active duty officer, or a blue and gold officer (Navy). Candidates accustomed to regular physical activity should have no difficulty with the Candidate Fitness Assessment.

Letter of Assurance

If a candidate's record of achievement is truly outstanding, he or she could receive an early offer called a Letter of Assurance. This indicates the intent to extend an Offer of Appointment, provided all of the candidate's remaining requirements are successfully completed.

Offer of Appointment

In effect, this is the candidate's letter of acceptance. Generally, candidates will be notified by April 15, and they should notify the admissions office of their intention to accept or decline by May 1.

Appendix B: Common Data Set Terms Used in the Admissions and Financial Aid Process

The Common Data Set (CDS) initiative is a collaborative effort among data providers in the higher education community and publishers as represented by the College Board, Peterson's, and *U.S. News & World Report*. The CDS is a set of standards and definitions of data developed to improve the quality and accuracy of information provided to all involved in a student's transition into higher education (see Common Data Set in Additional Resources).

Common Data Set Definitions

All definitions related to the financial aid section appear at the end of this Appendix (see Financial Aid Definitions).

Items preceded by an asterisk (*) represent definitions agreed to among publishers that do not appear on the CDS document but may be present on individual publishers' surveys.

*Academic advisement: Plan under which each student is assigned to a faculty member or a trained adviser, who, through regular meetings, helps the student plan and implement immediate and long-term academic and vocational goals.

Accelerated program: Completion of a college program of study in fewer than the usual number of years, most often by attending summer sessions and carrying extra courses during the regular academic term.

Admitted student: Applicant who is offered admission to a degree-granting program at your institution.

*Adult student services: Admission assistance, support, orientation, and other services expressly for adults who have started college for the first time or who are reentering after a lapse of a few years.

American Indian or Alaska native: A person having origins in any of the original peoples of North America and who maintains cultural identification through tribal affiliation or community recognition.

Applicant (first-time, first-year): An individual who has fulfilled the institution's requirements to be considered for admission (including payment or waiving of the application fee, if any) and who has been notified of one of the following actions: admission, nonadmission, placement on waiting list, or application withdrawn (by applicant or institution).

Application fee: That amount of money that an institution charges for processing a student's application for acceptance. This amount is not creditable toward tuition and required fees, nor is it refundable if the student is not admitted to the institution.

Asian or Pacific Islander: A person having origins in any of the original peoples of the Far East, Southeast Asia, the Indian Subcontinent, or Pacific Islands. This includes people from China, Japan, Korea, the Philippine Islands, American Samoa, India, and Vietnam.

Associate's degree: An award that normally requires at least 2 but less than 4 years of full-time equivalent college work.

Bachelor's degree: An award (baccalaureate or equivalent degree, as determined by the Secretary of the U.S. Department of Education) that normally requires at least 4 years but not more than 5 years of full-time equivalent college-level work. This includes *all* bachelor's degrees conferred in a 5-year cooperative (work-study plan) program. (A cooperative plan provides for alternate class attendance and employment in business, industry, or government; thus, it allows students to combine actual work experience with their college studies.) Also, it includes bachelor's degrees in which the normal 4 years of work are completed in 3 years.

Black, non-Hispanic: A person having origins in any of the Black racial groups of Africa (except those of Hispanic origin).

Board (charges): Assume average cost for 19 meals per week or the maximum meal plan.

Books and supplies (costs): Average cost of books and supplies. Do not include unusual costs for special groups of students (e.g., engineering or art majors), unless they constitute the majority of students at your institution.

Calendar system: The method by which an institution structures most of its courses for the academic year.

*Career and placement services: A range of services, including (often) the following: coordination of visits of employers to campus; aptitude and vocational testing; interest inventories, personal counseling; help in résumé writing, interviewing, launching the job search; listings for those students desiring employment and those seeking permanent positions; establishment of a permanent reference folder; career resource materials.

Carnegie units: One year of study or the equivalent in a secondary school subject.

Certificate: See *postsecondary award, certificate,* or *diploma.*

Class rank: The relative numerical position of a student in his or her graduating class, calculated by the high school on the basis of grade point average, whether weighted or unweighted.

College-preparatory program: Courses in academic subjects (English, history and social studies, foreign languages, mathematics, science, and the arts) that stress preparation for college or university study.

Common Application: The standard application form distributed by the National Association of Secondary School Principals for a large number of private colleges who are members of the Common Application Group.

***Community service program:** Referral center for students wishing to perform volunteer work in the community or participate in volunteer activities coordinated by academic departments.

Commuter: A student who lives off campus in housing that is not owned by, operated by, or affiliated with the college. This category includes students who commute from home and students who have moved to the area to attend college.

Contact hour: A unit of measure that represents an hour of scheduled instruction given to students. Also referred to as clock hour.

Continuous basis (for program enrollment): A calendar system classification that is used by institutions that enroll students at any time during the academic year. For example, a cosmetology school or a word processing school might allow students to enroll and begin studies at various times, with no requirement that classes begin on a certain date.

Cooperative housing: College-owned, -operated, or -affiliated housing in which students share room and board expenses and participate in household chores to reduce living expenses.

Cooperative (work-study plan) program: A program that provides for alternate class attendance and employment in business, industry, or government.

***Counseling service:** Activities designed to assist students in making plans and decisions related to their education, career, or personal development.

Credit: Recognition of attendance or performance in an instructional activity (course or program) that can be applied by a recipient toward the requirements for a degree, diploma, certificate, or other formal award.

Credit course: A course that, if successfully completed, can be applied toward the number of courses required for achieving a degree, diploma, certificate, or other formal award.

Credit hour: A unit of measure representing an hour (50 minutes) of instruction over a 15-week period in a semester or trimester system or a 10-week period in a quarter system. It is applied toward the total number of hours needed for completing the requirements of a degree, diploma, certificate, or other formal award.

Cross-registration: A system whereby students enrolled at one institution may take courses at another institution without having to apply to the second institution.

Deferred admission: The practice of permitting admitted students to postpone enrollment, usually for a period of one academic term or year.

Degree: An award conferred by a college, university, or other postsecondary education institution as official recognition for the successful completion of a program of studies.

Degree-seeking students: Students enrolled in courses for credit who are recognized by the institution as seeking a degree or formal award. At the undergraduate level, this is intended to include students enrolled in vocational or occupational programs.

Differs by program (calendar system): A calendar system classification that is used by institutions that have occupational/vocational programs of varying length. These schools may enroll students at specific times depending on the program desired. For example, a school might offer a 2-month program in January, March, May, September, and November; and a 3-month program in January, April, and October.

Diploma: See *postsecondary award, certificate,* or *diploma.*

Distance learning: An option for earning course credit at off-campus locations via cable television, Internet, satellite classes, videotapes, correspondence courses, or other means.

Doctor's degree—research/scholarship: A Ph.D. or other doctor's degree that requires advanced work beyond the master's level, including the preparation and defense of a dissertation based on original research, or the planning and execution of an original project demonstrating substantial artistic or scholarly achievement. Some examples of this type of degree may include Ed.D., D.M.A., D.B.A., D.Sc., D.A., or D.M, and others, as designated by the awarding institution.

Doctor's degree—professional practice: A doctor's degree that is conferred upon completion of a program providing the knowledge and skills for the recognition, credential, or license required for professional practice. The degree is awarded after a period of study such that the total time to the degree, including both preprofessional and professional preparation, equals at least 6 full-time equivalent academic years. Some of these degrees were formerly classified as *first-professional* and may include chiropractic (D.C. or D.C.M.); dentistry (D.D.S. or D.M.D.); law (L.L.B. or J.D.); medicine (M.D.); optometry (O.D.); osteopathic medicine (D.O); pharmacy (Pharm.D.); podiatry (D.P.M., Pod.D., D.P.); veterinary medicine (D.V.M.); and others, as designated by the awarding institution.

Doctor's degree—other: A doctor's degree that does not meet the definition of a doctor's degree—research/scholarship, or a doctor's degree—professional practice

Double major: Program in which students may complete two undergraduate programs of study simultaneously.

Dual enrollment: A program through which high school students may enroll in college courses while still enrolled in high school. Students are not required to apply for admission to the college in order to participate.

Early action plan: An admission plan that allows students to apply and be notified of an admission decision well in advance of the regular notification dates. If admitted, the candidate is not committed to enroll; the student may reply to the offer under the college's regular reply policy.

Early admission: A policy under which students who have not completed high school are admitted and enroll full-time in college, usually after completion of their junior year.

Early decision plan: A plan that permits students to apply and be notified of an admission decision (and financial aid offer if applicable) well in advance of the regular notification date. Applicants agree to accept an offer of admission and, if admitted, to withdraw their applications from other colleges. There are three possible decisions for early decision applicants: admitted, denied, or not admitted but forwarded for consideration with the regular applicant pool, without prejudice.

English as a second language (ESL): A course of study designed specifically for students whose native language is not English.

Exchange student program—domestic: Any arrangement between a student and a college that permits study for a semester or more at another college in the United States without extending the amount of time required for a degree. See also *study abroad*.

External degree program: A program of study in which students earn credits toward a degree through independent study, college courses, proficiency examinations, and personal experience. External degree programs require minimal or no classroom attendance.

Extracurricular activities (as admission factor): Special consideration in the admissions process given for participation in both school- and nonschool-related activities of interest to the college, such as clubs, hobbies, student government, athletics, performing arts, and so forth.

First professional certificate (postdegree): An award that requires completion of an organized program of study designed for persons who have completed the first professional degree. Examples could be refresher courses or additional units of study in a specialty or subspecialty.

First professional degree: An award in one of the following fields: chiropractic (D.C., D.C.M.), dentistry (D.D.S., D.M.D.), medicine (M.D.), optometry (O.D.), osteopathic medicine (D.O.), rabbinical and Talmudic studies

(M.H.L., Rav.), Pharmacy (B.Pharm., Pharm.D.), podiatry (Pod.D., D.P., D.P.M.), veterinary medicine (D.V.M.), law (L.L.B., J.D.), divinity/ministry (B.D., M.Div.).

First-time student: A student attending any institution for the first time at the level enrolled. Includes students enrolled in the fall term who attended a postsecondary institution for the first time at the same level in the prior summer term. Also includes students who entered with advanced standing (college credit earned before graduation from high school).

First-time, first-year (freshman) student: A student attending any institution for the first time at the undergraduate level. Includes students enrolled in the fall term who attended college for the first time in the prior summer term. Also includes students who entered with advanced standing (college credits earned before graduation from high school).

First-year student: A student who has completed less than the equivalent of 1 full year of undergraduate work; that is, less than 30 semester hours (in a 120-hour degree program) or less than 900 contact hours.

Freshman: A first-year undergraduate student.

*Freshman/new student orientation: Orientation addressing the academic, social, emotional, and intellectual issues involved in beginning college. May be a few hours or a few days in length; at some colleges, there is a fee.

Full-time student (undergraduate): A student enrolled for 12 or more semester credits, 12 or more quarter credits, or 24 or more contact hours a week each term.

Geographical residence (as admission factor): Special consideration in the admission process given to students from a particular region, state, or country of residence.

Grade point average (academic high school GPA): The sum of grade points a student has earned in secondary school divided by the number of courses taken. The most common system of assigning numbers to grades counts 4 points for an A, 3 points for a B, 2 points for a C, 1 point for a D, and no points for an E or F. Unweighted GPAs assign the same weight to each course. Weighting gives students additional points for their grades in advanced or honors courses.

Graduate student: A student who holds a bachelor's or equivalent and is taking courses at the postbaccalaureate level.

*Health services: Free or low-cost on-campus primary and preventive health care available to students.

High school diploma or recognized equivalent: A document certifying the successful completion of a prescribed secondary school program of studies, or the attainment of satisfactory scores on the Tests of General Educational Development (GED), or another state-specified examination.

Hispanic: A person of Mexican, Puerto Rican, Cuban, Central or South American, or other Spanish culture or origin, regardless of race.

Honors program: Any special program for very able students offering the opportunity for educational enrichment, independent study, acceleration, or some combination of these.

Independent study: Academic work chosen or designed by the student with the approval of the department concerned, under an instructor's supervision, and usually undertaken outside of the regular classroom structure.

In-state tuition: The tuition charged by institutions to those students who meet the state's or institution's residency requirements.

International student: See *nonresident alien.*

Internship: Any short-term, supervised work experience usually related to a student's major field, for which the student earns academic credit. The work can be full- or part-time, on- or off-campus, paid or unpaid.

*Learning center: Center offering assistance through tutors, workshops, computer programs, or audiovisual equipment in reading, writing, math, and skills such as taking notes, managing time, taking tests.

*Legal services: Free or low-cost legal advice for a range of issues (personal and other).

Liberal arts/career combination: Program in which a student earns undergraduate degrees in two separate fields, one in a liberal arts major and the other in a professional or specialized major, whether on campus or through cross-registration.

Master's degree: An award that requires the successful completion of a program of study of generally 1 or 2 full-time equivalent academic years of work beyond the bachelor's degree. Some of these degrees, such as those in theology (M.Div., M.H.L./Rav.) that were formerly classified as *first-professional*, may require more than 2 full-time equivalent academic years of work.

Minority affiliation (as admission factor): Special consideration in the admission process for members of designated racial/ethnic minority groups.

*Minority student center: Center with programs, activities, and/or services intended to enhance the college experience of students of color.

Nonresident alien: A person who is not a citizen or national of the United States and who is in this country on a visa or temporary basis and does not have the right to remain indefinitely.

*On-campus day care: Licensed day care for students' children (usually age 3 and up), usually for a fee.

Open admission: Admission policy under which virtually all secondary school graduates or students with GED equivalency diplomas are admitted without regard to academic record, test scores, or other qualifications.

Other expenses (costs): Include average costs for clothing, laundry, entertainment, medical (if not a required fee), and furnishings.

Out-of-state tuition: The tuition charged by institutions to those students who do not meet the institution's or state's residency requirements.

Part-time student (undergraduate): A student enrolled for fewer than 12 credits per semester or quarter, or fewer than 24 contact hours a week each term.

*Personal counseling: One-on-one or group counseling with trained professionals for students who want to explore personal, educational, or vocational issues.

Postbaccalaureate certificate: An award that requires completion of an organized program of study requiring 18 credit hours beyond the bachelor's; designed for persons who have completed a baccalaureate degree but do not meet the requirements of academic degrees carrying the title of master.

Post-master's certificate: An award that requires completion of an organized program of study of 24 credit hours beyond the master's degree but does not meet the requirements of academic degrees at the doctoral level.

Postsecondary award, certificate, or diploma: Includes the following three Integrated Postsecondary Education Data System (IPEDS) definitions for postsecondary awards, certificates, and diplomas of varying durations and credit/contact hour requirements:

> *** Less than 1 academic year:** Requires completion of an organized program of study at the postsecondary level (below the baccalaureate degree) in less than 1 academic year (2 semesters or 3 quarters) or in less than 900 contact hours by a student enrolled full-time.

> *** At least 1 but less than 2 academic years:** Requires completion of an organized program of study at the postsecondary level (below the baccalaureate degree) in at least 1 but less than 2 full-time equivalent academic years, or designed for completion in at least 30 but less than 60 credit hours, or in at least 900 but less than 1,800 contact hours.

> *** At least 2 but less than 4 academic years:** Requires completion of an organized program of study at the postsecondary level (below the baccalaureate degree) in at least 2 but less than 4 full-time equivalent academic years, or designed for completion in at least 60 but less than 120 credit hours, or in at least 1,800 but less than 3,600 contact hours.

Private institution: An educational institution controlled by a private individual(s) or by a nongovernmental agency, usually supported primarily by other than public funds, and operated by other than publicly elected or appointed officials.

Private for-profit institution: A private institution in which the individual(s) or agency in control receives compensation, other than wages, rent, or other expenses for the assumption of risk.

Private nonprofit institution: A private institution in which the individual(s) or agency in control receives no compensation, other than wages, rent, or other expenses for the assumption of risk. These include both independent nonprofit schools and those affiliated with a religious organization.

Proprietary institution: See *private for-profit institution.*

Public institution: An educational institution whose programs and activities are operated by publicly elected or appointed school officials and which is supported primarily by public funds.

Quarter calendar system: A calendar system in which the academic year consists of three sessions called quarters of about 12 weeks each. The range may be from 10 to 15 weeks. There may be an additional quarter in the summer.

Race/ethnicity: Category used to describe groups to which individuals belong, identify with, or belong in the eyes of the community. The categories do not denote scientific definitions of anthropological origins. A person may be counted in only one group.

Race/ethnicity unknown: Category used to classify students or employees whose race/ethnicity is not known and whom institutions are unable to place in one of the specified racial/ethnic categories.

Religious affiliation/commitment (as admission factor): Special consideration given in the admission process for affiliation with a certain church or faith/religion, commitment to a religious vocation, or observance of certain religious tenets/lifestyle.

***Religious counseling:** One-on-one or group counseling with trained professionals for students who want to explore religious problems or issues.

***Remedial services:** Instructional courses designed for students deficient in the general competencies necessary for a regular postsecondary curriculum and educational setting.

Required fees: Fixed sum charged to students for items not covered by tuition and required of such a large proportion of all students that the student who does *not* pay is the exception. Does not include application fees or optional fees such as lab fees or parking fees.

Resident alien or other eligible noncitizen: A person who is not a citizen or national of the United States and who has been admitted as a legal immigrant for the purpose of obtaining permanent resident alien status (and who holds either an alien registration card [Form I-551 or I-151], a temporary resident card [Form I-688], or an arrival-departure record [Form I-94] with a notation that conveys legal immigrant status, such as Section 207 Refugee, Section 208 Asylee, Conditional Entrant Parolee, or Cuban-Haitian).

Room and board (charges)—on campus: Assume double occupancy in institutional housing and 19 meals per week (or maximum meal plan).

Secondary school record (as admission factor): Information maintained by the secondary school that may include such things as the student's high school transcript, class rank, GPA, and teacher and counselor recommendations.

Semester calendar system: A calendar system that consists of two semesters during the academic year with about 16 weeks for each semester of instruction. There may be an additional summer session.

Student-designed major: A program of study based on individual interests, designed with the assistance of an advisor.

Study abroad: Any arrangement by which a student completes part of the college program studying in another country. Can be at a campus abroad or through a cooperative agreement with some other U.S. college or an institution of another country.

*Summer session: A summer session is shorter than a regular semester and not considered part of the academic year. It is not the third term of an institution operating on a trimester system or the fourth term of an institution operating on a quarter calendar system. The institution may have two or more sessions occurring in the summer months. Some schools, such as vocational and beauty schools, have year-round classes with no separate summer session.

Talent/ability (as admission factor): Special consideration given to students with demonstrated talent/abilities in areas of interest to the institution (e.g., sports, the arts, languages).

Teacher certification program: Program designed to prepare students to meet the requirements for certification as teachers in elementary, middle/junior high, and secondary schools.

Transfer applicant: An individual who has fulfilled the institution's requirements to be considered for admission (including payment or waiving of the application fee, if any) and who has previously attended another college or university and earned college-level credit.

Transfer student: A student entering the institution for the first time but known to have previously attended a postsecondary institution at the same level (e.g., undergraduate). The student may transfer with or without credit.

Transportation (costs): Assume two round trips to student's hometown per year for students in institutional housing or daily travel to and from your institution for commuter students.

Trimester calendar system: An academic year consisting of three terms of about 15 weeks each.

Tuition: Amount of money charged to students for instructional services. Tuition may be charged per term, per course, or per credit.

*Tutoring: May range from one-on-one tutoring in specific subjects to tutoring in an area such as math, reading, or writing. Most tutors are college students; at some colleges, they are specially trained and certified.

Unit: A standard of measurement representing hours of academic instruction (e.g., semester credit, quarter credit, contact hour).

Undergraduate: A student enrolled in a 4- or 5-year bachelor's degree program, an associate's degree program, or a vocational or technical program below the baccalaureate.

*Veteran's counseling: Helps veterans and their dependents obtain benefits for their selected program and provides certifications to the Veteran's

Administration. May also provide personal counseling on the transition from the military to a civilian life.

*Visually impaired: Any person whose sight loss is not correctable and is sufficiently severe as to adversely affect educational performance.

Volunteer work (as admission factor): Special consideration given to students for activity done on a volunteer basis (e.g., tutoring, hospital care, working with the elderly or disabled) as a service to the community or the public in general.

Wait list: List of students who meet the admission requirements but will be offered a place in the class only if space becomes available.

Weekend college: A program that allows students to take a complete course of study and attend classes only on weekends.

White, non-Hispanic: A person having origins in any of the original peoples of Europe, North Africa, or the Middle East (except those of Hispanic origin).

*Women's center: Center with programs, academic activities, and/or services intended to promote an understanding of the evolving roles of women.

Work experience (as admission factor): Special consideration given to students who have been employed prior to application, whether for relevance to major, demonstration of employment-related skills, or as explanation of student's academic and extracurricular record.

Financial Aid Definitions

Financial aid applicant: Any applicant who submits any one of the institutionally required financial aid applications/forms, such as the Free Application for Federal Student Aid (FASFA).

Financial need: As determined by your institution using the federal methodology and/or your institution's own standards.

Indebtedness: Aggregate dollar amount borrowed through any loan programs (e.g., federal, state, subsidized, unsubsidized, private; excluding parent loans) while the student was enrolled at an institution. Student loans cosigned by a parent are assumed to be the responsibility of the student and should be included.

Institutional and external funds: Endowment, alumni, or external monies for which the institution determines the recipient or the dollar amount awarded.

Need-based aid: College-funded or college-administered award from institutional, state, federal, or other sources for which a student must have financial need to qualify. This includes both institutional and noninstitutional student aid (grants, jobs, and loans).

Need-based scholarship or grant aid: Scholarships and grants from institutional, state, federal, or other sources for which a student must have financial need to qualify.

Need-based self-help aid: Loans and jobs from institutional, state, federal, or other sources for which a student must demonstrate financial need to qualify.

Non-need-based scholarship or grant aid: Scholarships and grants, gifts, or merit-based aid from institutional, state, federal, or other sources (including unrestricted funds or gifts and endowment income) awarded solely on the basis of academic achievement, merit, or any other non-need-based reason. When reporting questions H1 and H2,* non-need-based aid that is used to meet need should be counted as need-based aid.

Note: Suggested order of precedence for counting non-need money as need-based:
Non-need institutional grants
Non-need tuition waivers
Non-need athletic awards
Non-need federal grants
Non-need state grants
Non-need outside grants
Non-need student loans
Non-need parent loans
Non-need work

Non-need-based self-help aid: Loans and jobs from institutional, state, or other sources for which a student need not demonstrate financial need to qualify.

Scholarships/grants from external sources: Monies received from outside (private) sources that the student brings with them (e.g., Kiwanis, National Merit scholarships). The institution may process paperwork to receive the dollars, but it has no role in determining the recipient or the dollar amount awarded.

Work-study and employment: Federal and state work-study aid and any employment packaged by your institution in financial aid awards.

---

* **Authors' Note:** H1 and H2 refer to earlier worksheet questions that are contained in a pdf on multiple college Web sites as well as the Common Data Set Initiative.

Appendix C: 10 Useful Web Pages for College Research

	Web Address	Research Notes
1.	http://www.utexas.edu/world/univ/state/	State-by-state guide to homepages of colleges. Click on any state. Links are provided to all colleges within that state.
2.	http://collegesearch.collegeboard.com/search/index.jsp	Multisearch Web site allows you to search colleges by major, location, campus life, activities, sports, and financial aid. Also includes a college quickfinder that allows you to search by college name. Private, public, and religious schools are included.
3.	http://www.act.org	Important Web site for students taking the ACT for college admission. Also offers educational and career planning through their EPAS program.
4.	http://www.commonapp.com/	Offers information related to nearly 400 colleges (e.g., the Common Application, admission requirements, admission deadlines). An essential tool in applying to colleges on the Common Application.
5.	http://www.a2zcolleges.com/Majors/	Offers a list of college majors. Leads to colleges in the United States that offer programs in that major. Students can choose from subjects they are interested in: for example, click on Biology or Veterinary Science. Does not, however, give career choices under each subject.

	Web Address	Research Notes
6.	http://www.ed.gov/about/inits/list/whhbcu/edlite-list.html	A listing of historically Black colleges (by state). Click on the colleges. Lists 2- and 4-year colleges (private and public). Department of Education is author of Web site. Click on useful resources. Leads to links—one is the United Negro College Fund.
7.	http://www.hispaniconline.com/	*Hispanic Magazine* lists the top 25 colleges for Latinos. Lists tuition, percentage of Latino students, student–faculty ratio, setting, and type of school.
8.	http://colleges.usnews.rankingsandreviews.com/best-colleges/rankings/national-universities/campus-ethnic-diversity	Lists campus ethnic diversity.
9.	http://www.ncaa.org/	Essential information for any student wanting to play college sports. Also home of the National Collegiate Athletic Association (NCAA) Eligibility Center.
10.	http://www.fafsa.ed.gov/	Provides information regarding the procedure of acquiring federal student aid.

References

Achieve. (2008, April). *Making college and career readiness the mission for high schools: A guide for state policymakers.* Achieve and The Education Trust, April 2008. Retrieved from http://www.achieve.org/files/MakingCollegeandCareerReadinesstheMissionforHighSchool.pdf

ACT, The 2011 http://www.act.org/aap/

Akos, P. (2010). Promoting successful school transitions: School counselor advocacy and leadership. Workshop. Retrieved from http://www.schoolcounselor.org/content.asp?contentid=470

ASCA (American School Counselor Association). (2005). *The ASCA National Model: A Framework for School Counseling Programs, Second Edition.* Alexandria, VA: Author.

Auerbach, S. (2002). Why do they give the good classes to some and not to others? Latino parent narratives of struggle in a college access program. *Teachers College Record, 104,* 1369–1392.

Baker, W. F., & O'Malley, M. (2008). *Leading with kindness: How good people consistently get superior results.* New York: AMACOM, a division of the American Management Association.

Bandura, A. (1986). *Social foundation of thought and action: A social cognitive theory.* Englewood Cliffs, NJ: Prentice Hall.

Baughman, J. L. (1940). Henry R. Luce and the rise of the American news media. Retrieved from http://www.pbs.org/wnet/americanmasters/database/luce_h.html

Bear, G. G., Kortering, L. J., & Braziel, P. (2006). School completers and noncompleters with learning disabilities: Similarities in academic achievement and perceptions of self and teachers. *Remedial and Special Education, 27,* 293–300.

Binghamton University. (2010). Take control of your college essay. Retrieved from http://www2.binghamton.edu/admissions/college-essay.html

Bodilly, S. J., Chun, J., Ikemoto, G. S., & Stockly, S. (2004). *Challenges and potential of a collaborative approach to education reform.* Washington, DC: RAND Corporation.

Boston College. (2006). Writing the "perfect" essay. Maintained by the Office of Undergraduate Admissions. Retrieved from http://www.bc.edu/admission/undergrad/process/tips/s-perfectessay.html

Brooks, D. (2008, May 2). The cognitive age. *The New York Times,* p. A21.

Brooks, D. (2010, July 8). The medium is the medium. New York Times, Op. Ed. Page. Retrieved from http://www.nytimes.com/2010/07/09/opinion/09brooks.html?scp=1&sq=the%20medium%20is%20the%20medium&st=cse

Carleton College. (2009). Essay tips. Retrieved from http://apps.carleton.edu/admissions/apply/essay_tips/

Carr, J. A., & Rockman, I. F. (2003, September). Information-literacy collaboration: A shared responsibility. *American Libraries, 34*(8), 52–54.

Carr, N. (2010, June 5). Does the Internet make you dumber? *Wall Street Journal,* W1.

Ceja, M. (2004). Chicana college aspirations and the role of parents: Developing educational resiliency. *Journal of Hispanic Higher Education, 3,* 338–362.

Chan, D., Schmitt, N., DeShon, R. P., Clause, C. S., & Delbridge, K. (1997). Reactions to cognitive ability tests: The relationship between race, test performance, face validity perceptions, and test-taking motivation. *Journal of Applied Psychology 82*(2), 300–310.

Chinien, C., & Boutin, F. (2001). Qualitative assessment of cognitive-based dropout prevention strategy. *High School Journal, 85,* 1–11.

College Board 2011 www.collegeboard.com

Collins, D.E., Weinbaum A.T., Ramon, G., Vaughan, D. (2009). Laying the groundwork: The constant gardening for postsecondary access and success. *Journal of Hispanic Higher Education*, Oct. 2009, 8(4), 394–417. Retrieved from http://jhh.sagepub.com/content/8/4/394

Colorado College. 2010. Applying to Colorado College. Retrieved from http://www.coloradocollege.edu/admission/firstyear/evaluation.asp

Common Application. 2011. https://www.commonapp.org/CommonApp/default.aspx

Common Data Set Definitions. (2010–2011). Stanford University, University Communications. Retrieved from http://ucomm.stanford.edu/cds/definitions.html

Dahir, C. (2000, May). The national standards for school counseling programs: A partnership in preparing students for the new millennium. *National Association of Secondary School Principals. NASSP Bulletin*; 84, 616; 68–77.

Daniel, E. (1997, July 6–11). High school to university: What skills do students need? In *Information rich but knowledge poor? Emerging issues for schools and libraries worldwide*. Research and Professional Papers presented at the 26th Annual Conference of the International Association of School Librarianship held in conjunction with the Association for Teacher-Librarianship in Vancouver, British Columbia, Canada, 53–61.

Deci, E.L., & Ryan, R.M. (1985). *Instrinsic motivaiton and self-determination in human behavior*. New York: Plenum.

Deci, E. L., & Ryan, R. M. (2002). *Handbook of self-determination research*. Rochester, NY: University of Rochester Press.

Dedmond, R. (2008, April). Launching students into their decade of transition. *Techniques*, April 2008. Retrieved from http://www.acteonline.org/uploadedFiles/Publications_and_Online_Media/files/files-techniques-2008/Thm1.pdf

Economic Times. (2008, July 25). China surpasses US in Internet use. *Economic Times*. Retrieved from http://economictimes.indiatimes.com/Infotech/Internet_/China_surpasses_US_in_internet_use/articleshow/3279347.cms

Education Week. (2010). Diplomas 2010. Graduation by the Numbers. Retrieved from http://edweek.org/media/ew/toc/2010/06/10/index.html

Elliott, E. S., & Dweck, C. S. (1988). Goals: An approach to motivation and achievement. *Journal of Personality and Social Psychology, 54*(1), 5–12.

Fann, A., McCafferty Jarsky, K., & McDonough, P. M. (2009). Parent involvement in the college planning process: A case study of a P–20 collaboration. *Journal of Hispanic Education, 8*(4) 374–393.

Field, S., & Hoffman, A. (1994). Development of a model for self determination. *Career Development for Exceptional Individuals, 17,* 159–169.

Finn, J. D., & Rock, D. A. (1997). Academic success among students at risk for school failure. *Journal of Applied Psychology, 82,* 221–234.

Fitzgerald, M. A. (2004, March/April). Making the leap from high school to college: Three new studies about information literacy skills of first-year college students. *Knowledge Quest, 32*(4), 19–24.

Fitzpatrick, C. (2008). Using technology to optimize learning. In W. Merriman & A. Nicoletti (Eds.), *Understanding and teaching today's students.* Washington, DC: National Catholic Educational Association, 89–108.

Fitzpatrick, C., & Lienert, C. (2009). Future direction for technology in schools. In W. Merriman & A. Nicoletti (Eds.), *Using technology in 21st century schools.* Washington, DC: National Catholic Educational Association, 168–187.

Fitzpatrick, C., & Mucciardi, M. (2005). Learning with interactive media: Characteristics of its impact in three different environments. In S.P. Schaffer and M.L. Price (Eds). *Interactive convergence: Critical issues in multimedia.* London: Inter-disciplinary Press. Retrieved from http://inter-disciplinary.net/publishing/id-press/ebooks/interactive-convergence-criticalissues-inmultimedia

Fitzpatrick, C., Mucciardi, M., & Sierra, C. (2002). Breaking ground in technology development: A school/college partnership focusing on the infusion of standards-based technologies into practice. Paper presented at the Annual Meeting of the Professional Development Schools (Orlando, FL, March 7–10). ED468153. Retrieved from http://www.eric.ed.gov/PDFS/ED468153.pdf

Forgan, J. W., & Vaughn, S. (2000). Adolescents with and without LD make the transition to middle school. *Journal of Learning Disabilities, 33,* 33–43.

Friedman, T. (2005). *The world is flat: A brief history of the twenty-first century.* New York: Farrar, Strauss and Giroux.

Fromme, K., Corbin W. R., & Kruse, M. I. (2008, September). Behavioral risks during the transition from high school to college. *Developmental Psychology, 44*(5). Retrieved from http://www.library.manhattan.edu:2642/ehost/detail?vid=8&hid=109&sid=5a93472c-dc2e-43a0-a51f-64c48237562d@sessionmgr113&bdata=JnNpdGU9ZWhvc3QtbGl2ZQ%3d%3d#db=aph&AN=34447946

George, P. S. (2000). The evolution of middle schools. *Educational Leadership, 58*(4), 40–44.

Globalization101. (2007). What is globalization? Retrieved from http://www.globalization101.org/What_is_Globalization.html

Grantmakers for Education. (2010). From access to success: A funders guide to ensuring more Americans earn postsecondary degrees. Retrieved from http://edfunders.org/downloads/GFEReports/GFE_FromAccessToSuccess_FundersGuide.pdf

Greene, J. P., & Winters, M. A. (2005, February). *Public high school graduation and college-readiness rates: 1991–2002.* Manhattan Institute for Policy Research. Education Working Paper 8. Retrieved from www.manhattaninstitute.org/html/ewp_08.htm

Hart, P., & Associates (2005). *Rising to the challenge: Are high school graduates prepared for college and work?* Study conducted for Achieve, a nonprofit organization for education reform, Washington, DC. Retrieved from http://www.achieve.org/rising tothechallenge

Herbert, R. (2008, May 17). Hard roads ahead: The toll high schools are imposing on America's future. *New York Times,* p. A17.

Hertzog, C. J., Morgan, P. L., Diamond, P. A., & Walker, M. J. (1996). Transition to high school: A look at student perceptions. *Becoming, 7,* 6–8.

Hoffman, L. M., & Nottis, K. E. (2008). Middle school students' perceptions of effective motivation and preparation factors for high-stakes tests. National Association of Secondary School Principals. *NASSP Bulletin, 92*(3), 209–223.

Holland, J. L. (1994). *Self-directed search: Form R (4th ed.).* Odessa, FL: Psychological Assessment Resources, Inc.

Horn, L., & Berktold, J. (1999). *Students with disabilities in postsecondary education: A profile of preparation, participation, and outcomes* (National Center for Education Statistics No. 187). Washington, DC: U.S. Department of Education. Retrieved from http://nces.ed.gov/pubsearch/pubsinfo.asp?pubid=1999187

Horn, L., & Nevill, S. (2006). *Profile of undergraduates in U.S. postsecondary education institutions: 2003–04: With a special analysis of community college students* (NCES 2006–184). Washington, DC: U.S. Department of Education. Retrieved from http://nces.ed.gov/pubsearch/pubsinfo.asp?pubid=2006184

Hossler, D., Schmidt, J., & Vesper, N. (1998). *Going to college: How social, economic, and educational factors influence the decisions students make.* Baltimore: Johns Hopkins University Press.

How-to-study.com. (2011). Your preferred learning style. Retrieved from http://www.how-to-study.com/study-skills/en/other-helpful-articles/49/your-preferred-learning-style/

Immelt, J. (2006, March 17). A CEO's responsibilities in the age of globalization. *Globalist* magazine. Retrieved from http://www.theglobalist.com/Storyid/aspx?StoryId=5183

Islam, R. L., & Murno, L. A. (2006, November). From perceptions to connections: Informing information literacy program planning in academic libraries through examination of high school library media center curricula. *College and Research Libraries, 67*(6), 492–514.

Jeynes, W. (2007). The relationship between parental involvement and urban secondary school student academic achievement: A meta-analysis. *Urban Education, 42*(1), 82–110.

Johnson, J., Rochkind, J., Ott, A., & DuPont, S. (2009). *With their whole lives ahead of them.* A study for the Bill and Linda Gates Foundation by Public Agenda. Retrieved from http://www.publicagenda.org/files/pdf/theirwholelivesaheadofthem.pdf

Kao, J. (2007). *Innovation nation.* New York: Free Press.

Kaplan. (2010). Would you score better on the SAT or the ACT? Retrieved from http://www.kaptest.com/satactpractice

Kelly, A. P., Schneider, M., & Carey, K. (2010). *Rising to the challenge: Hispanic graduation rates as a national priority.* American Enterprise Institute for Public Policy Research. Papers and Studies: March 18, 2010. Retrieved from www.aei.org/paper/100093

Kravets, M.B., & Wax, I.F. (2008). *Learning disabilities*, 9th edition. New York: Random House.

Leana, F.C. (2009). I believe in magic. *Journal of College Admissions*, Fall 2009. Retrieved from http://findarticles.com/p/articles/mi_qa3955/is_200910/ai_n42857122

Lent, R. W., Brown, S. D., & Hackett, G. (1994). Toward a unifying social cognitive theory of career and academic interest, choice, and performance. *Journal of Vocational Behavior, 45*, 79–122.

Levine, M. (1997). Introduction. In M. Levine & R. Trachtman (Eds.), *Making professional development schools work: Politics, practice, and policy.* New York: Teachers College Press.

Lewin, T. (2010, July 23). Once a leader, U.S. lags in college degrees. *The New York Times*, N–A10. Retrieved from http://www.nytimes.com/2010/07/23/education/23college.html?_r=1

Matorana, J., Curtis, S., DeDecker, S., Edgerton, S., Gibbons, C., & Luck, L. (2001). Bridging the gap: Information literacy workshops for H.S. teachers. *Research Strategies*, 18: 113–120.

McIntosh, K., Flannery, K. B., Sugai, G., Braun, D. H., & Cochrane, K. L. (2008). Relationships between academics and problem behavior in the transition from middle school to high school. *Journal of Positive Behavior Interventions*, Fall 2008 *10*(4), 243–255.

Mizelle, N. B., & Irvin, J. L. (2000). Transition from middle school into high school. *Middle School Journal, 31*(5), 37–61.

Morgan, P. L., & Hertzog, C. J. (2001). Designing comprehensive transitions. *Principal Leadership, 1*(7), 10–18.

National Association for College Admission Counseling. (NACAC) (2008). *Fundamentals of college admission counseling*, 2nd edition. Dubuque, IA: Kendall/Hunt Publishing.

National Merit Scholarship Corporation. www.collegeplanningsimplified.com/NationalMerit.html.

National Merit Scholarship Program 2011 Annual Report, p. 9. www.nationalmerit.org/nmsp.php

National Merit Selection Indexes 2011 www.collegeplanningsimplified.com/NationalMerit.html

Naviance. (2010). Palos Verdes Peninsula High School Named Naviance 2010 Innovative Program of the Year. Retrieved from www.naviance.com/archives/1561

Newman, B. M., Lohman, B. J., Newman, P. R., Myers, M. C., & Smith, V. L. (2000). Experiences of urban youth navigating the transition to ninth grade. *Youth & Society, 31*, 387–416.

Newman, B. M., Newman, P. R., Griffen, S., O'Connor, K., & Spag, J. *Adolescence*, (2007), Fall *42*(167), 441–459.

Oliva, M. (2004). Reluctant partners, problem definition, and legislative intent: P-20 policy for Latino college success. *Journal of Hispanic Higher Education, 3*, 209–230.

Onishi, N. (2008, June 4). Rush to study abroad splits Korean families. *Herald Tribune*, p. 2.

Ostrower, F. (2005). The reality underneath the buzz of partnerships: The potentials and pitfalls of partnering. *Stanford Social Innovation Review*, April, 34–41.

Owen, P. (2010). A transition checklist for high school seniors. *School Library Monthly*, V; XXVI, 8 April, 20–23.

Owen, P. L., & Oakleaf, M. (2008, October 22–24). Using evidence to bridge the 12–13 gap. (Presentation). Ohio Educational Library Media Association Annual Conference, Columbus.

Pandora, C. (2004, October 20–22). Library research skills: High school to college transition. (Presentation). Ohio Educational Library Media Association Annual Conference, Columbus.

Pew Hispanic Center/Kaiser Family Foundation. (2004). *National survey of Latinos: Education*. Washington, DC: author. Retrieved from http://pewhispanic.org/files/reports/25.pdf

Pontin, J. (2008, July/August). The future of Web 2.0. *Technology Review*. Cambridge: MIT. Retrieved from https://www.techologyreview.com/infotech/20918/?a=f

PSAT/NMQT. 2011. www.college board psat.com and www.collegeboard.com/student/testing/psat/prep.html.

Quarton, B. (2003). Research skills and the new undergraduate. *Journal of Instructional Psychology, 30*(2), 120–124.

Ravitch, D. (2000). *Left back: A century of failed school reforms*. New York: Simon & Schuster.

Reents, J. N. (2002). Isolating ninth graders. *School Administrator, 59*(3), 14–19.

Roberts, D. F., & Foehr, U. G. (2008). Trends in media use. In J. Brooks-Gunn & E. Hirschborn Donahue (Eds.), *Children and electronic media, 18*(1). Retrieved from http://www.futureofchildren.org/pubs-info2825/pubs-info_show.htm?doc_id=674322

Sanders, M. G. (2005). *Building school-community partnerships*. Thousand Oaks, CA: Corwin Press.

Seely, J. (2000 March/April). Growing up digital: How the Web changes work, education, and the way people learn. *Change*, March/April, 2000. Retrieved from http://www.johnseelybrown.com/Growing_up_digital.pdf

Segal, C. (2010). *Motivation, Test Scores, and Economic Success*. Retrieved from http://www.econ.upf.edu/~segal/SegalMotivationTestScoresJuly2010.pdf

Shirky, C. (2010, June 4). Does the Internet make you smarter? *The Wall Street Journal*, p. W–1.

Shore, R. (2008). *The power of pow! Wham! Children, digital media, and our nation's future. Three challenges for the coming decade*. New York: The Joan Ganz Center at Sesame Workshop. Retrieved from http://www.joanganzcooneycenter.org/pdf/Cooney_Challenge_advance.pdf

Slavin, R.E. (1999). Educating young students at risk of school failure: Research, practice, and policy. In R. Stevens (Ed.) *Teaching in American Schools* (pp. 103–119). Upper Saddle River, NJ: Prentice-Hall.

Smith, W. L., & Zhang, P. (2009, June). Students' perceptions and experiences with key factors during the transition from high school to college. *College Student Journal, 43*(2), 643–657.

Southern Methodist University. Altshuler Learning Enhancement Center. *How is college different from high school?* Retrieved from http://smu.edu/alec/transition.asp

Stage, E., & Hossler, D. (1989). Differences in family influences on college attendance plans for male and female ninth graders. *Research in Higher Education, 30*, 301–314.

Stanford University. (2010). Freshman requirements & process: Essays. Retrieved from http://www.stanford.edu/dept/uga/application/freshman/essays.html

State University of New York at Binghamton. (2010). Retrieved from http://www2.binghamton.edu/admissions/apply/freshman/get-started.html

Steinberg, J. (2010, March 3). Graduates fault advice of guidance counselors. *The New York Times*, National Edition, p. A20.

Subrahmanyam, K., & Greenfield, P. (2008). Online communication and adolescent relationships. In J. Brooks-Gunn & E. Hirschborn Donahue (Eds.), *Children and electronic media*, 18(1), Spring 2008. Retrieved from http://www.futureofchildren.org/futureofchildren/publications/docs/18_01_06.pdf

Super, D. E. (1990). A life-span, life-space approach to career development. In D. Brown & L. Brooks (Eds.), *Career choice and development: Applying contemporary approaches to practice*. San Francisco: Jossey-Bass, 11–20.

Tang, M., Wei, P., & Newmeyer, M. (2008). Factors influencing high school students' career aspirations. *Professional School Counseling*, June 2008, *11*(5), 285–295.

Timpane, R. M., & White, L. S. (Eds.). (1998). *Higher education and school reform*. New York: John Wiley.

Torrez, N. (2004). Developing parent information frameworks that support college preparation for Latino students. *The High School Journal, 87*, 54–59.

Turner, T. (2008). Interview on *Meet the Press*, with Tom Brokaw. Nov. 30. Retrieved from http://www.msnbc.msn.com/id/27983385/ns/meet_the_press/.

U.S. Department of Labor. (2006). *America's dynamic workforce*. Washington, DC: U.S. Dept. of Labor, p. 23. Retrieved from http://digitalcommons.ilr.cornell.edu/cgi/viewcontent.cgi?article=1292&context=key_workplace&sei-redir=1#search=%22U.S.+Department+of+Labor.+%282006%29.+America%C3%A2%C2%80%C2%99s+dynamic+workforce.%22

University of Michigan. (2010). Tips for writing a great essay. Retrieved from http://www.admissions.umich.edu/essay/tips/

University of Texas at Austin. (2010). Tips on essay writing. Retrieved from http://bealonghorn.utexas.edu/freshmen/admission/essays/index.html

W. K. Kellogg Foundation. (2005). *Pursuing opportunities through partnerships: Higher education and communities*. Morgantown: West Virginia University Press.

Wallis, C. (2006, December 10). How to bring our schools out of the 20th century. *Time* magazine in partnership with CNN. Retrieved from http://www.time.com/time/magazine/article/0,9171,1568480-4,00.html

Weinbaum, A. T., Allen, D., Blythe, T., Simon, K., Seidel, S., & Rubin, C. (2004). *Teaching as inquiry: Asking hard questions to improve student achievement.* New York: Teachers College Press.

Wheelock, A., Bebell, D., & Haney, W. (2000a, November 2). Student self-portraits as test-takers: Variations, contextual differences, and assumptions by motivation. *Teachers College Record* (ID Number: 10635). Retrieved from http://www.library.manhattan.edu:2159

Wheelock, A., Bebell, D., & Haney, W. (2000b, November 2). What can student drawings tell us about high stakes testing in Massachusetts? *Teachers College Record* (ID Number: 10634). Retrieved from http://www.library.manhattan.edu:2159

Wilson, B. (2008). Media and children's aggression, fear, and altruism. In J. Brooks-Gunn & E. Hirschborn Donahue (Eds.), *Children and electronic media, 18*(1). Retrieved from http://www.futureofchildren.org/pubs-info2825/pubs-info_show.htm?doc_id=674322

Wise, B. (2008). *Raising the grade: How high school reform can save our youth and our nation.* San Francisco: Jossey-Bass.

Zakaria, F. (2008). *The post American world.* New York: W.W. Norton.

Additional Resources

A2ZColleges.com, Majors: http://www.a2zcolleges.com/Majors/

ACT: http://www.act.org

American School Counselor Association: http://www.schoolcounselor.org

College Admission Essay: http://www.college-admission-essay.com/comprehensive.html

College Admissions Essays: http://www.collegeadmissionsessays.com/

College Board for counselors: http://www.professionals.collegeboard.com/educator/k-12-counselor

College Board Scholarship Search: http://www.apps.collegeboard.com/cbsearch_ss/welcome.jsp

College Board: http://www.collegeboard.com

College Board's College Search: http://www.collegesearch.collegeboard.com/search/index.jsp

College Board's PSAT Web site: http://www.collegeboard.com/student/testing/psat/prep.html

College Board's SAT Web site: http://www.sat.collegeboard.com/home

College Scholarships.org: http://www.collegescholarships.org

Common Application, The: http://www.commonapp.org

Common Data Set: http://www.commondataset.org

Cornell University, Office of Minority Educational Affairs: http://www.omea.cornell.edu

Counselor-O-Matic review of tools: http://www.technewsworld.com/story/40056.html?wlc=1231621966

Counselor-O-Matic—Princeton Review: http://www.theprincetonreviewk12.com/index.php

Department of Education's Family Policy Compliance Office (FPCO): http://www.ed.gov./policy/gen/guid/fpco/index.html

Education Update: http://educationupdate.com/index.html

Encyclopedia of Mental Disorders: http://www.minddisorders.com/Del-Fi/index.html#ixzz0W0fYGCWQ

FAFSA: http://www.fafsa.ed.gov

Fastweb: http://www.fastweb.com/

Foundation Center: http://www.fdncenter.org

LASSI (Learning and Study Strategies Inventory): http://www.hhpublishing.com/_assessments/LASSI/

Mach 25: http://www.collegenet.com/mach25/app

My College QuickStart. https://www.quickstart.collegeboard.com

MyRoad. https://www.myroad.collegeboard.com/

NACAC for Counselors: http://www.nacacnet.org/Pages/default.aspx

National Association for College Admission Counseling (NACAC): http://www.nacacnet.org

National Association of State Student Grant and Aid Programs: http://www.nassgap.org

National Center for College Costs: http://www.collegecosts.com

National Center for Transforming School Counseling: http://www2.edtrust.org/EdTrust/Transforming+School+Counseling/main

National Merit Scholarship Program: http://www.nationalmerit.org/nmsp.php

Naviance for counselors: http://www.naviance.com/products/workspacek12/index.html

Naviance: http://www.naviance.com

PSAT: http://www.collegeboard.com/student/testing/PSAT/prep.html

Quintessential Careers: http://www.quintcareers.com/college_application_essay.html

SAT Subject Tests: http://www.sat.collegeboard.com/practice/sat-subject-test-preparation

Scholarship Resource Network (SRN) Express: http://www.srnexpress.com/index.cfm

SUNY Binghamton: http://www.sunybinghamton.edu/eop

Index

CD Contents

Chapter 4: The Move to High School: Making the Transitioning to 9th Grade Successful
- Exercise on Establishing Goals for First Semester
- Executive Functioning Exercise
- Prioritizing Study Schedule

Chapter 6: Motivation and Testing: Learning About Standardized Testing and Using It to Get Motivated About the College Process (10th–11th Grades)
- Your Results on the Initial Practice PSAT
- Tips for Counselors
- PSAT Performance Exercise
- Initial Student Plan for Standardized Testing

Chapter 7: Assisting Students in Career Exploration
- Exercise on Personality Type and Learning Style
- Exercise on Majors and Careers
- Exercise on Career Requirements

Chapter 8: Advising Students in College Research (11th Grade)
- Junior-Year Form for Standardized Testing
- Engineering Degree Specializations
- Exercise on Majors and Careers
- Exercise to Evaluate Colleges after Visits
- Exercise on College Matches

Chapter 9: Empowering Students in Their Essay Writing (11th–12th Grades)
- Personal Essay Questions from the Common Application
- Personal Essay Exercise: Events
- Personal Essay Exercise: People
- Writing a Rough Draft
- Tips to get the Attention of the Admissions Committee

Chapter 10: Assisting Students in Constructing the Final List of Colleges (12th Grade)
- Senior-Year Standardized Testing Form
- Sample Activities/Resume Sheet
- Exercise on Evaluating College Visits
- Exercise on College Matches